ECONOMICS AND SOCIETY: No 2

Social and Business Enterprises

ECONOMICS AND SOCIETY SERIES
General Editor: Professor C. D. Harbury

1. ECONOMICS IN SOCIETY: *A Basic Course*
   by D. T. King and G. D. Hamilton

ECONOMICS AND SOCIETY SERIES

Social and Business Enterprises

An Introduction to Organisational Economics

by

J. S. BOSWELL

Senior Lecturer in Managerial Economics
The City University

London   George Allen & Unwin Ltd
Ruskin House   Museum Street

First published 1976

© George Allen & Unwin Ltd 1976

ISBN   0 04 338078 6 hardback
        0 04 338079 4 paperback

Printed in Great Britain
in 10 point Times Roman type
by Clarke, Doble & Brendon Ltd
Plymouth

Preface

This book shows how micro-economics can be used to clarify and stimulate thinking about organisations and their decision making. Unlike many texts in this field, its scope is wide, covering business enterprises, local authorities and a variety of public and voluntary organisations. It is neither highly abstract nor technical nor merely descriptive. And in highlighting the central theme – the fruitful interaction between abiding economic ideas and contemporary organisational problems – it draws heavily on brief case studies based on actual experience.

Among students the principal users are expected to be second and third year undergraduates in polytechnics and universities who are preparing for degrees in economics, other social sciences, management and business studies or public/social administration. It is assumed that, normally speaking, such students will already have completed a first year introductory course in economics. To get the most out of the book some factual knowledge of contemporary business, local government and social institutions would also be desirable. The book should also be a suitable introductory text for postgraduate students at business schools and in social administration and for students of these various subjects at technical colleges or colleges of further education.

For the general reader, as for the student with little or no previous economics, it should be emphasised that the treatment is relatively simple and also non-mathematical. Although some previous economics is desirable, it is not essential provided such students pursue extra reading elsewhere (on which suggestions are made). The author believes that applied micro-economics can be made stimulating and useful for the post-experience reader who is able and willing to take trouble, regardless of his or her previous formal education. However, the material in this book is very concentrated. The reader may find it best to read through the book fairly quickly once and then to read it again more carefully.

To consider the economics of business, public and voluntary organisations within the ambit of a single book, even an introductory one, may seem novel and risky. Conventionally, one branch of micro-economics concentrates on markets, prices and business firms, another on public sector finance, social cost–benefit analysis,

etc. This split between 'business' and 'public' is historically under-
standable and appears to be convenient. The field is so vast that
some division of labour may seem essential if studies are not to
become unmanageable or lose their cutting edge. Nonetheless the
author firmly suggests that in trying to understand organisational
economics the 'business/public' split has become more of a liability than an asset.

There are several reasons for this assertion. First, the allocation
systems within which businesses, local authorities and the rest
operate are remarkably interdependent, interrelated and even overlapping, as we shall see. Second, even where major contrasts exist,
fruitful comparisons can be made. Indeed, stimulus and advance
in both micro-economics and management positively require such
cross-fertilisation and juxtaposition. Third, the 'business/public'
split has the disadvantage of over-emphasising extreme distinctions
or polar cases, for example 'private versus public goods', 'competition versus control', 'markets versus planning'. This often means
unrealistically ignoring whole swathes of activity which lie between.
It also exacerbates schisms and misunderstandings between sectors.
But, perhaps most important, the economic logic of choice is
basically the same throughout. Precisely the same economic principles are to be found in all types of organisation, public, semi-
public, charitable and voluntary, market and business, large and
small. In varying mixtures and degrees the same economic concepts are applicable to the decision making of, say, a chemical company, a local amenity society, a borough council, a corner shop or
a symphony orchestra.

Some economics texts in these fields tend to be very abstract.
They expound in detail the theories, concepts and models thought
to be applicable but do not clearly relate these to the decision
making workface. Then there are the technique orientated books.
These devote much space to institutional facts or the detailed
technical jobs done by economists who actually work in organisations. For example, the precise statistical techniques and practical
problems in deriving cost or demand functions or measuring social
costs may be described in detail.

There is a place for both kinds of approach; but not here. For
our purposes abstract exposition conveys neither the priorities of
problems in the real world nor the flavour of decision making. For
introductory purposes a mainly technical and descriptive bias is
hardly better. This can easily disguise the essentially integrated
character of organisational decision making. It can over-stress
esoteric skills to the detriment of the general economic approach

to fundamental strategy and policy. The reader is bogged down in administrative functions, techniques and facts which are highly specialised, perhaps even ephemeral. So this book tries to avoid being abstract *or* technical *or* merely descriptive. More positively, it seeks to concentrate on the interaction between two factors: on the one hand, a few economic ideas which are fundamental, relatively abiding and above all relevant and, on the other hand, organisational situations and problems which are typical, of central importance and also realistically conveyed.

The book is arranged as follows. The first three chapters are introductory. Chapter 1 outlines the meaning and scope of organisational economics. Chapter 2 emphasises the interconnections, overlaps and contrasts between the allocation systems of business, public and voluntary enterprises. It glances at what some particularly stimulating contemporary economists have said about the interplay, on these micro levels, of power and coercion, self-interested exchange and social benevolence. Chapter 3 gives a bird's-eye view of the generic economic approach to decision making and the logic of choice as applied to organisations.

The bulk of the book then discusses more specific applications. Chapters 4, 5, 6 and 7 outline the practical uses – relative to all kinds of organisation, business, public and voluntary – of four main groups of economic ideas: marginalism; opportunity cost; time, risk and uncertainty; and the theme of size and efficiency. We then turn to some more distinctive problems of business and social enterprises. In relation to firms, economic approaches are used to illuminate profit policies, problems of market knowledge and big business budgeting and planning systems (Chapters 8 and 9). In relation to local authorities and social and voluntary enterprises, the problems of obtaining resources through social pricing and grants are discussed and then the problems of allocating these resources 'efficiently' and 'fairly' (Chapters 10 and 11). Finally, the last chapter glances at wider social issues. The author outlines a personal interpretation of the uses of micro-economics in thinking about some contemporary problems of social conflict and organisational reform.

There is a liberal use of short case studies. Some of these derive from published data about particular organisations. Most of the case studies, however, are drawn from the author's and other people's experience. These specially constructed cases represent isolated pieces of events drawn from a wide variety of organisations, suitably put together, shuffled, simplified and stylised. Any resemblances to particular organisations are coincidental. These cases are shorter than is the case in some texts on decision making, being designed to stimulate thinking in a general sense rather than to provide practice in 'problem solving'. They spring from many years of experience, ranging across small and large firms, local authorities and voluntary organisations, and involving work at different levels and in varying roles. The cases also draw on many conversations which the author has had over these years with people in factories, offices, boardrooms, bureaucracies and local communities and with observers of these scenes. Both the case studies and the general shape of the book have been helped, too, by numerous discussions with undergraduate, postgraduate and post-experience students of organisational economics at the City University over the past few years. Detailed acknowledgement of the help received from all these people would be impracticable, but the author is deeply conscious of his debt to them.

J. S. Boswell

July 1975

Contents

12 *Contents*

Figures

Chapter 1

What is Organisational Economics?

First of all, we take economics to be that social science which studies the employment, production and distribution of scarce resources which have competing uses. We take an 'organisation' to be a system of consciously co-ordinated activities of two or more persons explicitly created to achieve specific ends.[1] Both of these definitions are complex and full of problems. For immediate purposes, however, only a few clarifications are necessary. It is important to make clear that we are concerned with organisations of an intermediate kind, namely those below the level of national government but above that of the individual household or family. This principally means private firms, nationalised industries, local authorities and charitable and voluntary enterprises. Such organisations are all particularist. That is to say, within a given nation state they all pursue sectional interests in varying degrees. Together they account for most of our employment in Western societies, most of our physical production, a large part of our public and welfare services, and much of our social life. The resource allocating systems and behaviour of such intermediate organisations have traditionally been the lifeblood of micro-economics.

ORGANISATIONS VIEWED ECONOMICALLY

By their nature organisations, even quite small ones, are highly intricate. They can be studied as formal and informal systems, from the viewpoints of structure or process, using static or dynamic models, sociologically, psychologically, politically, managerially. Like these other approaches, economics necessarily abstracts from a complex reality. From all the rich complexities of organisational development and activity economics picks out a single guiding theme. Although this theme is a partial one, and certainly makes no pretence of explaining organisations as a whole, it is vital and all-pervasive.

Economics views an organisation's decision making as an act of choice which deploys resources of manpower, managerial skill, money and materials which are usually scarce. Such choice consequently diverts these resources from other uses to which they could be put, either by the organisation itself or by others. In one well-tried model, economics sees the organisation as a transformation system, taking precious human, material and financial resources (the 'inputs'), working on them in various ways and then performing various activities, distributions or services (the 'outputs'). Thus the organisation makes difficult choices in deploying resources internally. It also relates dynamically to the environment, on the one hand taking resources and imposing costs and, on the other, providing goods or accomplishing tasks which may benefit the community. But at all points the organisation is influencing the disposition of scarce resources.

Let us take a simplified illustration. A large company, a local authority or a charity is considering major changes in its activities, perhaps as part of some annual budgeting or planning exercise. Note that the concept of such decisions taken explicitly and at a single, definable point of time may already be an abstraction. In practice, the organisation's decision making will probably be more messy and fragmented than this implies. But accepting the simplification for the moment, there are many angles from which the strategic decisions under consideration can be viewed. The decisions can be regarded as a problem of human relations, psychology or communications. For example, who actually makes such decisions in the company, local authority or charity? Whom do they consult and why? What influence is played by formal and informal pressures, behaviour patterns, organisational structures or morale? Again, the decisions can be viewed technologically. What are the physical production possibilities of producing and delivering the relevant goods and services? For example, the company may be considering buying new equipment or making a new product, the local authority may be trying to decide priorities between public housing or services for the elderly. Technical problems will then arise of just how much can be done with given sets of resources, for example the physical capacity of plant to turn out products and of land to sustain building densities. A further and related aspect is that of quantifiability. Accountants will be on hand to measure and advise on cash flows. Statisticians and operational researchers may be needed to manipulate the quantifiable data mathematically as an aid to decision making.

These human, technical, accounting and quantitative aspects are important and we will often refer to them. But the economic view-point is different. It concentrates single-mindedly on what happens – relative to scarce resources – in, and as a result of, the very act of choice. In particular, how pressurised or scarce are the resources under consideration relative to the organisation's goals *or* society's? Such scarcity will incidentally be measured only imperfectly by their money prices, if any. Are the decision makers aware of the other uses to which the resources could be put, at least by the organisation? How far is their decision making about the resources rational, clear, explicit and consistent in terms of the sheer logic of choice? How will the efficiency of their choice be judged by themselves, by their peers or by society? What people are going to benefit or lose out by the choice relative to other alternatives? What other choices might be made if, for example, the internal decision making process was organised differently, for example if the organisation were differently owned or controlled or larger or smaller, or if the activities were co-ordinated by grants and taxes rather than markets, or the other way round? And what predictions can be made about resource allocations under these varying conditions?

To return to our simplified example. In pursuing major changes the company, local authority or charity may well have to recruit more people, get hold of more land, raise cash from government, the capital market or supporters. In so doing it will almost certainly divert these resources from other organisations and other existing or possible uses. Having got hold of the resources, the organisation will then use them more or less fully – in a very inefficient case just sitting on them for long periods! Alternatively, the people in charge may feel that they have enough resources just for the moment and of course they may simply be unable to get any more anyway. But in both the last cases, in deciding to pursue one activity rather than others, the organisation will be making a further diversion of resources, this time 'internally'. For example, the company could produce more refrigerators but at the cost of fewer washing machines, the local authority more housing but at the cost of fewer public libraries or refuse collections. For that matter the charity could help more people in Newcastle but perhaps fewer in Biafra. Moreover, the element of sacrifice and choice may also relate to time. If big investments in new factories or housing are decided upon, in the long run this should respectively help the company or people on the housing waiting-list. But in the short run it is likely to mean sacrifices, perhaps less cash for the company's

B

shareholders or workers, fewer current services for the local authority's ratepayers.

These are only a few of the economic issues that will arise. Moreover, in each case economics will have a lot to say about such questions as, how big are the actual sacrifices, gains or trade-offs? How can they be measured? Should they be made explicit and if so by whom? Not least, what concepts can help in deciding what is the 'best' thing to do – and then, afterwards, whether the 'best' thing has been done?

SCOPE OF ORGANISATIONAL ECONOMICS

We should now be more precise about the scope of our subject. First, we cannot consider organisations and their decision making from economic viewpoints without paying careful attention to the allocation systems within which they are set. The concept of an allocation system may need clarifying. Allocation systems are not, of course, separate from social systems but simply represent a way of looking at social systems, whether these be co-operatives, clubs, municipalities, corner shops or giant businesses. The concept of an allocation system helps us to look at social systems from the specific viewpoint of how they carry out their economic role, that of allocating scarce resources. An important part of our subject – and a persistent theme of this book – is the classification, comparison and understanding of these allocation systems. This includes the interplay of power and coercion, exchange and self-interest, and social benevolence, working through complex systems of markets and grants, bureaucracies and electoral choice.

Next, our subject brings us closer to the guts of decision making in boardroom, council chamber or director's office. In deciding on important changes, organisations are not only bounded by wider social systems, they are also influenced by their own objectives. But economic problems also arise about these objectives. To imagine that economics is only about 'means' and never about 'ends' is of course completely false. For not only will an organisation's objectives interrelate with its allocative environment, at any point of time its objectives are extremely unlikely to be mutually consistent. On the contrary, they will often conflict. Just as a national economy is caught in the toils of choices or trade-offs between, say, full employment and stable prices or between public and private consumption, so a business may have constantly to juggle its short-term profit against long-term profit objectives. So, too, a public body at grass-roots level may be torn between its speed and efficiency objectives, say, and the need to consult local opinion. Therefore, in a real sense corporate objectives, also, have to be economised. Relative to available resources, various trade-offs between objectives will exist. Although the final choice of objectives is the prerogative of decision makers rather than economists, the latter frequently contribute advice on what priorities or combinations of organisational objectives may be possible.

Organisations are complex systems in which component parts relate to each other and also to the whole, and in which decisions about the short-run, the medium-run and the long-run are inextricably intertwined. Organisations are also open-ended systems, closely related to their outside environments of suppliers, customers, local citizens, central government etc. Even apparently small decisions are often highly general in their implications. For example, the decision inside a large company whether to replace a little old warehouse in Piddlington relates to its requirement for stock-holding. The company's stock-holding system may have been wrung through a computer but the levels of stocks anticipated relate to its production plans and, more particularly, to its estimates of future sales. Still more important, the company's estimates of future sales relate in turn not only to its market forecasts but also to its market strategy. What share of the market is it aiming at and why? Finally, market strategy relates to overall strategy and objectives. How does the company see its constraints and opportunities, whether in terms of finance, labour and other resources, competition, political forces or managerial abilities and aims? All these questions clearly interlock. Moreover, the interlocking character of organisational activities extends no less to, say, a large local authority, a hospital or a housing association.

An advantage of micro-economics is that it offers principles in the light of which virtually all types of decisions can be viewed. These economic concepts are few in number and broad in scope, yet also sufficiently clear-cut to create some order out of a complex scene. Each of the main micro-economic principles can be applied, in varying degrees and forms, to virtually all sorts of decisions. But they also provide ways of looking at decision problems which are interestingly distinct. So a lot of attention must be given to these basic ideas and how they can be used in practice both by student observers trying to make sense of organisations from the outside and by the internal decision makers.

Finally there is the wider social dimension. As explained so far, organisational economics mainly concentrates on the existing activities and objectives of organisations and on how they can pursue these more efficiently. But the social effects of organisational actions, for both good and ill, cannot be ignored in an interdependent society. This is so whether or not such effects are taken into account by the organisations themselves. If organisations pollute the atmosphere, ruthlessly conflict with each other to the detriment of public objectives, pursue corrupt or unethical practices or ride roughshod over workers, consumers or local citizens, such actions are of critical concern. Micro-economics has long studied and debated such issues, mainly under the headings of market and economic power, externalities, distributional impacts and the social choice of allocation systems. Micro-economics also offers a necessary and stimulating framework within which some of the moral questions at stake can be discussed and within which the practical problems of reforming existing organisations – and perhaps developing socially desirable *new* ones – can be clarified. These wider social issues cannot be lost sight of, even if space forbids more than a brief mention of them.

Chapter 2

Markets, Bureaucracies, Gifts

As mentioned in the last chapter, allocation systems represent a way of looking at bigger social systems. An allocation system is the method by which any sort of social system, be it a family, tribe, municipality or business, obtains, produces and distributes resources. But there is no simple way to sum up the allocation systems used by any organisation, however small. Even the systems employed by a tiny shop round the corner cannot be contained within the simple market concepts of 'buying' and 'selling'. Still less can the allocative processes of vast businesses like ITT or ICI be wholly subsumed under the label of 'markets'. Nor can the expenditure decisions of, say, the Greater London Council be neatly encapsulated in the conventional categories of citizen choice exercised through the ballot box. On the contrary, a given type of social system, whatever its size and sector, has to employ several types of allocation system in deploying resources. Moreover, these allocation systems interrelate in complex ways.

In this chapter we outline a classification of allocation systems which emphasises the interconnections, overlaps and contrasts between business, public and voluntary organisations. We glance briefly at some stimulating contemporary economic ideas about the interplay – in and around such organisations – of allocation systems based on power, self-interested exchange and social benevolence. These ideas help to illuminate the scene within which organisational decision making, to be discussed in the following few chapters, is set. The ideas are reviewed in broad outline: a note on further reading, with a list of their main expositors, will be found at the end of the chapter.

CLASSIFYING ALLOCATION SYSTEMS

A very useful framework for considering complex allocation systems has been suggested by the distinguished American economist

Kenneth Boulding.[1] Boulding suggests that in any society there are basically three methods of organising human activity. One 'social organiser' is coercion, using threats and fear. This corresponds to someone saying, in effect, 'You do this because I tell you or else . . .' The second social organiser, which Boulding calls 'integration', relies on love, loyalty or goodwill, and corresponds to someone saying, 'I do this with you or for you because I *want* to'. And, according to Boulding, the third organiser is based on exchange, implying a contractual or conditional relationship, namely, 'If you do this for me, but *only* if, then I will do that for you'. As Boulding remarks, these are polarisations and, at least in their purer forms, rare. But essentially his argument is that in any social system the three organising principles of coercion, integration and exchange are all present, although in widely varying mixtures and forms. For example, even in the family, where integration and affection play such a big role, coercion is also found. In business life, where exchange relationships are most highly developed, both coercion and integration are also evident. In government, as Boulding suggests, the mixture is particularly rich. Thus people obey governments partly because they fear punishment if they don't (coercion), partly because they identify with governments and their aims as a

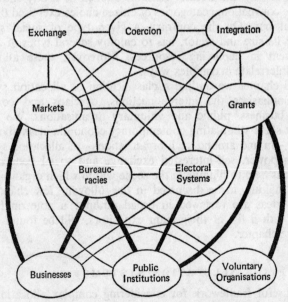

Figure 1 Interacting allocation systems

result of altruism, patriotism or public spirit (integration), and partly also because they see that in return for taxes and obedience to laws, government after all provides things they need and desire (exchange).

This three-angled perspective on allocation systems will recur several times in this book. The accompanying diagram (Figure 1) extends the Boulding framework downwards into the areas we are concerned with. Just below the Boulding triad itself are the two main allocative systems characteristic of developed societies, namely markets (whereby goods and services are exchanged for money) and grants (whereby goods and services are transferred in one-way fashion from some people to others, by families, private gift making or government). However, in complex societies, neither markets nor grants can operate without intricate support and control systems. Bureaucracies, i.e. administrative and hierarchical systems of officials, are essential. Economists as well as sociologists and political scientists have found that bureaucracies tend to develop a life of their own and to exert a strong and distinctive influence on the allocation of resources, whether in business, government or even in the voluntary sector. So bureaucracies represent another form of allocative system, whether or not this is explicitly recognised. So, too, in political democracies, do systems of electoral choice. The economic implications of different types of election systems, and particularly of majority voting, have been considerably discussed by modern economists. However great the gap between democratic theory and practice, however crude the operation of choice through the ballot box and however great or small its final effects, the voting system represents yet another way of influencing the allocation of resources.

The bottom tier of the diagram shows the three types of organisation we are concerned with, namely businesses, public institutions and voluntary organisations. The lines connecting all of these elements symbolise interactions or mutual influences between them. The heavy lines represent the more obvious primary links. Thus businesses primarily operate through markets and bureaucracies; public institutions through elective systems, bureaucracies and grants; voluntary organisations through grants and, sometimes, bureaucracies. However, the three types of organisation have *some* links with all types of allocation system. For example, businesses both receive grants (mainly from government) and make them; local authorities depend heavily for their resource inputs on the factor markets for labour, capital, materials and land; and voluntary organisations also make market purchases as well as frequently having close relationships with local authorities and other public bodies. These examples certainly do not exhaust the interactions which exist between the different types of allocation systems and organisations, nor the many ways in which resources actually flow between them. Moreover, to return to the Boulding triad at the top, all three types of organisation reflect varying mixtures of exchange, coercion and integration. For the purposes of our argument at this point, the important question is, *what* mixtures and *how*? Let us turn to what some contemporary economists have said about the interplays in particular sectors.

POWER IN BIG BUSINESS AND MARKETS

As every elementary economics student knows, under perfect competition, if this existed, the individual firm would have no power over markets. A firm would merely be one among many sellers of a homogeneous product in a market where no one firm could exert major leverage over price, quality or anything else. The impersonal forces of supply and demand, operating through the interactions of buyers and sellers, would determine prices. This highly abstract concept of perfect competition is by no means useless. In a few cases it is approximated in the real world, if only very roughly. It has played an essential part in the development of economic thinking. Moreover, the concept of perfect competition is useful as a benchmark for determining degrees of market power. For, insofar as the conditions for perfect competition are departed from, as they always are in some degree, firms can clearly be said to possess such power. Yet it is a familiar point that the theory of perfect competition, at least as a way of explaining how things happen, has steadily retreated over the past half-century or more. For that matter, so has the other polar concept of a pure, ultra-powerful monopoly. Instead, applied economists now mainly address themselves to the real-life situations that lie between, to the almost universal phenomenon of firms which have genuine but imperfect market control.[2]

Thus economists increasingly study oligopoly pricing, price leadership, entry forestalling and advertising. They have developed theories and made observations about the varying situations of modern industry where competitors are few and market shares large, and in which competition is pursued through marketing, product differentiation, innovation and indirect substitutes, as well as price. Even for small firms the earlier theories have had their wings clipped. So far as large corporations are concerned, it is the forms, uses and implications of market power that now occupy the centre of the stage. But economists are divided on how to interpret the trend. Empirical knowledge is still inadequate. Reliable economic histories of modern big businesses are few. The things we want to know are often buried within mounds of aggregated data, lost in the mists of discretion or forgetfulness or obfuscated, wittingly or otherwise, in personalised memoirs or bland official histories. Certainly no central, generally accepted theory of big business behaviour has yet ascended the throne once occupied by perfect competition. But a number of stimulating theories exist, providing clashes of opinion and hypothesis which may prove to be essential for progress. No student of economics and organisations can afford to neglect these theories, tentative, provocative or conflicting as they may seem.

To illustrate the clash of economic ideas, let us take a mythically named but typical giant company, the Universal Foods Corporation. UFC is a large public company with substantial interests in food manufacturing, processing and distribution, controlled by professional managers. The company has recently introduced an innovation, chicken fingers. UFC backroom boys had been researching this idea for some time. The company's product development department had checked that it was technologically viable. The market researchers had investigated likely consumer reactions to chicken fingers and felt these would be good, provided there was a first-class advertising campaign. The board of UFC needed some persuasion to adopt the chicken fingers idea. There were some apparently reasonable alternative uses for the company's spare funds at the time. But the directors finally accepted that chicken fingers would be a profitable and useful addition to the company's existing range of convenience foods. The introduction of chicken fingers required careful and co-ordinated planning. UFC had already secured a foothold in chicken rearing and the company used its enormous buying power to ensure large and economic supplies. New processing facilities to manufacture the fingers were laid down. The company's distributive outlets were alerted and a massive advertising campaign involving newspapers and television was conceived. Within one year UFC had substantially increased their general market share of chicken products. Chicken fingers obtained widespread acceptance. The new product seemed to be profitable and successful.

Now there are two sharply delineated economic interpretations of what happened here.[3] The first may be loosely described as the 'Galbraithian'. According to this interpretation the Universal Foods

Corporation deploys massive power. Its sheer size, its oligopoly or quasi-monopoly position in various markets, its vertical links with supply and distribution, its ability to innovate and differentiate its products and to advertise and persuade the public – these are seen as representing a formidable combination. According to the Galbraithian view, UFC pretty well decides what it wants to do and then plans the market. It is able to achieve what it wants, basically for two reasons. First, the view is that under modern conditions consumers can be persuaded more easily. Relative affluence makes it easier to manufacture new and more refined consumer wants and to win acceptance by subtle psychological appeals (the 'dependence effect'). The influence of mass advertising in getting acceptance of something like chicken fingers is envisaged as strong. But secondly, according to the Galbraithian interpretation, the progress of big companies like UFC has become virtually written into the development of modern society. The big corporations have ensured, in a general sense, that their objectives are, in effect, those of society. Through their ramified power over consumers, small firms and government, as well as markets, the large corporations have ensured that business growth and the proliferation of new consumer wants are uncritically accepted by most people as socially virtuous and, very important, that other priorities are relatively less emphasised. Therefore, the path of UFC in persuading the consumer to buy its new product is eased by the conventional wisdom that associates 'progress' with such developments and by the operation of a system that muffles the issue of what *else* could be done with the resources which are now devoted to manufacturing, distributing, advertising and consuming chicken fingers.

But there is, of course, another sharply delineated interpretation of events. According to the critics of Galbraith, far from creating a new consumer want out of nothing, the UFC is essentially drawing out desires which already existed in latent or inchoate form. After all, it may be said, market research had to be used to verify whether consumers would accept chicken fingers. Moreover, advertising is assumed to be less influential than Galbraith suggests. Advertising messages may get to the wrong people or be misunderstood or forgotten or accepted but ignored, or just plain resisted. In the face of these obstacles, UFC's advertising of chicken fingers must have struck a genuine chord. After all, so this interpretation continues, big business power cannot be all that triumphant because it sometimes, perhaps even frequently, meets with striking reverses. It is conceivable that chicken fingers might have followed such precedents as the collapse of the Ford Edsel, the $425 million General Dynamics lost on the Convair 880, the $100 million Du Pont lost on Corfam, and so on. According to the critics of Galbraith, such misjudgements and inefficiencies on the part of big corporations are significant, although often hidden. Even admitting that UFC has indeed won a strong market position for itself with chicken fingers, the critics would ask, how secure is this market power anyway? How long will it be before UFC's competitors catch up or think of something better? If UFC is so highly profitable, is it not possible that some other giant company will enter its traditional markets? Alternatively, if UFC's market power leads it to become slothful and complacent, is it not possible that it might actually be taken over by another company? In any case, so the argument goes, Galbraith exaggerates the wider political power of big businesses (note the plural). Faced with giant government, trade unions and public opinion, the top management of UFC are far from being in control of events. On the contrary, they certainly feel, and to a considerable extent probably are, vulnerable to government scrutiny and public criticism, as well as business competition, nationally and perhaps also internationally. To cap it all, the critics of Galbraith may add a further point which is rather more of a value judgement. If it is felt to be moral or democratic that consumers should, broadly, get what they desire, then they may say that on the above reasoning chicken fingers cannot really be criticised as a 'bad thing' anyway.

Thus we appear to have a clear-cut choice between two radically different factual interpretations of the allocation systems within and surrounding a company like the Universal Foods Corporation. One interpretation concentrates on the external power of UFC, the other on its fallibility and vulnerability. For the Galbraithian what matters is the planning power of UFC's bureaucracy, for the anti-Galbraithian the power, actual or potential, of the market. As always, of course, it is possible to build bridges between the two positions and to take some sort of middle view. For example, it may be said that some of the differences between the two positions are more apparent than real, perhaps even a matter of the difficult semantics surrounding the word 'power'. It is possible to say that if consumers occasionally act 'independently' and reject something like chicken fingers – or even if an individual giant like UFC is brought low by some combination of competition and recession, union militancy and governmental power – this does not destroy Galbraith's hypothesis as to a *general* 'dependence effect'. It can be said that, although a high consumption society well serves their purposes, at least in a general sense, companies like UFC hardly create, but tend much more to be caught up in, this system. It is also possible to argue that each case of market power must be judged on its merits, implying that at this stage in our knowledge no sweeping generalisations are possible in any case. Indeed, the latter position probably particularly appeals to many economists. Industrial economists have long applied a series of measures – largely derived from the theory of perfect competition, as mentioned above – in order to assess the relativities of market power. Their analysis enables us not only to compare degrees of market power but also to make some tentative predictions about its likely consequences, in particular sectors. It may be argued that this is a serviceable enough approach without indulging in sweeping hypotheses about the general supremacy of either big business power or market forces.

When it comes to studying a particular case like UFC, the pragmatic, non-generalising approach has strong merits. On the other hand, our understanding of social forces requires more than intricate measuring devices. Bold hypotheses and synoptic views – and the debates to which they give rise – may be helpful both in clarifying our perspective and in advancing the frontiers of understanding. It is hard to see where we would be today, for example, without the purist extremism of the theory of perfect competition. It may be that the Galbraithian theory, together with the counter-reaction to that theory, will serve something of the same purpose. It may even be that in understanding the complexities of the dynamic relationship between a company like UFC and its markets, theories of corporate dominance and of external constraints are both indispensable. So the reader is advised to keep these wider theories in view as he observes the intricacies of business allocation systems. He should indeed find them positively helpful in deciding for himself where the balance of truth lies.

But the fruitful clash between hypotheses is not restricted to the dimensions of market power. It also relates to the internal allocation systems of big businesses. In a world where a single company may command more resources than many nation states, for economists to be concerned with the internal resource flows and allocations of giant corporations needs no justification. To return to UFC, one of the most striking phenomena is the way in which the decision to allocate the company's resources to chicken fingers is taken and then carried through. Let us suppose that the chicken fingers development was expected to cause a massive upheaval inside the company, and that in fact it did so. Suppose, for example, that some other division, say the Fish Division, got much less money as a result;

that other alternative developments which company people believed in were held back; that the balance of power at middle management levels was substantially affected; that workers had to be persuaded to accept new methods; and that trade union co-operation had to be obtained. Given that such problems are likely to be important, how were they overcome? Do companies like UFC secure such massive resource dispositions mainly through internal coercion, financial incentives or voluntary goodwill? Can any generalisations about big business social systems be developed in the interests of predicting how resources will be internally allocated?

Here again economists have varied and often conflicting ideas. Some see the internal dynamics of large corporations as pluralist, even indeterminate. One pluralist interpretation would emphasise the functional diversities which exist within a company like UFC, for example between buying, manufacturing and selling, the difficulties of maintaining morale in large concerns and the allocative importance of such factors as 'sentiment, snobbery, taboo, myth, fetish, ritual, herd instinct or the "gentleman ideal" '.[4] According to this sort of view, perhaps, corporations can be 'typed' but few overall generalisations made. Another pluralist view suggests only the most general of formulations, a 'position–personality–bargaining configuration', varying from one corporation to another as well as over time.[5] But other economists attribute the big corporation's feats of internal co-ordination to one or other of the allocative principles of coercion, exchange and integration. Some see such co-ordination achieved through a quasi-market system. According to this view, top management successfully deploy a complex system emphasising internal competition and financial sanctions and inducements. Another view sees internal co-ordination achieved by 'canalising rules and the acceptance of common goals'.[6] For Galbraith the 'technostructure' of a company like UFC embraces not only its top men but all who contribute information and expertise to important decisions (like that on chicken fingers). For Galbraith this technostructure achieves a high degree of cohesion because their concerns for personal power, security, financial rewards or public repute give them an enormous common interest in the corporation's growth. We shall return to many of these themes later.

EXCHANGE AND SELF-INTEREST IN POLITICS

The reader will note that the theories of big business power we have just glanced at tend to share one feature. In their efforts to explain and predict they burst the bounds of ideas related purely to exchange. In order to make sense of both the internal allocative systems of big firms and their relationships with markets – including such phenomena as administered prices, market sharing, non-price competition and long-term business planning – the theories lean more or less heavily on the concept of power. Indeed, some economists have quite explicitly used political categories to explain allocative behaviour in business and markets. But paradoxically, some other economists have engaged in a contrary process. They have transported the concepts of exchange and self-interest, traditionally used in analysing markets, into a very different field – that of government.

Again let us start out from a stylised but typical example, this time drawn from the world of local government. The municipal authority in Middletown has just made a public statement about its current and long-term resource allocations in housing, social services, the environment and other local services. A year ago the governing party fought a highly successful election campaign and gained a decisive majority at the town hall. Their programme, which subsequent research showed as having an important effect on voters in this politically marginal area, included an attack on 'town hall extravagance' and pledges of 'substantial cuts in bureaucratic spending at the town hall'. The victorious party also promised, very significantly, 'better services for the elderly and handicapped'. Another plank in their manifesto was the creation of a new park in an over-crowded area – a pledge which appeared to swing a lot of votes in that area in their favour. The newly-elected representatives swept into the town hall and council chamber full of enthusiasm for their ideas.

The ensuing few months were spent in hammering out implementation plans with the council's officials. This proved a sobering experience. The council's senior officers were very cautious about both the proposed expenditure cuts and the expensive new projects. First the committee chairmen and then their council supporters were disappointed to find that on both fronts the scope for manœuvre was much less than they had thought. There followed strong disagreements on priorities. Broadly, each department of the council formed up behind its committee chairman in an effort to advance its own services. The fact that the pledges towards the elderly and the new park were to some extent conflicting crystallised a battle for resources between social services and public recreation. Both sides sought allies, informal coalitions were formed among both council officers and politicians, the clash was intensified by a power struggle between the two main committee chairmen. Finally a compromise was hammered out after intense debate both at top politician–officer level and in the majority party caucus meeting. When the final accouncements were made it appeared that the park had been postponed, that the cuts in administrative spending and staff were to be minimal and that social services for the elderly and handicapped were to be expanded but less fully than had been promised and hoped.

What economic theories can be used to shed light on such events? From the viewpoint of allocative systems, what is the interplay between Middletown electors, council politicians and town hall officials? If the final allocation is viewed as a complex transaction involving all three groups, what is the division of power between them in determining the flow of resources and what is the relative importance in this transaction of coercion, solidarity and exchange? Faced with the allocative decisions of hundreds of Middletowns, what sort of hypotheses and predictions are possible?

As already mentioned, some contemporary economists believe that the resource allocations of public institutions like the Middletown council can usefully be regarded as exchange or quasi-market transactions. According to this view, citizens have preferences or desires for services for themselves – or demands for public goods – and are primarily self-interested. Government and elected authorities are then viewed as a machine or artifact for achieving these individually conceived citizen desires. The citizen hands over his vote, plus rates and taxes, in return for individual gains for himself and his family through public services. The politician, who is also assumed to be mainly self-interested in seeking votes and power, is envisaged as a sort of 'political entrepreneur', trader or middleman, operating within a quasi-market characterised by supply and demand for political favours. As one version puts it, the politician receives votes, campaign contributions and voluntary help (his 'revenues') in return for pledging commitments to his electors and supporters, plus the expenditure of his time and energies (his 'costs').

In some versions of this voter–politician 'mutual gain' model the final resource allocations actually resulting from the transaction are seen as 'democratic' or 'acceptable', in others this situation is posited as an ideal. Sometimes an ideal situation of mutual gains is related to the celebrated condition of 'Pareto optimality' or of never, in effect, making some people better off at the expense of others. Whatever the refinements, the basic idea is of a self-interested exchange transaction between citizen voters and politicians, with public officials as agents or executives.

The voter–politician mutual gain interpretation may carry us quite a long way in explaining the resource allocations of the Middle-town Council. Perhaps the victorious political party thought a good deal about the sort of pledges which would gather votes in certain critical areas. Hence, perhaps, the proposal for a new park. Perhaps, too, many voters decided to vote for this party mainly because they saw it providing direct benefits to themselves and their families. In other words an awareness of the sort of desires felt by local citizens in an area like Middletown might enable us to predict to some degree (*a*) what political parties would offer the citizens and (*b*) what the latter would eventually receive, although (*a*) might be easier to forecast than (*b*).

On the other hand, the voter–politician mutual gain model has limitations. For one thing, as we shall see in a moment, it tends to leave out the interests of a third critical figure, the public official. More fundamentally, the assumptions of 'self-interest' and 'indivi-dualism' on which the theory rests are somewhat vulnerable. Sub-stantial chunks of political reality are left apparently unexplained. Voters' instincts, habits and social loyalties; the role of both envy and benevolence; the apparent importance of ideology for many politicians; the fact that public investment decisions often involve benefits for future generations with whom no possible 'exchange' can be envisaged; the phenomenon of political courage – these and other factors are neglected. Alternatively, if the theory attempts to incorporate such wider motivations into a generalised utility func-tion, it risks becoming merely tautologous ('citizens and politicians try to maximise their desires . . .').

One problem, the omission of the public official, is readily met by another version of the theory. This introduces the self-interest of the bureaucrat as another (perhaps major) allocative influence. To quote a major protagonist of this theory, 'bureaucratic officials in general have a complex set of goals including power, income, prestige, security, convenience, loyalty (to an idea, an institution or the nation), pride in excellent work, and desire to serve the public interest'. But for predictive purposes it is considered fruitful to assume that 'regardless of the particular goals involved, every official is significantly motivated by his own self-interest even when acting in a purely official capacity'.[7] On this assumption, insofar as the bureaucrat has an important role in decision making, certain predictions are ventured about allocative behaviour inside public organisations. For example, the power structure of the bureaucratic system itself is stressed, as also is the importance of non-monetary coalitions, bargains and exchanges both between individual bureau-crats and between departments.

When bureaucratic self-interests are added to those of both voters and politicians, some complex and perhaps displeasing results are predicted. For example, if the bureaucrats are very powerful, so it is said, producer interests are likely to dominate over client or citizen ones. Too much emphasis may be laid on empire-building, on entry restrictions or quasi-monopolistic practices on the part of the professionals, on prestige projects, on public services which the experts think are 'best' for people, rather than on what people want themselves. Again, if both market *and* democratic-political signals are lacking, the bureaucrats may be compelled to impose implicit rationing systems, for example long queues, irritable reactions to clients' requests or even subtle forms of bribery.

The bureaucratic self-interest models have some negative value. They help to dispel any idea of government as a smooth, disembodied machine, devoid of private motives and pressures. They accord with some of the findings of political scientists on the internal allocative behaviour of public bureaucracies.[8] They bring to light, often mercilessly, certain side-effects, and even perversities, of bureaucratic systems for allocating resources, whether in local government, other public agencies or voluntary organisations. They usefully highlight the important question of whether bureaucracies are the servants or masters of democratically elected bodies. But the bureaucratic self-interest theory also has limitations. Like the other self-interest/exchange theories it neglects the political importance of two key phenomena, coercion and altruism. And it misses out virtually completely on a critically important aspect of public affairs, that of attempted or real redistributions of resources between social groups.

REDISTRIBUTION AND GRANTS: COERCION OR ALTRUISM

The reader will recall the Middletown Council's desire to improve services for the elderly and handicapped and also to create a new park in an overpopulated area. Such pledges are the stuff of politics and in this case the victorious party had swept to power partly on the strength of them. Economically speaking, the pledges implied a redistribution of resources to these two things from other actual or potential council services. Whether or not such an actual redistribution was made explicit in the elections, it was certainly implicit. Once it became clear to the politicians that neither more services for the elderly nor the new park could be financed by cuts in administration, the redistributive element became more marked. If the

c

pledges were to be honoured, there would have to be cuts in some existing social services, delays in other future projects, increases in local taxation or some combination of these measures. Whatever the method, there would be a redistribution towards the elderly, the handicapped and the area without parks – probably, in effect, from younger and able-bodied citizens, from the people already enjoying green spaces and from the general run of better-off ratepayers.

The important point is that insofar as the Middletown Council went ahead with the pledges, it was performing its role as part of the welfare state public grants economy – that of taking resources from people who are considered to be 'fortunate' in some way in order to steer these resources towards the 'less fortunate'. It is a major weakness of the quasi-market and exchange theories of government that they do not come to grips with this massive phenomenon of real or attempted public redistribution. The attempt of public authorities like those in Middletown to obtain 'fairer' distributions is inadequately explained. Nor are any predictions made as to the likely direction, overall, of such redistributive efforts.

Several economic theories now try to rectify this omission. One influential view attributes public redistributive efforts to a combination of the self-interested motives of both politicians and voters, the mechanics of majority voting and the possibility of coercion. According to this view, in order to get elected, politicians have to appeal to some majority or other by offering them benefits at the expense of a minority. This seems plausible enough but the problem is to predict which income groups are likely to be the gainers and losers. One version of the theory maintains that the majority likely to be benefited is the 50 plus n per cent of the *lowest* income groups. It is admitted that in practice redistribution from the richer minority to this poorer majority may well be slow. For example, there may be ignorance about who are in fact the poorest people – some distress has a habit of being hidden away in forgotten basements – and moreover the rich may use their position to obstruct the process. Nonetheless the key prediction here is that in a democracy there will be constant, self-interested pressures to redistribute resources coercively, through taxation and grants, from rich to poor. Another version, on the other hand, makes less egalitarian predictions, denying that it is the poorest who will benefit. Instead, it posits a coalition of the *middle* income groups effectively creating a majority at the expense of both the very rich and the very poor. Proponents of both versions have cited some of the evidence on actual redistribution to support their views. Unfortunately, this evidence is too limited and conflicting for any firm conclusions to be drawn either way.

But the self-interest plus coercion theories of redistribution do not hold undisputed sway among economists. There is another interpretation which seeks to relate public redistribution to strikingly different motives, those of altruism and generosity. The role of altruism and solidarity in allocation systems has been discussed by economists more frequently than is commonly thought.[9] First, the major premise is that individuals often (mostly) derive some utility from increases in other people's resources insofar as they clearly perceive the latter as poorer than they themselves are. It is then suggested that this is a possible explanation of the redistributive intentions and achievements of modern governments. Whereas the coercion theory suggests that in a democracy voting coalitions compel transfers to themselves from the rest of society, according to the altruism theory the process of redistribution is more benign. Not only is redistribution more likely to help the poorest, assuming their poverty is clearly perceived (a hypothesis shared with one version of the coercion theory, as we have seen), but also, more strikingly perhaps, such redistribution is viewed as something which the better-off are generous enough to vote willingly for.

To return to Middletown, the altruism theory may accord with experience to some degree. Perhaps a fair proportion of younger and able-bodied voters – including those with no elderly relatives in the area – were genuinely attracted by the pledge to help the old and the handicapped. Perhaps, too, some of the people enjoying green spaces were prepared to support a new park for those with none. Of course, if faced with an actual direct choice between such altruism and their own interests, these relatively public-spirited voters might tend to prefer their own interests. However, by then the decision would probably not be theirs but that of elected representatives partly returned on these pledges. Whether politicians elected on such pledges have more benevolent utility functions than their electors – and how far they dislike promise-breaking – is debatable. A possible strength of the altruism theory is that at the margin relatively altruistic voters and/or politicians may sometimes have more power than their actual numbers may suggest. But of course this point may also apply to a self-interested minority holding the effective balance of power.

In its sweeping form, and applied to governmental redistribution, the altruism theory seems contestable. It appears, alas, too good to be true. For example, the theory is hard to square with data on the tax-avoiding proclivities of the better-off or the highly unequal wealth distributions of societies where the poor lack votes. Under present conditions the coercion theory – which sees any public re-

distribution towards the poor mainly as a tribute exacted from
generally reluctant taxpayers – may be somewhat more realistic.

Is the altruism theory stronger in the field of *voluntary* giving?
Quantitatively speaking, voluntary gifts are not insubstantial. In the
United States, for example, private philanthropic grants of money
– mainly gifts by individual citizens and organisations to charity,
social welfare, churches, education and the arts – have been
estimated to represent between 2 per cent and 3 per cent of GNP
(this of course excludes the far larger field of intra-family giving).
Although reliable estimates are lacking, labour grants, namely implicit or explicit gifts of time through voluntary service, appear to
be important, perhaps more so in some ways than money grants.
A wide range of voluntary organisations depend wholly or partly
on grants. In Britain, voluntary gifts of money, labour and other
resources (and in many cases also grants from the public sector)
help to sustain organisations as diverse as churches, arts enterprises,
amenity societies, Dr Barnardo's and Oxfam, hospitals and schools,
housing associations, neighbourhood groups and the National Trust.
This allocative system is often discussed under the heading of the
'economics of philanthropy'. Among the issues already raised are
the amount of voluntary giving, whether money gifts tend to be
income elastic, how redistributive philanthropic gifts are, particularly towards the poorest, and how cost effective in terms of the
objectives of donors and charitable organisations. Once again, too,
economists have raised the question of whether voluntary gifts
are best explained and predicted under the heading of exchange,
coercion or benevolence.

Kenneth Boulding has suggested that voluntary gifts are an
integrating force in the building up of organisations. Although
admitting that such gifts may often reflect elements of exchange,
perhaps even of coercion, Boulding hypothesises that 'one of the
most important aspects of the grants economy is the role it plays
in the building up of integrative structures and communities – that
is, groups of people who have some feelings of identification and
benevolence toward each other'.[10] Boulding distinguishes three main
types of situation that serve this role. First, simple one-way transfers
of resources where positive feelings arise between giver and
recipient. Second, simple reciprocity involving a two-way transfer
between persons, simultaneously or separated by intervals of time.
(Such reciprocal giving is often non-contractual and unconditional,
in Boulding's view, and therefore to be distinguished from exchange,
although in practice the lines may be blurred.) Third, 'serial
reciprocity', where a gift from A to B creates a general sense of

obligation on the part of B, who may then give something to C, and so on. Such serial reciprocity may be infectious, with ripple effects involving more and more people and justifying the term 'reciprocity multiplier'. Obviously, the gifts may take the form of money, physical objects or time.

Although conceding that gifts can involve condescension, 'pathologies' and 'dependence traps', Boulding hypothesises that their solidarity-reflecting and creating properties are probably dominant. He also suggests that as compared with the narrow, self-interested and usually two-party relationships of exchange – and the vertical, hierarchical and authoritarian relationships of command – gift relationships are more likely to be multi-party, horizontal and associative.

Boulding's integrative theory of voluntary gifts has interesting ramifications well beyond the field of charities and voluntary organisations. Observation suggests that integrative giving reflects through into almost all types of organisation, if only subtly and dilutedly. For example, an organisation makes gifts to its employees, partly in order to boost corporate morale. Employees make gifts of extra work beyond normal lines of duty or working hours. In a more implicit but real sense, people make gifts to an organisation they work for when they accept less than normal market rewards. In many situations workers are willing and able to give time and effort towards voluntarily helping each other on the job. All these types of gifts may reflect elements of background coercion or disguised exchange. But, by and large, they seem more likely to spring from affection, loyalty, generosity, friendship and gregariousness. Insofar as they do, such gifts probably contribute towards the bonds which are required for an organisation to function efficiently, to avoid disputes, to cope with crises or even to exist at all.

CONCLUSIONS

In this chapter we have outlined a conceptual framework for understanding micro-allocation systems derived from the ideas of Kenneth Boulding. This framework emphasises the comprehensive sweep of modern micro-economics. Contrary to the impression often conveyed by elementary textbooks, economists are not only concerned with the organising principle of exchange and its embodiment in markets. Important as both exchange and markets are, the parallel importance of coercion and integration as methods of allocating resources must be fully reckoned with. So must the vast resource dispositions which occur, whether in traditional or developed societies, through grants and by means of the choice mechanisms of bureaucracy and politics. The pre-classical economists regarded these bureaucratic, political and redistributive systems as well within the purview of economics. Over recent years, recognising their great importance, economists have increasingly worked on them. Since this has not yet percolated through to popular consciousness, even among many who have studied basic economics, the practical concern of economics with all types of scarce resource allocation has still to be stressed. The conceptual scheme derived from Kenneth Boulding's triad of social organisers is suggested as a useful device for this purpose.

Next, the common threads running through all types of allocation systems have been emphasised. It has been argued that the organising principles of exchange, coercion and solidarity are ubiquitous. Each of these percolates through, often in implicit, marginal or even disguised forms, to businesses and markets, public institutions and voluntary organisations. Exchange does not have to be monetary, market-mediated or even explicit but may be evident, for example, in horse-trading between officials or deals between pressure groups and politicians. Coercion need not be barked out in some powerful boss's resource directives to his subordinates but may occur in markets featuring grossly unequal power, in predatory actions by business or labour monopolies or in intrusive advertising. Indeed, coercion occurs in precautionary giving, where grants are handed over to people to prevent them from resorting to revolution, violence or theft. As for solidarity, in a sense this underpins all allocative systems without exception and many in quite dominant ways, as suggested. It has been shown that, far from rigidly dividing allocation systems into separate and autonomous boxes, many modern economic theories pursue a free trade policy of liberally transferring interpretations from one economic sphere to another, for example using political categories to interpret markets and vice versa. The reader can elaborate easily enough for himself on these varying patterns of exchange, coercion and integration. It is important to realise how a lively sense of their interactions can enrich our understanding of micro-allocation systems.

We have glanced briefly at some of the more ambitious ideas of contemporary economists on these systems. Such ideas take the form of hypotheses, theories or models with the object of portraying underlying forces, sketching synoptic pictures and making predictions. The Galbraithian perspective on big business power; the more traditional view of competition and market constraints; the exchange interpretations of politics; the theories relating public redistribution to either coercion or generosity; the Boulding hypothesis on integrative gifts – all of these represent highly simplified abstractions. Such theories deliberately throw away close fidelity to detail in order to predict, hypothesise or at least stimulate. In the same manner as the theory of perfect competition in its day, they act as a cutting edge against which a complex reality can be tested. As with any theories in the social sciences, they tend to be highly tentative and they cry out for further debate, checking and verification. Meantime, of course, they often conflict and perhaps this is all to the good. Space has forbidden more than the briefest mention of these theories. To do justice to them the reader is particularly recommended to the texts listed at the end of this chapter. He may also find it fruitful to try to apply some of them to organisational situations with which he is familiar.

In this chapter we have stressed what is often called positive economics, that is the attempt to describe and predict what actually happens to scarce resources and why. But micro-allocation systems cannot be divorced from the human purposes they serve. A decision-making unit not only uses a mixture of allocative principles and systems, it also has some choice, more or less constrained, on what mixture would be best for its purposes. A business, a local authority or a voluntary agency must decide, as a matter of deliberate policy, what overall mixture of exchange, coercion and integration is feasible and desirable for itself. This problem comes to a head in the choice of a planning and budgeting system. It relates to critical issues of organisational size, control, efficiency, centralisation and decentralisation. We shall return to the choice of allocation systems within business and social organisations in later chapters – and to the overall social choice of systems right at the end.

Our final point leads us to the immediately ensuing chapters. Whatever allocation system is used, an organisation's actual decision making can be more or less efficient. Whatever the mixture of coercion, exchange and solidarity, whether the institutions are those of markets or grants, bureaucracy or electoral choice, whether the resource allocator is a business, a public institution or a voluntary enterprise or a sub-unit of any of these, the detailed process of decision making can be more or less rational, logical and consistent. One role of micro-economics is to study the systems within which such decisions take place, as we have seen. But another is to propose concepts in the light of which the decisions can be taken more efficiently. It is to this question that we now turn.

Note on Further Reading

This chapter has covered a lot of important ground very rapidly. It has also mentioned significant theories without referring to their main expositors. The following list has therefore been compiled to help the reader and includes most of the classic expositions. Many of these are indispensable to any serious student of modern economics.

Power in business and markets
   K. W. Rothschild (ed.), *Power in Economics*, Penguin Modern Economics Readings, Harmondsworth, Penguin, 1971. Includes essays by, for example, H. Albert, J. Pen, M. D. Reagan, J. K. Galbraith and A. Hunter.
   Allan G. Gruchy, *Contemporary Economic Thought: The Contribution of Neo-Institutionalist Economics*, London, Macmillan, 1973. A useful introduction to the relevant thinking of, in particular, Veblen, Schumpeter, J. M. Clark and Gardiner Means.
   Joseph Schumpeter, *Capitalism, Socialism and Democracy*, 3rd edition, London, Allen & Unwin, 1961. Still a classic and full of penetrating and provocative insights on market power.
   J. M. Clark, *Competition as a Dynamic Process*, Washington, Brookings Institution, 1961. The classic exposition and defence of the theory of 'workable competition'. A 'middle of the road' view.
   F. M. Scherer, *Industrial Structure and Market Performance*, Chicago, Rand McNally, 1970. Usefully summarises empirical work bearing on the degrees, forms and uses of market power.
   Paul A. Baran and Paul M. Sweezy, *Monopoly Capital: An essay on the American Economic and Social Order*, Harmondsworth, Penguin, 1968. A Marxian interpretation.
   John Kenneth Galbraith, *The New Industrial State*, London, Hamish Hamilton, 1967.
   John Kenneth Galbraith, *The Affluent Society*, 2nd edition, London, Hamish Hamilton, 1969.
   G. C. Allen, *Economic Fact and Fantasy: A Rejoinder to Galbraith's Reith lectures*, Institute of Economic Affairs, 1969. A stimulating defence of competition against Galbraith's strictures.

Exchange and self-interest in politics
   James M. Buchanan and Gordon Tullock, *The Calculus of Consent: Logical Foundations of Constitutional Democracy*, Ann Arbor, University of Michigan Press, 1962. The major statement of this theory.
   K. J. Arrow, *Social Choice and Individual Values*, 2nd edition, New York, Wiley, 1963. A classic abstract work on the theory of social choice.
   Anthony Downs, *Inside Bureaucracy*, Boston, Little, Brown, 1967. The bureaucratic self-interest theory stimulatingly applied to the allocative behaviour and development of public organisations.
   W. A. Niskanen, *Bureaucracy and Representative Government*, Chicago, Aldine-Atherton, 1971. An economic theory of the behaviour of bureaux particularly in relation to representative political institutions.

Redistribution and grants: coercion or altruism?
   A. J. Culyer, *The Economics of Social Policy*, London, Martin Robertson,

1973. Contains a useful summary of modern positive theories of redistribution (Chapter 4).

H. M. Hochman and G. E. Peterson (eds), *Redistribution through Public Choice*, Columbia University Press, 1974. Contains some useful essays.

Anthony Downs, *An Economic Theory of Democracy*, New York, Harper & Row, 1957. The self-interest plus coercion theory of redistribution.

Kenneth E. Boulding, *The Economy of Love and Fear: A Preface to Grants Economics*, Belmont, California, Wadsworth Publishing Co Inc., 1973. Includes a statement of the altruism theory of redistribution and many stimulating ideas on the grants economy more generally.

F. G. Dickinson (ed.), *Philanthropy and Public Policy*, New York, National Bureau of Economic Research, 1962. Useful essays on the economics of the voluntary sector, particularly by Vickrey and Boulding.

Raymond Firth (ed.), *Themes in Economic Anthropology*, London, Tavistock Publications, 1967. See Chapter 1 where Firth discusses 'the economics of the gift' in relation to traditional societies.

Institute of Economic Affairs, *The Economics of Charity*, IEA Readings 12, London, IEA, 1973. These more theoretical essays apply neo-classical thinking to the subject.

R. H. Tawney, *The Acquisitive Society*, London, Victor Gollancz, 1937. A classic exposition of public service and co-operative themes.

General

Kenneth E. Boulding, *Economics as a Science*, New York, McGraw-Hill, 1970. Stimulatingly illustrates the sweep and widely varying uses of modern economics.

Chapter 3

Economics and Decision Making

The economic approach to decision making revolves around four basic axioms which are to a large extent interdependent. First, decision making is rational. Second, decision makers have explicit goals. Third, decision making involves careful evaluation of all relevant costs and benefits. And fourth, in trying to attain their goals, decision makers seek to optimise. It must straightaway be made clear that economists do not regard these axioms as describing what always happens in fact. That the canons of rationality, goal stipulation, cost benefit evaluation and optimisation are sometimes, perhaps often, departed from in the real world of affairs is admitted. There is, too, a constant problem of reconciling the necessary speed of decision making with the desirability of measured data and deliberation. Economists believe, however, that these approaches to decision making are feasible, that they are pursued at least to an extent which makes possible certain predictions about organisational behaviour, and, most important for our purposes, that the active pursuit of these approaches can help organisations to be more efficient.

RATIONALITY

Of the four axioms, that of rationality has the most philosophical difficulties, although these cannot detain us here. Suffice it to say that economics has a gut interest in the idea of human beings as capable, within various limits, of exercising choices which are cognisant, deliberative and effective. Without such assumptions as to human abilities to reason and to exercise control over affairs, not only economics but also the sciences more generally, and indeed ethics itself, would fall to the ground. Determinism and economics must necessarily be radically opposed. The rationality axiom of economics admits constraints, but insists on the possibility of choice; it is, indeed, an axiom of constrained or bounded choice. It assumes that organisational decision makers are human beings who can know, assess probabilities, reason, control and learn. They are not puppets, lunatics or solipsists.

In some earlier economic theories the conditions of knowledge and rationality appeared to be extravagantly overstated. For example, the businessman was pictured as confronting so clear a perspective of supply and demand, of both costs and revenues, that in conditions of competition he could equate marginal costs and revenues in such a way as to maximise his profits, in the process contributing to an ideal equilibrium of affairs (see Chapter 4). Sometimes this super-knowledge was ascribed to public decision makers, too. In some welfare economics theories, public decision makers were assumed to be so potentially cognisant of the preferences of all members of society that they could contemplate precisely optimal policies which might benefit some or all citizens and, what is more, upset none. Although such theories may still serve wider purposes, clearly they are light years removed from the direct experiences of decision makers. Particularly since the 1920s, however, with the writings of Knight, Shackle, Keynes and many others, economists have not just recognised but extensively discussed the phenomena of risk, probability and uncertainty. The economic theory of decision making now encompasses the all-too-obvious fact that there are many, many things that businessmen, bureaucrats or politicians do not and cannot know. Even the past and present they can 'know' only partially. As for the future, the bright light of pure certainty is rare, perhaps almost to vanishing point. Instead, the decision maker is faced with a spectrum of atmospherics, ranging from light mists to almost pitch darkness. Costs, prices, business and market conditions, the political and economic environment, strikes, windfalls, natural disasters – on all of these there may be probabilities in varying degrees and possibilities more or less foreseeable, but no more.

However, any notion that decision making rationality is destroyed by such risks and uncertainties must be vehemently denied. On the contrary, the economic theory of decision making asserts that the treatment of risk and uncertainty itself can, and should, be rational. Decision makers can make proper use, so it is claimed, of probabilities ascertained from the past. Even in relation to mere possibilities they can order and clarify their own thinking in many fruitful ways (see Chapter 6).

STIPULATION OF GOALS

The second basic axiom of the economic theory of decision making is that decision makers possess consciously formulated and explicit goals which they pursue in their decision making and use as yardsticks of its effectiveness. Economics does not try to explain why decision makers have particular sorts of goals (part of the province of sociology and psychology), still less does it define which goals are morally 'best' (the realm of ethics). What economics does is to assume that such goals exist in specifiable form and that they influence allocative choices in ways that enable predictions to be made. Thus if an economist assumes that A-type organisations have B-type goals, he may predict C-type consequences for the allocation of resources. For example, that familiar prediction, the lower the market price of something, generally speaking the higher the demand for it, depends on the assumption that decision makers, in this case buyers in markets, have the 'self-interested' goal of preferring terms more advantageous to themselves or, in other words, that they tend to prefer to buy more at lower prices than at higher. Since economists have found that this particular generalisation about buyers' goals helps to predict the actual behaviour of markets, they have naturally grown rather attached to it. But it is at this point that some serious misunderstandings about the economic theory of decision making start to arise. For the overall goals of organisations, as distinct from, say, those of buyers in markets, are highly complex. Indeed, the dominant objectives of organisations are often unclear, diverse and conflicting. If economists are to make predictions about organisational behaviour, they have to make assumptions about organisational goals, frequently on the basis of slim evidence. What goals, then, do economists assume businesses, nationalised industries, local authorities or voluntary organisations to have?

Historically, one theme has hogged the economic limelight, at least since the eighteenth century, that of individual self-interest related to material gain. The classical and neo-classical economists of the nineteenth and early twentieth centuries concentrated on the behaviour of markets. In markets, so they assumed, the dominant goal of decision makers was material self-interest, namely, to 'buy cheap and sell dear'. For businesses this translated into an assumed desire for maximum profit. The profit-maximising goal of businesses was an assumption to which virtually all the well-known economists broadly subscribed, whether in tones of neutrality, approval or dislike, from Adam Smith, Ricardo and Marx to Marshall and Keynes.

But many economists went still further. They sought to apply the underlying theme of material self-interest to public sector decisions too. As part of what became known as 'welfare economics', a related goal was posited for the public authorities, that of seeking to maximise the aggregated self-interests of large numbers of individual citizens. True, the basic contention here was normative rather than positive. Whereas the goals of business and individual self-interest were held largely to explain market behaviour as a fact, the notion of public authorities as agents of citizens' individual gains was presented as more of an ideal. But, in one way or another, individual self-interest, largely or exclusively in the pursuit of material resources, continued to be the decision making goal for organisations (as well as individuals) which economists postulated most often in their efforts to explain and predict.

Nor is it difficult to see why. For one thing most economists continued to concentrate on markets and there, at least, the assumptions of self-interested and maximum profit-seeking goals appeared to have a reasonable track record in helping to explain and predict events. In a wider sense these hypotheses also had much plausibility. A minimum of material resources has long been a necessary precondition for higher pursuits, indeed for human existence. Introspection and observation alike suggest that the motives of individual or family self-interest are, to say the least, strong. It must be faced, too, that many economists soon developed strong vested interests in the profit maximising idea – as a basis for theories of perfect competition or, sometimes, as a stick with which to attack the capitalist system. Whatever the reasons, the results were clear. The economic theory of decision making came to be associated in many people's minds with one particular set of goals. For example, it was widely thought that something called the 'economic theory of the firm' assumed that businesses always sought maximum profit above all else. It was widely imagined that economics was only interested in such public decision making goals as conduced towards the material wealth of individual citizens, or that economic theories of voluntary and social organisations related solely to self-interested or material interpretations of these organisations' goals.

This view is now a caricature. As indicated in Chapter 2, economists have considerably enlarged the repertoire of organisational goals which they need to stipulate for their work. Thus, in relation to businesses, economists now predicate many other goals besides short-term, or even long-term, profit maximisation – notably growth, managerial rewards and power, stable profits, continued control by existing owners and retention or increase in market share.[1] For example, Baumol has argued that firms seek to maximise not their profits but rather their sales (total revenue), subject to profits being at least adequate to secure further capital from the market. Baumol's model of sales maximisation subject to a profit constraint has been very influential. Other economists have produced models on the assumption that the top executives of companies will try to maximise their own interests. Williamson has suggested that, subject to profits being adequate to satisfy shareholders, top managers will seek in varying mixtures to increase the staff under their control (empire building), their self-determined emoluments (both cash and fringe benefits) and also 'discretionary profits' (the element of profits they can control). Marris has usefully synthesised many of the quantitative models which make widely varying assumptions about managerial motives and utility functions. Marris himself has argued persuasively in favour of pluralist approaches but with a strong emphasis on the apparent importance and predictive utility of objectives related to corporate growth and managerial power. All of which simply amounts to saying that there is certainly no single accepted 'economic theory of the firm' based on profit maximising assumptions or indeed anything else. Moreover, this pluralism is even greater when it comes to public authority decision making. The widely varying assumptions made by contemporary economists about the objectives of citizens, politicians and public officials – in terms of material self-interest, power and vote getting, empire building, distributive justice, help for the less privileged and social altruism – were mentioned in Chapter 2.

Two further points need to be made about goals. First, there is the patent fact that organisations have multiple goals. Economists tend to cope with this problem in several ways. For example, in quantitative models one of an organisation's goals is regarded as dominant, with the others introduced as constraints. But in a more fundamental sense economic analysis is often precisely about the degree of consistency or 'trade-off' which may exist between different and often widely contrasted organisational goals. Second, the economic theory of decision making is not restricted to the dizzy heights of strategy and of dominant or overriding goals. It is also concerned with the microscopic logic of small decisions. The problem may be something as down-to-earth as appointing a foreman, scheduling meals on wheels for old people or deciding on suppliers of envelopes. Provided the decision means that scarce resources will move one way rather than another, however infinitesimally, the theory applies. But with many decisions the initial difficulty is one of correctly defining the problem. It is only when the problem has been clearly defined that an appropriate goal can be identified. That is why, in so many books on management loosely adhering to the economic approach, the first stage in decision making is specified as 'problem formulation'. This emphasis is perfectly correct.

EVALUATION OF COSTS AND BENEFITS

The third axiom of the economic theory of decision making, that the decision maker seeks to evaluate all relevant costs and benefits, poses great difficulties, both intellectual and practical. For what is the meaning of these slippery words 'cost' and 'benefit'? What costs and benefits are 'relevant'? Just those that can be quantified, or others as well? Just the costs and benefits affecting the organisation, or those affecting other people too? How do we actually perform the 'careful evaluations', particularly where the items we are concerned with appear to be measurable in principle but hardly in practice, measurable but not commensurable, or not even measurable at all?

Let us start with the definition of 'costs' and 'benefits'. These are relative terms, dependent on people's behaviour and opinions. The fundamental point is that, faced with scarce resources in relation to our complex and often conflicting objectives, we are constantly having to make choices between one object or activity and another. Such choices are usually implicit. They are not necessarily deliberate or even conscious. What is important is that as a result of myriads of such choices certain things begin to emerge as fairly consistently more highly valued than others. Generally or widely accepted rankings appear. People's preferences become ascertainable, not in terms of theories, dreams or pretences but in terms of their actual choices at the margin of decision making where one thing has to be sacrificed to another. People's preferences emerge, first and foremost, in their ordinary social behaviour, for example in allocations of time between various pursuits. But there are other arenas in which their preferences are indicated, if only imperfectly. One such arena is markets. Another is voting patterns at elections. Another is opinion surveys. Yet another is the decisions which people entrust to elected representatives or others who are felt to be specially qualified. In some of these arenas money is available as a proxy indicator of people's preferences, in others not. Note, too, that there is no implication that the valuations are necessarily morally correct, a problem for ethics or political theory rather than economics. What economics insists on is that people's practical valuations or preferences should be made explicit, clarified, tested and, so far as is possible, measured.

Against this background it becomes easier to define costs and benefits. *Benefits* are things practically valued as 'good' by citizens, consumers, electors or legitimate authorities. Clearly, there may be conflicts about what is or is not a benefit in particular cases which economics can no more resolve than any other social science, although it can certainly clarify how far the conflict is apparent or real. *Costs* are things which the same constituencies regard as 'bad' or view as requiring recompense. Here, too, the same potential conflicts may occur. But costs can be (*a*) the benefits lost as a result of doing one thing rather than another, (*b*) the resources used up as a result of particular decisions (for example, raw materials or people's time spent on making things) or (*c*) other burdens or penalties inflicted on people (for example, noise, unhappiness). Such distinctions are far from academic. (*a*) are opportunity costs, of which more in Chapter 5, (*b*) and (*c*) are actual or historical costs. Both costs and benefits can be classified according to whether they are internal or external. *Internal costs and benefits* directly affect the organisation and those with whom it has transactions while *external costs and benefits* affect other people or interests. *Social costs and benefits* embrace the 'bads' and 'goods' affecting everybody concerned, including, incidentally, future generations, and so they cover both the internal and external items. And all of these types of costs and benefits may be further subdivided. For example, they may or may not be financial in the sense of commanding money prices and they may also be tangible or intangible, quantifiable or unquantifiable. Although the reader should not worry too much about these definitions at this stage, he may find it helpful to ask himself a few questions. For example, what would be an instance of, say, an historical, internal, non-financial cost, or of an external, tangible, quantifiable benefit?

The economic theory of decision making now ventures upon its most critical and hazardous step, that of asserting that all relevant costs and benefits should be carefully evaluated. What does this apparently sweeping assertion mean for organisations? For costs and benefits which are internal and also financial, careful evaluation means, above all, forecasting. Organisations frequently make assumptions about market, economic and political conditions affecting their future cash flows. These assumptions need to be made explicit, debated and, more often than not, tested by research. Once obtained, the future cash flow estimates, whether these relate to sales, local tax proceeds, government subsidies or grants, may need to be adjusted to allow for time and risk (see Chapter 6). But organisations also spend money on items like research and development, training, employee welfare and advertising and public relations. Depending on the sector, they hope such outlays will produce successful innovations, higher skills, better employee morale, fewer strikes, higher sales or contributions, an improved public image or more votes. Financial and non-financial returns of this kind tend to be long-term, subtle and hard to pin down. Nonetheless the economic theory of decision making assumes that these items, too, should be subjected to forecasting and analysis. Sometimes statistical analysis of past relationships, for example on the behaviour of employees, buyers or voters, may be appropriate; sometimes direct surveys of these groups. Frequently all that can be done is to consult the best available expert opinions inside or outside the organisation. Whatever the technique, so the theory claims, subjective judgement should be reinforced or tested by research, reason and debate.

But the economic theory of decision making does not end there. It asserts that the same processes of testing, reasoning and explicit valuation should extend to the social costs and benefits affecting wider communities. If anything, many economists nowadays assert this more formidable social task with greater zeal. It is, of course, primarily a task for public and social organisations. For if decision makers have the obligation and objective of serving wider social interests, it is arguably all the more important that they should trace out the likely human consequences of these decisions and, secondly, consult the attitudes and preferences of the communities involved. The latter means looking at the explicit and implicit choices which people make in all sorts of situations, whether in their reactions to price changes, in their day-to-day social behaviour, in their voting decisions at elections or directly through special opinion surveys. Here the object is to get behind organisational decision makers' opinions in search of what the people themselves would choose. Economics suggests the problems and priorities that lie along this difficult path of consulting people's valuations. It concentrates on methods for so doing, notably in relation to cost–benefit analysis (see Chapter 11).

OPTIMISING

We now come to the final decisional theme, that of optimising. Having formulated the problem and stipulated the goals, having also identified the alternatives and estimated or shadow-priced the relevant costs and benefits, the decision maker now has to choose. To state a decision rule of universal and almost pious correctness is easy: the decision maker should choose that course of action which optimises. For organisations such an optimal alternative will be one that (*a*) minimises costs for a given set of benefits, (*b*) maximises benefits for a given set of costs or (*c*) maximises the ratio of benefits to costs. For society the same formula applies except that all social costs and benefits, whether internal or external to particular interests, would be included. The problem, however, is how to make such general formulas operational, given that varying degrees and types of quantifiability apply and also that some important costs and benefits may be intangible and only quantifiable imprecisely or not at all.

From the viewpoint of quantitative optimising, organisational decisions tend to fall into four main zones, as follows.

In zone 1 pure quantitative analysis can be very useful and even decisive. Here the problem is determinate, being specifiable in purely quantitative and commensurable terms. Technically speaking, there is an objective function or variable that the decision maker wishes to maximise or minimise, say net income or sales as the maximand, internal financial costs as the minimand. There are also constraints or limitations in the situation, for example in the supply of labour, machines, funds or raw materials, and these, too, can be expressed quantitatively. Where multiple goals exist, some can be reduced to constraints, leaving just one goal as the objective function. Finally, non-quantifiable elements in the situation are likely to be peripheral. This is the zone in which precise mathematical solutions – or at least ranges of possible solutions – are possible. The mathematics involved ranges from simple arithmetic to mathematical programming of varying degrees of sophistication. Typical examples of the sort of decisions which fall within this category are 'cheapest buy' problems, stock control, use of transport and delivery fleets, production scheduling and replacement of machinery.

In zone 2 of decision making pure quantitative analysis can be useful, subject to reservations. Here the various elements of the problem are still both quantifiable and commensurable but are non-determinate and subject to change and uncertainty. Although such situations can be illustrated or modelled mathematically, the real-world assumptions behind the models are fragile and vulnerable to risk. Often, too, important unquantifiable aspects arise. Quantification is both feasible and desirable, but in such a manner as to clarify and illustrate rather than actually 'solve' a problem as in zone 1. The methods used may include mathematical models as in zone 1, statistics, ranging from simple extrapolation and curve-fitting to multiple regression, techniques related to input–output analysis, and discounted cash flows. Typical decisions in this zone involve forecasts of future financial flows, for example of costs, sales or profits, rate income, government grants or charitable contributions, estimates of demand and supply in markets.

In zone 3 quantitative analysis of a mixed character can be useful alongside other approaches. Precise solutions may still apply to sub-elements of the problem as in zone 1 above, so may models as in zone 2. But important factors affecting the decision are incommensurable (for example, the quantities may be financial, physical and human). Some quantification may be ordinal rather than cardinal, as with simple ranking systems. There may be important disagreements or uncertainties over moral values so that even where quantities can be assigned – for example on the distributional impacts of different social policies – weightings cannot be applied except by political fiat. Finally, as in zone 2, important unquantifiable elements arise. The methods used on zone 3 problems include social indicators, distributional impact statements and shadow-pricing, related either to past behaviour (markets, elections, work choices, time allocations etc.) or current attitudes (tested through opinion surveys). The decisions might relate to expenditures on advertising, public relations or staff training, issues of manpower planning, wages and collective bargaining, expenditure priorities of voluntary and charitable enterprises, and of public authorities, particularly in such areas as health, education, housing and social services.

Finally, in zone 4 quantitative analysis of any kind is peripheral. Typical examples would be ad hoc, 'one-off' decisions authorising small expenditures and also, very important, the hiring, firing or promotion of individual staff. Even here, though, the frequent importance of past quantitative analysis in the decision maker's mind should not be forgotten.

A major issue is to identify how far quantifiable analysis is able to go. The neo-classical theory of the firm envisaged a simplified and knowable world in which single-minded and clear-eyed decision makers would respond in Pavlovian fashion to external stimuli, as superior fact-collectors and calculators. In business the calculus would be one of profit maximising, in the public sector it would take the form of collapsing the measurable utilities of millions of citizens into a gigantic, quantified 'social welfare function'. Such ideas of super-knowingness in a brightly lit, predictable world have played a considerable part in the development of economics in general and the economic theory of decision making in particular. They have fuelled the quantitative optimising idea which lies behind a significant development in modern management: the application of mathematics to decision making through the techniques of operational research. However, modern economics has become much more aware of the diversities, uncertainties and perversities of the decision making world. The predictive or explanatory power of an abstract economic hypothesis or theory, which could still be great, is distinguished from its immediate utility at micro-levels, which may be small. Risk and uncertainty, ignored by earlier theories, are increasingly discussed. Thus, to revert to the four zones of decision making mentioned above, economists connected with the world of affairs are unlikely to see business planning and investment decisions as lying within the tidy area of determinate solutions (zone 1) and even less likely to see social expenditure decisions involving cost–benefit analysis as falling within zone 1 or even zone 2.

Unfortunately, however, some of the older misconceptions persist. Students whose economic diet has been dominated by the earlier models of neo-classical micro-economics, perhaps with little time or taste for anything else, still yearn for a tidy, elegant world in which problems of the zone 1 type predominate. Non-economist practical men still identify economics with half-understood and hazy notions of 'economic laws' and geometric curves and then regard it, quite plausibly, as largely irrelevant to them. Those whose acquaintance with modern economics is restricted identify the economic theory of decision making with either (a) the extravagant claim that all decisions can, or should, lie within zone 1, or (b) the narrow view that only decisions of the zone 1 type are really of economic concern. The former idea ascribes to economics a sort of quantitative imperialism, the second would deny its basic rationale and, for practical purposes, consign it to a strait jacket. But neither idea is correct. The economic theory does not imply that quantification can extend everywhere in identical form, still less that it can swamp the decision making process. The notion that economic reasoning stops short somewhere in the spectrum is even more grotesque. On the contrary, the ideas of rationality, goal formulation, cost–benefit evaluation and optimising are applicable to all forms of decision making without exception, although in widely varying forms.

THE INCREMENTALIST ATTACK AND MANAGERIAL REALITIES

The economic theory of decision making has undergone some mis-conceived attacks. But there is one line of real or implied criticism of it that must be taken seriously, that of incrementalism. Incre-mentalism derives from various modern administrative theories, although it has venerable antecedents. Although mainly concerned with public administration, incrementalism is regarded as widely relevant. Basically, incrementalism puts together the problems of risk and uncertainty, the practical difficulties of quantification, the plurality and mobility of decision makers' goals, the non-explicitness of much decision making, the realities of human and social conflict, and other factors. Its main hypothesis is that 'administrative policy characteristically involves a continuation of past policies with the least possible, i.e. incremental, modification to suit changing cir-cumstances'. Completely rational decision making is impossible, so decision makers have to 'make do' with decisions that 'get by', the easiest being those that merely follow past precedent.[2] Incre-mentalists maintain that this is what actually happens and that it is likely to persist. Some incrementalists regret this and advocate improvements. Others argue that incrementalism is not only 'more realistic' than the economic approach but also more rational – and even morally or politically preferable.

The phraseology of incrementalism is illuminating: 'satisficing', or the pursuit of minimal or acceptable standards, rather than optimising; 'guiding norms and relationships' rather than 'goals'; 'balancing efforts', the art of 'appreciation', or mixed judgement about facts and values, rather than the weighing up of alternatives; the search for 'better solutions' rather than the best. More provoca-tively, the American economist, Charles Lindblom, has attacked the economic theory of a 'root', 'rational-comprehensive' or synoptic model for decision making. Lindblom has offered some pithy phrases like the 'branch method', 'successive limited comparisons', 'disjointed incrementalism' or 'partisan mutual adjustment' as better descriptions of what administrators actually do. He has also stimulatingly argued that, in typical conditions of irrationality, partial knowledge and social conflict, the rationalistic effort to define overall goals and to get everybody to agree on such goals may even be counter-productive. It may often be better to fudge such issues deliberately and to concentrate on specific, limited policies on which people can more easily agree. In a pluralist society like America, in Lindblom's view, where so many interests enter the bargaining process, such an approach 'could secure a more comprehensive regard for the values of the whole society than any attempt at intellectual comprehensiveness'.[3]

As a description of the facts, incrementalism appears to have some validity. Studies of managerial work suggest that rationalistic approaches of a formal and elaborate kind are often quite impracticable. A recent study has observed that the activities of top decision makers in both business and public administration are fast-paced, highly fragmented and variable in mood, orientated towards crises, articulated through bargaining and verbal rather than written contacts, with a strong preference for informal rather than formal information systems. 'The pressure of the job does not encourage the development of a planner, but of an adaptive information manipulator who works in a stimulus–response environment and who prefers live action.'[4]

On the other hand, the incrementalist interpretation can easily be pushed too far. Although decisions are often taken hurriedly, informally and with apparent irrationality, past experience and rational thinking are frequently implicitly distilled in the decision makers' minds. The study just quoted went on to maintain that decision makers develop mental constructs which are non-verbalised and undocumented but often highly elaborate: both models of systems and plans which are 'loose, flexible and implicit'.[5] What managers say they do in ad hoc decision making does not necessarily fully mirror their own mental processes, either at the time or previously. Nor does it necessarily capture their use of the information gathering and explicit model building of analysts and planners in their organisations. The alleged opposition between incrementalism and the economic theory is sometimes purely semantic. For example, almost any sort of change can be described as 'incremental'. The language of 'pluralistic goals', 'guiding norms', 'marginal improvements' or 'quasi-optimising' may be opposed to the earlier economic models. But as a description of what actually happens it shades almost imperceptibly into the flexible modern approaches of economics as outlined above.

It is over the normative aspects that the real clash occurs. When it comes to helping and improving decision making, incrementalism wears thin. Critics maintain that it is too conservative and complacent a theory to cope with the frequent need for comprehensive analysis, radical breakthroughs and fundamental change. In its desire to improve the world as well as to understand it, economics is dedicated to two fundamental norms: that decision making should aim to be as rational as possible and that the valuations and preferences of all parties are important and should be assessed, again so far as possible. What is 'possible' in particular cases is, of course, always arguable. But constantly to attempt improvement is fundamental. To rest content with present ways of doing things is not good enough. On a deeper level, too, the claim of some incrementalists that ad hoc bargaining is actually a 'better' way of resolving problems in a 'pluralist society' is open to dispute. Stemming from the *realpolitik* tradition of Machiavelli, Hobbes and Metternich, this view tends to rationalise the status quo, to sanctify the present weightings of power. It is possible to argue that it fails to provide explicitly for the interests of the inarticulate and powerless, that it under-emphasises the frequent need for collective interest policies in such matters as defence, pollution, population or incomes, and that it ignores the question of ethical principles, for example over responsibilities to future generations and distributive justice. Such normative inadequacies are grave.

Incrementalism usefully stresses the constraints of time and political pressure in an imperfect, risk-laden and fast-moving world. It is these conditions that form part of the challenge with which the economic approach to decision making is faced. Conflicts between the need for urgency and the desirability of more information are persistent and often acute. For example, information and analysis may be rigorous and comprehensive but over-costly and too late to be useful – or it may be partial and hurried but relevant and timely. In considering the search for more information the costs of delay must always be weighed against the benefits of greater accuracy in decision making. Indeed, the cost–benefit evaluation of extra information itself is a ceaseless and difficult task. But this most emphatically does not mean that basic principles are, let alone should be, lost sight of. On the contrary, so far from being abandoned in the interests of a facile pragmatism, ideals and concepts for improving decision making should be pursued all the more vigorously. It is simply that their practical applications demand flexibility, imagination and skill.

Note on Further Reading

For fuller treatments of the economic approach to decision making in business see: Joel Dean, *Managerial Economics*, Englewood Cliffs, N.J., Prentice-Hall, 1957, and C. I. Savage and J. R. Small, *Introduction to Managerial Economics*, London, Hutchinson, 1967.

There is no precisely comparable text for the public sector but a good extended introduction to the theory of cost–benefit analysis is: E. J. Mishan,

Cost–Benefit Analysis: An Informal Introduction, 2nd edition, London, Allen & Unwin, 1975.

On the role of quantitative analysis see: H. Theil, J. C. G. Boot and T. Kloek, *Operations Research and Quantitative Economics: An Elementary Introduction*, New York, McGraw-Hill, 1965, and W. J. Baumol, *Economic Theory and Operations Analysis*, 2nd edition, Englewood Cliffs, N.J., Prentice-Hall, 1965. A particularly useful introduction will be found in the relevant sections of D. C. Hague, *Managerial Economics*, London, Longmans, 1971.

For a useful survey of the issue of economic and related approaches to decision making versus incrementalism see: The Open University, *Approaches to the Study of Public Administration*, Part 2, 'The administrative process as a decision-making and goal-attaining system' and Part 3, 'The administrative process as incrementalism', Milton Keynes, The Open University Press, 1974.

Chapter 4

Marginalism

Among their many roles organisational decision makers have to act as micro-resource manipulators and tacticians. They try to juggle their activities so as to secure the best mixture in pursuing their objectives. They trim their sails, now one way and now another. They wonder whether to do a bit more here, a bit less there. This detailed balancing of trade-offs – a workaday, housekeeping aspect of management – is a universal and continuous process. Essentially, what the marginal analysis does is to sharpen and improve it. Although the formal theories of marginalism as developed by many economists within the last century have frequently been highly abstract and esoteric, their practical message is valid and clear. Marginalism suggests that the trade-off process is best pursued by means of strictly relevant data, quantification and optimising formulas. In a perfectly rational and predictable world, organisations of every kind would be both willing and able to do these things. In practice, marginalism can be attained only partially. But its firm and clear-eyed pursuit – in more or less modified forms – is essential for rational management.

DEFINITIONS OF FINANCIAL COSTS

First, we need a few conventional definitions of financial costs (with apologies to readers who are already familiar with them). *Direct costs* are costs which can be allocated directly to a particular product or activity, for example the wages of workers involved in it. *Indirect costs* are costs which cannot be so allocated, ranging from the chief executive's salary to electric light and heat in a large plant. Another term for indirect costs is *overheads*. The distinction between direct and indirect costs must not be confused with another distinction, that between fixed and variable costs. *Fixed costs* are costs that do not vary as a result of any decisions being made, *variable costs* are those that do. The decisions in question are usually in connection with levels of output, but they may also be decisions about order-taking, making or buying things, investment or disinvestment. It should be noted, first, that direct costs may sometimes be fixed (for example, an organisation may not want to sack the workers directly involved in something even though production is greatly reduced). Conversely, indirect costs may sometimes be variable (for example, public relations expenditures). A second point to note is that the distinction between fixed and variable costs is often difficult to make. For example, in relation to output variations there is an important class of *semi-variable costs*. These semi-variables may be costs which stay put over big output ranges but then suddenly go up in a major jump, as when two foremen are needed instead of one. Alternatively, semi-variables are costs which are part fixed and part variable, the outstanding example here being depreciation of a physical asset, some of which is due to straight obsolescence, some to actual use. The third point to note about fixed and variable costs is obvious, although important. This is that they are, of course, related to the time period in question. The longer the period of time, the more costs become variable. So the fixed–variable distinction is linked with two other relative terms, namely the *short run* (when some costs vary, others do not) and the *long run* (all costs vary).

The reader's patience is still needed for some more definitions. *Sunk costs* represent resources that have been consumed or used up as a result of previous decisions. *Unit costs* are simply another name for average costs, i.e. total costs divided by the number of units. *Standard costs* are estimates of what future cost will or should be, based on previous experience and various standards of achievement which may be set in the organisation. Standard costs are frequently related to a 'normal' level of activity in relation to capacity, as compared with, say, 'peak' or 'off-peak' levels. Finally, a central concept of this chapter, *marginal cost*. In the strict sense this means the cost change associated with a one-unit change in output. It is necessary to emphasise that the question, 'What is one unit?' is, often complex. In the case of a railway system, for example, 'one unit' might relate to a single passenger (although in this case the marginal cost will probably be virtually nil), a particular train service or a branch line. The problem is complicated by indivisibilities.

These definitions, together with those in Chapter 3, by no means exhaust important cost concepts as used by accountants or economists. With the vital exception of opportunity costs, however (see Chapter 5), they cover most of the costs which are relevant to the economic analysis of organisations and their decisions.

MARGINALISM FROM THE GROUND UP

To illustrate the role of marginalism within a conventional cost framework, let us turn to a simple example, production costs in a small printing works. There is no particular reason why we should take a printing works rather than, say, a cosmetic factory or a supermarket, or for that matter a social service department or a swimming bath, except that common principles may be brought out more clearly. The X printing works employs 300 people, produces a wide variety of printing jobs and has a careful and apparently quite efficient accounting system. The company's accountants produce a series of estimates of costs for the next year. To do this they have to make assumptions about likely future sales

Table 1 *Hourly cost for vertical press*

Investment: £12,000
Floor area: 300 square feet
Maximum possible working hours: 52 weeks × 40 hours
= 2,080 hours
Normal working hours, allowing for holidays: 1,900 hours

Direct costs	£
Labour, 2 men at £2·00 × 2,080 hours	8,320
National insurance, company pensions, etc	1,300
Power	60
Depreciation (10% of investment)	1,200
Repairs (1% of investment)	120
	11,000

Indirect costs	
Rent (£3·50 × 300 square feet)	1,050
Administrative overheads (80% of direct costs)	8,800
Insurance	150
	10,000

Total cost for next 12 months	21,000

Hourly cost of press in relation to level of capacity working	
100% production capacity, 1,900 hours	11·05
80% production capacity, 1,520 hours	13·82
60% production capacity, 1,140 hours	18·42
40% production capacity, 760 hours	27·63

and also about the amount of machinery and labour required to achieve those sales (the former task being by far the most difficult, but of this more in Chapter 8). Using these estimates, they then calculate a critical figure: the average hourly machine costs for the next year. Table 1 shows how the hourly cost is calculated for one particular bit of machinery in the works.

The X company uses these figures in making decisions, for example on whether to accept a printing order involving the vertical press and what price to charge for it. In the case of a particular order a further estimate has to be made. This is the number of machine hours that would be required on the vertical press, taking into account the important human factors and the company's experience of how their workers normally perform on such a job. The total cost of the order would then equal the hourly machine costs multiplied by the estimated time for the job (plus, of course, the cost of materials).

Now an economist would be inclined to raise all sorts of questions about this process, but the one that particularly concerns us here is quite simply, how useful are these cost data for decision-making purposes? The trouble with many accounting systems is that the very act of labelling and valuing things may produce a false sense of security and precision. So the economist will not be very impressed with such groupings as direct, indirect and overhead costs, terms which may be tainted with rigidity, however useful they may be for purely historical purposes. Instead, he will want to know whether the cost data are able to indicate what will happen when managers need to manipulate things, to make changes. For example, suppose the company is thinking of varying production as a result of a particular decision. Is information available on which costs would vary as a result and which would not? The above schedule is not much use here. For some direct costs will vary directly with output, others will not. Only part of labour costs is likely to go up and down with output since the firm may be unwilling to lay people off. A major part of power and depreciation will not be sensitive to output variations; but, conversely, some of the administrative expenses *might* be. And so on. Such points must be able to be disentangled if a cost system is to serve the purpose of helping decision making as well as recording the past. In this case, what is apparently lacking is the ability to distinguish both variable and marginal costs.

More than anything else, it is Company X's method of pricing its products that brings this issue into focus. Let us suppose that the managing director, Mr Robinson, says that the company's policy is to charge the full cost of each job, together with a 'fair profit' or 'mark-up' on top. Referring to Table 1, the price for a job would be: the average hourly machine costs multiplied by the estimated time for the job, plus the cost of materials (i.e. the total cost of the job), plus the company's normal mark-up. In the judgement of Mr Robinson and his company this procedure is entirely accurate, fair and convenient. It appears to be the policy pursued by competitor firms. In practice, there is some flexibility in applying it. The official mark-ups are slightly higher for first runs of any jobs requiring creative work, slightly lower for small jobs where this might attract big new custom. Thus to some extent the competitive situation in printing is reflected through to pricing even though the firm are strongly attached to the idea that prices should reflect the full costs for each job plus a 'fair profit'. Moreover, the firm advance some further reasons for full cost pricing, namely that alternative pricing methods would mean frequent price changes which would be troublesome to operate and unwelcome to customers; that competition on quality rather than price is anyway the important thing in this industry; and that to charge either a lot more or a lot less than full cost would be 'unethical'.

Now let us assume that Mr Robinson wants the business to do better and is reasonably open-minded about ways of achieving this. To facilitate discussion with him, it would be essential first of all to know more about the competitive conditions in his locality and section of the printing trade. In particular, it would be necessary to know how responsive demand is to changes in prices. Let us make the reasonable assumption that for some of Company X's products, A, an increase or decrease in price would not make much difference to sales whereas for others, B, it would make a considerable difference, in fact a more than proportional difference. Mr Robinson's claim that non-price competition is the determining factor really only applies with force to the A products. For the B products, possibly to some extent even for the A products, price competition is also likely to be of considerable importance, more or less, depending mainly on the extent of the price sensitivity of demand.

Subject to this critically important point, the following comments might be made to Mr Robinson. (1) Even now you are not pursuing an all-out full cost pricing policy. After all, profit mark-ups are pared down to get particularly favourable orders. In other words, the competitive situation is inescapable and for the sake of marginal benefits you are already pricing below 'full cost plus fair margin' in some cases. (2) This is a seasonal trade, with 'off-periods' when

lower capacity working means much higher unit costs. A thorough
going full cost policy would logically mean charging *more* at these
times. But you obviously do not do this, which suggests again that
rigid consistency in this matter would be unwise. Indeed, if anything, there might be an argument for actually charging regular
customers of B products at *below* full cost in off-periods. (3) This
last argument would apply even more strongly if there were a slump
in the trade. In such a situation it might be necessary to charge still
lower prices, perhaps even prices below marginal or variable costs.
If there were no alternative uses for the firm's resources, such a
policy would be justified and essential. (4) In some cases, where
demand is relatively price responsive, it might be wise to charge
below full cost anyway, indeed closer to marginal costs, assuming
that the firm is concerned about immediate profits. Why? Because,
insofar as demand is price sensitive, sales would then be more than
proportionally greater and profits would be higher.

Logically, these arguments are irrefutable, although you will be
unlikely to convince Mr Robinson of them all that easily. Assuming
you do finally convince him, of course, he is still entitled to say that
he prefers his present policy on the grounds that it is (*a*) 'easier',
(*b*) 'more conformable to the general pattern' or (*c*) 'more ethical'.
That is his privilege.

For argument's sake let us now assume that under the powerful
stimulus of increased competition and/or a depression in the trade
Mr Robinson has changed his mind. He is now keen to maximise
his profit or minimise his losses. Alternatively, he at least wants to
know what a short-term maximising policy would involve, even
though he may not always wish to pursue it. In this case a two-
pronged approach might apply. For A products, insofar as demand
is insensitive to price changes but dependent on special quality factors which Company X provides or could provide in the future, the
price could be what the market will bear – this of course requiring
very considerable judgement. For B products, insofar as demand is
sensitive to price changes, the price could be at least at the level of
marginal cost plus whatever the market will bear, again depending
on the competition. 'Full cost plus fair margin' would effectually
be abandoned. Instead, pricing would mainly depend on critical
estimates of (*a*) competitive pressures and (*b*) differential costs.
In the case of a particular order Company X would need to assess
the marginal impacts of various prices on sales and of various output levels on costs. Broadly, provided the former exceeded the
latter, the order would be worth taking. Company X might then
charge above the differential cost in this sense, but only to the

extent that competition seemed to allow. The sales margin over and above marginal cost would then represent a contribution to overhead and profit. In some cases obviously this contribution would be lower than in the previous situation, in other cases it would be higher. Overall, the firm would almost certainly be more profitable, if that was what it wanted. In broad terms, it would be pursuing, or at least aware of the implications of, a more marginalist sort of pricing policy.

The lessons from this simple example, which is fairly typical managerially, should be clear. In the first place Company X and Mr Robinson exemplify the influence of custom and accepted practice, the preference for stable prices and the use of ethical categories of 'fairness' to justify what is being done. To denigrate all this too glibly would be wrong. Secondly, however, there was some confused thinking about what was happening. The 'full cost plus fair profit' formula was trotted out despite the fact that this was not, and indeed could not be, rigorously applied; and the accounting classifications of cost were hardly designed to clarify many important choices that had to be made. Both of these features – a gap between managerial formulas and actual practice, and an internal data confusion which may at least partially explain that gap – are frequently found in all types of organisation. Thirdly, the example illustrates that marginal costs do not provide a rigid formula for pricing decisions but clarify them in an essential manner. It is sometimes thought that what is implied is that marginal cost should actually determine price. This is not so. What marginal cost does is to establish the extent to which, under varying assumptions about output and sales, an item contributes to the overall fortunes of a concern. It does not indicate what actual price should be charged but rather some of the critical parameters of pricing choice, the zones of danger, safety or reward. Fourthly, the case illustrates the subtle gradations of marginalism, the fact that it can be applied at varying degrees of intensity and certainly without explicit formulation.

Finally, the printing works case gives something of the flavour of marginalist reasoning in a managerial context. It shows how a questioning process can help management towards (a) awareness of what they are doing at the margin and of the trade-offs they are making, (b) appreciation of their need for sharper decision-oriented data, (c) more realistic formulas for certain decisions, in this case for pricing under varying degrees of competitive or economic pressure, and, as a by-product of all this, perhaps also (d) a clearer formulation of their objectives and strategy.

THE EQUIMARGINAL THEORY

So much for the approach to marginalism from the ground up. What about the more rarefied approach, starting from the ideal? First, some definitions. *Marginalism* in the strict sense means a concern with the effects of one-unit changes in quantifiable aggregates. Thus marginal *cost* as already mentioned, is the money cost increase associated with a one-unit increase in output. *Marginal revenue* is the revenue (money benefit) increase associated with a one-unit increase in sales. *Marginal productivity* is the ability of one extra unit of an input to increase production. *Marginal utility* or *disutility* is the extra satisfaction or benefit (dissatisfaction or cost) experienced by consumers or citizens as a result of a one-unit increase in goods or services consumed (burdens imposed). Theoretical neo-classical economics assumed, first, that these things are measurable. It added a crucial behavioural hypothesis, namely that businesses, organisations, consumers and individuals frequently (mostly? always?) seek to optimise their positions by minimising their costs and maximising their benefits. It then mixed this powerful potion and deduced an historically important idea, the *equimarginal principle*.

To illustrate the principle it is easiest to take a simplified version of the pricing problem already discussed in relation to Company X. Let us assume that Company X makes a single product, Y, knows exactly what effect price changes will have on Y's sales, and is pursuing maximum profit. Figure 2 shows the price of Y on the vertical axis, its output on the horizontal axis. The two curves then show what X's marginal costs and marginal revenues will be at varying levels of price and output. The area below the *MC* curve measures the total cost of producing any output. The area under the *MR* curve measures the total revenue from the sale of any output. The important point is that maximum profit would be attained when the *MC* and *MR* curves intersect at *P*. Why? Because if Company X produces more than this, say *OD*, marginal cost will exceed marginal revenue and the area *PFG* will represent a loss, to be deducted from the area *APC*. But if the company produces less, say *OZ*, then profit, *AHIC*, will be lower than it need be. Given the assumptions, the deduction necessarily follows.

The equimarginal theory can be extended theoretically in all sorts of directions. For example, it can be shown that a multi-product firm would maximise its profits by juggling its resources or inputs between its various products so as to achieve an optimum result. This result would be at a point where there were equal marginal net revenues

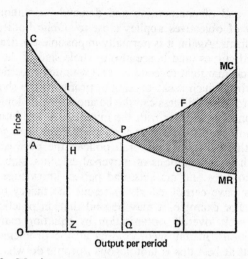

Figure 2 Maximum profit through equating marginal cost and marginal revenue

(profits) per unit of input from all the products. Again, why? Because at any other point the firm would be earning less profit than it might and could increase profit by shifting some resources from products with low marginal return to those with high marginal return. Again, in a very abstract sense the equimarginal principle can embrace the decisions of a public body as it tries to balance priorities between different expenditures. Assuming that the public body 'aims to maximise the satisfactions of citizens', its basic optimising formula would be clear: so to juggle expenditures on different public benefits that there is equality between the marginal satisfactions of citizens derived from all marginal expenditures. Equimarginal theory has generalised its formulas into almost every sphere including that of individual or consumer behaviour. Its kernel is the idea of an optimum or equilibrium point which is attained or attainable either partially (by particular individuals or organisations at micro levels) or generally (in the economy or society as a whole).

Now in practice there are all sorts of reasons why ultra-pure marginalism in this sense is extremely hard to apply. One gigantic obstacle stands in the way, namely the fact that the *overall* objectives of organisations can rarely, if ever, be reduced to purely quantitative terms. Some of the reasons for this have already been introduced in Chapter 3. Other, and closely related, reasons will be discussed later, notably the problems of risk and uncertainty

E

(Chapter 6) and of competition and demand estimation (Chapter 8). Plurality of objectives applies most to public bodies, but also to business firms. Again, it is normally impossible for firms to know their demand curves (and hence also a whole side of the conjuror's equation, their marginal revenue curves) with any precision. Indeed, not even a firm which seeks maximum profits in the short run can avoid this problem. Still less can the business seeking long-run profit maximisation as it wrestles with the mysteries of the future and the apparent conflicts between short-term and longer-term gain. Therefore, from the viewpoint of overall policies the pure equimarginal theory – with its assumptions of universal calculus, stability of attitudes, technologies and markets, and perfect knowledge – is hardly helpful. Nor have certain efforts to rescue the theory been wholly convincing. For example, it may be said that, in practice, decision makers do seek 'overall' optimisation by equating marginal costs and satisfactions, merely incorporating all the problems into their calculus. But at best this is tautologous ('people do what they want to do') and scarcely a guide to improvement.

Does this mean, then, that marginalism has no organisational uses? As already illustrated, the answer to this question is an emphatic 'no'. As so often in applied economics, 'the best' must not be allowed to become the enemy of 'the good'. The fact that a pure theory is unattainable (or perhaps even undesirable) hardly justifies relapse into a confused pragmatism. The overweening ambitions of the pure theory, in terms of top decision making and organisations as a whole, must be largely abandoned. Its quantified rigour, particularly in terms of an obsession with one-unit changes in output, must often be relaxed. But that is all. Stripped of these excesses, marginalism is perfectly serviceable and frequently vital. Some of the constructive uses of more general marginalist reasoning have already been glimpsed in relation to Company X. But even the milder and most essential axioms of such reasoning are frequently transgressed. So long as this is the case, vigorous evangelism is necessary.

ELEMENTAL PROBLEMS

To illustrate, here are some extreme managerial offences against marginalism covering a wide range of organisations in the United Kingdom:

(1) Some years ago an investigation found that when calculating the benefits from new investments a large number of quoted com-

panies included a proportion of their existing overhead expenses in the running costs of the new plant and machinery. Two-thirds of the firms included existing overheads of the factory and one-third included selling and distributive overheads.[1]

(2) The same survey found that 10 per cent of the companies even added the book value of assets that were to be scrapped to the capital cost of the plant and equipment which would replace it.[1]

(3) Similar errors in piling the past load of fixed or sunk costs onto future projects were made by the National Coal Board, the railways and some of the Area Gas Boards as recently as the late 1950s and early 1960s.[2]

(4) More recently, in trying to establish financial targets, a sizeable electrical concern enunciated the principle that 'no investment should be made in anything of which it is considered the company may have to divest itself in less than the depreciation period'.

(5) In making investment, order-taking and pricing decisions many small firms fail to distinguish between fixed and variable costs, lack reliable estimates of marginal costs and apply tradition-bound formulas.[3]

(6) Many expenditure decisions in local authorities and other public bodies are made in ignorance of the marginal impacts these decisions will have on costs, on particular activities and not least on the various groups of citizens involved. As one authority on the subject puts it: 'the traditional budget in local government provides information for control purposes, it is not intended to aid decision-making'.[4]

(7) A recent study on economic principles in the health services found in relation to hospitals that the main costing units of their accounts 'are far too broad' and, more generally, that 'the form in which financial information is currently assembled for accountancy purposes in the health services does not lend itself to discussion of medical priorities, because breakdowns of expenditure and costs are generally given for broad categories which are not sub-divided in such a way as to be of use in costing particular objectives of the service'.[5]

The point about these cases is that they offend the minimal canon of marginalist reasoning mentioned at the beginning of this chapter, namely the need for strictly relevant data. There is no possibility of balancing trade-offs if we do not even know what it is we are trading off – if our data on costs and benefits are crude and even misleading because (*a*) irrelevant data are included or (*b*) relevant detail is lacking, or (c) most likely both. Whatever the reasons for such managerial obscurity, it will tend, at one end of the organisational spectrum, to stymie business efficiency, sometimes to the detriment of consumers, at the other to obfuscate public choice and muddle or ignore important priorities of social need. Fortunately the situation is changing, although all too slowly. To get some idea of marginalism in action let us glance at some of the problems, priorities and recent advances, first in business and then in the public and social sectors.

MARGINALISM AND BUSINESS PRICING

A relevant issue is how far businesses are able and willing to take account of marginal costs and revenues in their pricing decisions. The evidence here is still inadequate. In the United States a survey in the 1950s found that giant corporations generally sought long-term profit. Within this framework, stability of prices and profit margins featured as the main pricing goal for some and competitive, or market-share oriented, pricing for others, although the dominant aim appeared to be a target return on investment, based on standard cost plus a target rate of profit. But this target price might be applied rigidly or flexibly and in the latter case various concessions to competitive conditions (and hence to marginal criteria) were made.[6] A much quoted study by James S. Earley was possibly significant because it concentrated on over 100 leading US companies which were also 'well managed'. This study found only a small minority rigidly applying full cost and equal margins on all products. 84 per cent of the firms said they modified their cost–price relationships to allow for competitive pressures from other companies, 79 per cent to allow for varying price elasticities of demand and 61 per cent to allow for varying fixed/variable cost ratios as between different products. The Earley study maintained that in these 'well managed companies' such tactical flexibility on pricing – influenced by commercial and (to a lesser extent) variable cost criteria, and assisted by marginal costing systems – was producing a form of marginalist behaviour 'on the wing': implicit, usually long-term profit oriented and very real.[7]

In this country the most recent detailed study was by Professor D. C. Hague. Although this covered only 13 (probably fairly enlightened) companies, its detailed discussion of the pitfalls and nuances of business marginalism is illuminating.[8] The Hague study found, naturally enough, that much depended on the nature of the products, their newness or oldness, varying competitive conditions, whether production was continuous, batch or one-off, and whether economic conditions were sunny or severe, as well as on varying attitudes and personalities in the firms.

(a) Of the 13 firms in the survey, three appeared to follow a rigid or rough and ready 'full cost' approach to pricing, sometimes with anomalies, without visible damage to the firm, mainly because competitive and economic conditions appeared to be relaxed.

(b) Three firms pursued flexible versions of 'full cost' (broadly, Company X's position, as discussed above), varying their 'full cost plus normal profit' formulas where appropriate to allow for market conditions, and occasionally also for cost–output relationships.

(c) In introducing a new product a surgical instrument company carefully estimated relevant costs for it and then applied a sophisticated formula to arrive at the price (effectively, marginal cost plus target return).

(d) A food manufacturer explicitly estimated marginal costs for its products but found this difficult insofar as many of them emanated from the same processes and therefore involved joint costs.

(e) Three engineering firms produced equipment on a contract basis, often 'one-off' or custom-built, and they also faced difficult trading conditions; both these factors tending to enforce a marginalist approach. For each contract or product variable costs were carefully separated out (cutting across the direct/indirect split, see above) and the marginal cost estimated. This was then normally used as a minimum price benchmark, indicating what contribution to fixed costs and profit higher prices than this would make, if attainable.

(f) A mass producer of a standardised product made careful forecasts of both demand and output, estimated costs at varying outputs at varying times of the year ('peak', 'normal' and 'slack') and separated out marginal costs for each line. This firm used a computer model to assist in decision making and was moving towards marginal cost per unit of output as a basis for determining prices.

Thus modified marginalism appeared to be fairly pervasive. Complete immunity seems only to have applied to the firms under (a). The rest of the companies exhibited a spectrum ranging from market-influenced marginalism of a very mild and implicit sort, (b), through an explicit addition of marginal cost criteria, (c) and (d), to a fairly complete marginal cost and competitive pricing policy, (e), with one company very close to the most elegant form, (f). Apart from management attitudes, marginalist pricing appeared to be favoured by the introduction of new products, by big fluctuations in output

and capacity utilisation due to 'lumpy' contracts or seasonal variations in demand, and by tougher and more competitive markets. On
management attitudes Professor Hague's study had some astringent
comments: 'the concept of marginal cost is simple and of great
benefit but still widely ignored and even more widely misunderstood'. It conceded that the allocation of indirect costs – and still
more the estimation of demand and price elasticities – posed considerable problems; and also that primitive 'rule of thumb' criteria
might sometimes suffice. But there appeared to be many needless
mistakes – for example a failure to adjust historical cost data to
allow for new developments, undue reliance on traditionalist
accounting systems, and inadequate linkage of estimates of sales,
output and costs. There were also crude misunderstandings of
marginalism and a widespread suspicion that salesmen and others
would merely seize on it as an opportunity to cut some prices 'too
low' simply in order to boost sales.

In the nationalised industries, conditions are somewhat different.
The question of whether the nationalised industries can or should
pursue marginalist pricing, and if so in what forms, partly depends
on technical factors: notably the character of their long-term investment programmes, their frequently major problems of varying
capacity utilisation and the extent to which they, too, are vulnerable
to long-term demand, uncertainties, competition and risks. But
nationalised industries' pricing is also strongly influenced, indeed
often dominated, by their overall financial targets and by ad hoc
governmental price interventions and political pressures. In practice,
marginalist pricing criteria have played some part. For example, in
the United Kingdom, long-term marginal costs have been taken into
account, if only broadly, in coal, gas and electricity pricing.
Nationalised industry pricing is even more a matter of compromise
than elsewhere. But that is not to say that marginalist criteria should
not play an important and perhaps increasing role.[9]

BUSINESS AND SOCIAL MARGINALISM: STRENGTHS AND WEAKNESSES

The last section discussed the use of marginalism in pricing
decisions. But, as already implied, marginalist information and
reasoning are necessary for a wide variety of business problems:
for example, whether or not to accept an order, to hire a piece of
equipment or use one's own, to sell off capital assets or to change
the product mix. In particular, marginalist data and thinking are
necessary for clear-sighted investment decisions (often, of course,

linked with pricing decisions). In each case, information systems should be able to provide data on the likely impacts of alternative decisions. That is to say, the data must cover both marginal costs and marginal benefits. This is not always easy. As we have seen, even to define the costs and benefits that are relevant to typical and important decisions can be a complex business. Then to disentangle these relevant costs and benefits is often difficult. The advance of more sophisticated accounting systems, providing data on marginal costs and oriented towards showing profit contributions, is helping to bring this about, although there is still a long way to go. But information on marginal costs and benefits is not even just a matter of accounting finesse, important though this is. It also involves intelligent forecasting of the conditions affecting future costs and benefits, particularly where the economic situation is volatile and in long-term investment decisions.

Marginalism in business is often identified with the notion of firms pursuing maximum profit. This interpretation is too crude. We shall be discussing profit objectives later. Suffice it to say here that for practical planning purposes the notion of 'maximum profit' is a will-o'-the-wisp. Business firms tend to pursue what they view as 'minimum', 'acceptable' or 'desirable' profits, both short-run and long-run. Such profit standards vary enormously, depending on the overall characteristics and objectives of the firm and its views on market constraints and opportunities, as also on ethical and political criteria. But whatever the profit policy, even short-term marginal analysis may be necessary for intelligent decision making. For a firm anxious to wrest short-term advantage in the interests of bare survival or capital gain, marginalism suggests how to obtain quick profits by tactical price and output adjustments. For a firm with ambitious profit targets in the longer term, such information may still be essential, even though the firm may very well decide that quick profits now would damage profits later, for example by endangering customer or public goodwill. If a firm sees profit objectives as conditional on high standards of ethical behaviour (doubtless for mixed reasons of enlightened self-interest and conscience), it should still know what marginal room for short-term profit manoeuvre it has. To be aware of the short-term financial advantages and disadvantages of alternative actions, even if one abjures the most immediately profitable, is essential for clear-eyed choice. Whatever the underlying attitude on profits, concern for the long-run profit implications of important decisions is likely to be crucial. Indeed, one can easily turn the problem upside-down and say that unless a firm properly estimates its scope for profit manœuvre, using both short-run *and* long-run marginal analysis, it does not even know what its overall profit policy is. So far from being sensible, let alone morally high-minded, avoidable ignorance of the marginal parameters of profit choice is more likely to be plain sloppy.

A cruder misunderstanding is to apply marginalist reasoning so as to decompose activities that are, or should be, integrated. Thus marginalism rightly splits down the enterprise into elements and sub-elements. This helps managers to see how far particular activities are (or are not) covering their variable costs, going on to contribute towards fixed costs or going still further to contribute towards profits. But a vulgar interpretation sometimes implies that the elements showing up 'badly' must necessarily be made more profitable or got rid of. For example, it is sometimes implied that 'cross subsidisation' is undesirable or that some nationalised industry, say, should dispense with 'loss makers'. Although this may well be justified, there are cases where it would be absurd. Such cases arise where there is a high degree of interdependence between the marginally 'bad' element and another marginally 'good' one. For example, sulphuric acid may be needed for a chemical process, a 'loss leader' in a supermarket may be useful in selling other items, a station car park may encourage commuters to go by rail. To argue that each of these elements should 'avoid losses', 'pay its way' or 'contribute to profit', regardless of its wider effects on the concern's system as a whole, would be ridiculous. On the contrary, any system of activities is likely to have 'loss making' as well as 'profit making' elements. Such complementarities or 'internalities' are ubiquitous. Here the role of marginalism is to disaggregate and illuminate interdependent systems but in the interests of integrating them better, not breaking them up.

In this chapter we have mainly discussed marginalism in the context of profit making enterprises. There the marginal costs and benefits being considered are normally purely internal ones. But marginalism equally embraces *external* costs and benefits wherever these are relevant to decision making (on the distinction between 'internal' and 'external' costs and benefits, see Chapter 3). For example, the decision whether or not to build a new underground railway only partly depends on the marginal effects on the costs and revenues of the railway system itself. It is necessary to take careful account of bigger marginal quantities: time savings to travellers on the new railway, the benefits of less congestion on the roads, the savings on alternative roads or on other transport projects that might otherwise be necessary. But the need for marginalism does not stop at this point. It extends well beyond the sphere of business, private or nationalised, and indeed well beyond items which are relatively easy to quantify financially.

Consider, for example, a hospital, school or local authority making allocative choices. A public or social organisation of this kind operates in a particularly mixed world of financial and non-financial calculation. Typically, its inputs will be financially quantified but not its objectives and outputs, at least not the important ones. We shall consider the quantification of outputs of public goods like health and social services later. Meantime the important point to note is that marginalist data and reasoning can apply as readily to non-financial quantities as financial ones. Suppose the costs (inputs) of an activity are financial, its benefits (outputs) non-financial but quantified in other ways. This implies a ratio of cost per unit of output, say cost per patient operation in a hospital. To go further, suppose that neither inputs nor outputs are properly regarded as financial, although both can be quantified. For example, consider a voluntary organisation like Task Force, a charity or a monastic community. Here the number of hours worked voluntarily by helpers or members (the inputs) normally can and should be related to the number of tasks performed or people helped (the outputs). In all such cases marginalism simply requires, again, that information on the cost–benefit (input–output) relationships be broken down and properly deployed in efforts to use resources more productively and to understand the impacts, for good or ill, of particular decisions.

As in business, so in the social sector marginalism can be interpreted ambitiously or moderately. A good example of an ambitious social use of marginalism would be in the area of public expenditures on health, transport and accident prevention. An important objective of such expenditures is to prolong or save human life. Supposing an effort is made, if only approximately, to quantify the extent to which each expenditure item or sub-item, say on kidney machines or road safety, is likely to contribute towards the saving of human life. Such estimates are essential for intelligent planning. Even in rough form, subject to wide margins of error and risk, they could be expressed in terms of the number of years of life saved. Now virtually everybody would agree that it is morally good to spend public money on saving human life. Most people would also agree that any money so spent should be designed to get the 'best value'. They might well agree that 'rough justice' suggests maximising the number of years of life saved overall – or at least avoiding a situation where vastly more is spent in saving one year of human life as a result of some types of expenditure compared with others. Yet at present not even the beginnings of such an effort at an economic and even-handed allocation are made. Instead, each agency implicitly assigns a valuation to human life separately, regardless of the others, let alone any overall norm. An ambitious social marginalism would suggest that this process of putting money valuations on human life should be made explicit and consistent throughout the public sector. As an economist well-versed in public expenditure problems puts it, planning is needed so that 'we do not find ourselves spending (say) £100,000 to prevent a loss of 100 man-years of life expectation on the railways, while on the roads (let us say) the corresponding figure is £1,000, for with the present diverse pattern we are not increasing the expectation of life of the community as a whole as much as we could even with the existing amounts of resources specifically devoted to this objective'.[10]

The reader should note that what is suggested here is an approximation to the equimarginal principle. Formally, and ideally, perhaps, the marginal benefits (years of life saved) per unit of input (£ spending) should be equal for all life-saving expenditures. A breathtaking objective this, even though a slightly closer approximation to it than now would be more humane and socially economic. But social sector applications of marginalism need not be so vaultingly ambitious. At present even the most elementary data on the costs and benefits of particular activities are frequently lacking. Consequently, the marginal impacts of decisions cannot be properly assessed. This applies to decision making by, say, welfare administrators, area health authorities, local authority social service committees or officials of charitable organisations. For example, suppose the social decision makers are wondering how to deploy social workers among different activities, whether to buy one item of medical equipment or another, whether to spend more on adventure playgrounds or holiday homes. An essential precondition is to be able to estimate how many people, of what kinds, in what areas and in what broadly specifiable ways, are likely to be affected. Moreover, such information should allow for overlaps so that in the case of a person being benefited by more than one adjacent activity the net numbers of beneficiaries are also known. Yet even such minimal information (let alone more complex data on the wider social implications) is frequently not available. The basic gospel of modified marginalism – its call for better information systems – is particularly relevant in the public, social and voluntary services.

A final word is necessary on the limitations of marginalism.

Essentially, marginalism is about the best deployment of existing resources within existing ambits of activities. It corresponds to the instinct for taking existing things to bits, seeing how they interrelate and making them work better. Tidy, careful and fair-minded, it finds echoes in the instincts of many engineers, accountants and public officials. Even its pure theory, enshrined in the equimarginal principle, is somewhat conservative. The equimarginalist manager would be like a conjuror, juggling his existing equipment ever more effectively, but not considering new sorts of conjuring, let alone other activities.

Modified marginalism is essential for answering the questions, 'Where are we now?' and 'How can we go one better?'. But on the wider strategic issues – 'Should we be here anyway?' and 'Where would be best?' – it is silent. Decision making without marginalism is merely blinkered. But decision making limited conceptually to marginalism is unlikely to be dynamic or creative.

Chapter 5
Opportunity Cost

In some ways the idea of opportunity cost is complementary to that of marginalism. Whereas marginalist reasoning in its useful modified form concentrates on keen adjustments and flexible improvements, opportunity cost reasoning is part of the very act of choice. Practical marginalism is essentially tactical but opportunity cost tends to be more strategically oriented, more critical and, in a sense, more radical. Of the two ideas it is also the more important. If marginalism in the pure sense is unattainable – and in the modified sense a matter of optional effort – opportunity cost is inescapable and perpetually pressing in on us, whether we like it or not. It is inherent in the whole human condition, fraught with triumph and tragedy. The critical question is whether we recognise it properly and apply its rationale with lucidity.

DEFINITION AND TYPES OF OPPORTUNITY COST

Opportunity cost is the value of the opportunity sacrificed, or the benefit forgone, as a result of not employing something in its best alternative use as seen by decision makers and/or society. James Buchanan expresses the contrast between historical and opportunity costs succinctly as a contrast between 'choice influenced' and 'choice influencing' costs.[1] In thinking about opportunity cost the key terms are 'alternatives', 'relinquishment', 'sacrifice' and 'displacement'. Relating these to individual experience, we may say that the opportunity cost of saving money is the benefit from the spending abstained from or postponed as a result. The opportunity cost of depositing money in a building society is measured by the return anticipated from investing in, say, government stock or perhaps equities. For a student the opportunity cost of taking a full-time course of education is the value, monetary or otherwise, from alternative activities he could pursue during the period of study; for a striker it is the value of earnings lost in the strike; for somebody helping a sick neighbour in the evenings it could be overtime earnings or the benefits of spending time with his family.

Although the basic opportunity cost idea is clear enough, there are some differences of emphasis in the way in which it is defined. In particular, most economists have emphasised opportunity cost as an objective concept, whereas some have concentrated on opportunity cost as a subjective experience of the decision maker. The subjectivist approach was perhaps expressed most strongly by Thirlby when he said that 'opportunity cost cannot be discovered by another person who eventually watches and records the flow'. It 'is not something which is objectively discoverable in this manner, it is something which existed in the mind of the decision maker before the flow began, and something which may quite likely have been but vaguely apprehended'. Thirlby refers to outcomes existing 'in the decision maker's imagination', to opportunity cost as 'ephemeral'. He says that 'the cost involved in a particular decision loses its significance with the making of decision because the decision displaces the alternative course of action'. 'The cost figure will never become objective, i.e. it will never be possible to check whether the forecast of the alternative revenue was correct because the alternative undertaking will never come into existence to produce the actual alternative revenue.'[2]

This subjectivist emphasis has some merit. It corresponds with the experience of many decision makers, particularly of the 'one-man band' or entrepreneurial kind, whose reasoning tends to be implicit, rapid and personal, whose management style is individualistic or authoritarian, who often tend to live for the moment and to regard their own activities and experiences as unique. A more substantial point, perhaps, is that opportunity costs tend to be elusive. They are usually very hard to discover in any precise sense, whether by decision makers or outsiders and whether before or after the event. Nonetheless, a pure subjectivism here risks solipsism. It contradicts the fact that we *do* commonly make judgements about the course of action pursued by others. Organisations' decisions *are* scrutinised from time to time, often after the event, sometimes before, by outsiders. We feel entitled to say that some are more efficient than others in terms of social, market or even their own criteria, to say that opportunity costs for society in some cases are needlessly high, and so on. Therefore, allowing for the possibilities of conflicting points of view, opportunity costs must be considered in these wider perspectives as well as in the mind of the decision maker (business or public) at the moment of choice.

Opportunity costs take a variety of forms. They must be divided into *internal opportunity costs*, (the benefits sacrificed by the organisations or individuals making the decisions) and *external*

opportunity costs, (the benefits lost by other organisations or individuals). Both these categories obviously subdivide according to
whether they involve money flows or not. But our definitions also
need to take into account the point already made about perception.
Since we are here concerned not with actual historical events, we
have to distinguish between opportunity costs as perceived before
the event and afterwards. We also need to take account of the fact
that opportunity costs may be perceived either by the decision
makers themselves or by outsiders. Table 2 should make these
distinctions clearer. Logically, there are sixteen aspects of opportunity

Table 2 *Classification of opportunity costs*

		Perceived ex ante		Perceived ex post	
		(a) Intern-ally	(b) Extern-ally	(c) Intern-ally	(d) Extern-ally
Monetary	External	1	5	9	13
	Internal	2	6	10	14
Non-monetary	External	3	7	11	15
	Internal	4	8	12	16

costs. Starting with column (*a*), opportunity costs at the moment of
choice as seen by the decision makers: businesses will tend to be
mainly concerned with 2 and 4, public decision makers with 1 and also
3. Even at the moment of decision, though, outsiders may have views:
column (*b*). For example, the government may well have opinions
regarding a large company's location decision. Because it perceives
external opportunity costs under 5 and 7, it may prefer the company to set up a big new factory at Y rather than Z for reasons
connected with, say, the environment or local employment. Other
outsiders may have opinions, too: for example, a major finance
house helping to finance the project is likely to have ideas on 6.
Then the final decision is made. Afterwards an intelligent organisation will try to apply hindsight: column (*c*). It will try to analyse
whether it correctly perceived the available alternatives at the time
and whether it was right to refuse those it did refuse (although such
an exercise can be daunting and politically sensitive). Once again,
too, outsiders may well have something to say: column (*d*). For
example, a quoted company may have the opportunity costs of its
decisions retrospectively scanned by stockbrokers, major investors
or financial journalists – or again by government. The majority

representatives on a local authority will probably have theirs criticised by the opposition party and varyingly appraised by their electors. No doubt, economists will be on hand to put their oar in as well! Thus opportunity costs are ubiquitous, the opportunity costs of a particular decision have several aspects, narrow or broad, inter-temporal and perceptual; and, moreover, these aspects may conflict. Opportunity costs are sometimes identified simply with financial or marketable items – or even as perceived purely internally and at the moment of choice – but none of these restrictions is correct.

ASSESSING OPPORTUNITY COSTS: QUANTITATIVE AND FINANCIAL PROBLEMS

In relation to organisational decisions, how should opportunity costs be assessed? How can they be handled in practice? In answering these questions we will concentrate on the point of view of decision makers at the moment of choice, in other words on opportunity costs perceived *ex ante* and internally (column (*a*) of the diagram). We will concentrate on enlightened practice (examples of defective opportunity cost thinking will come later). We will also outline the problems in ascending order of managerial difficulty. Broadly, this means starting with the most readily quantifiable sorts of situations and working upwards to the least quantifiable.

Let us start, therefore, with zone 1 determinate-type decisions as outlined in Chapter 3. In the case of an ultra-simple problem relating to physical outputs, opportunity costs are dazzlingly clear. Suppose two products, alpha and beta, can be produced from a piece of plant, Z, in various combinations as shown in Table 3.

Table 3 *Possible combinations of alpha and beta per Z hour*

Combinations	Number of units	
	Alpha	Beta
A	1,000	0
B	750	125
C	500	250
D	250	375
E	0	500

In this situation the opportunity cost of producing 1,000 units of alpha is quite simply 500 units of beta. If we move from combination B to combination C we shall produce 125 more units of beta but the opportunity cost will be 250 units of alpha. If we then jump back to combination A, the opportunity cost of producing 500 more units of alpha will be 250 units of beta and so on.

Even in this ultra-simple form of ratios between two physical outputs, opportunity cost reasoning may occasionally be glimpsed. Analogous problems may be faced by small and relatively self-sufficient communal units, for example, in certain peasant economies or, say, a kibbutz, a commune or monastery. In such cases material choices of this kind may be austerely simple, probably deliberately so, and monetary or market categories are kept at bay, more or less successfully. However, the main value of this problem is as a limiting case. The conditions attaching to it are, of course, highly exceptional, including (a) no constraints inside the system or complete freedom to vary the combinations of alpha and beta, (b) no money costs or prices, (c) no quantified objective to be aimed at, (d) only two variables, the products alpha and beta, (e) a linear production function, (f) all elements quantifiable, (g) exact simultaneity of alternatives, (h) their collective exhaustiveness and (j) all problems of risk and uncertainty correspondingly remote. The reader hardly needs to be reminded that in varying degrees these conditions will tend not to apply. As they are departed from, so opportunity cost reasoning may grow harder.

Let us assume, then, that at least some of the conditions are relaxed. In particular, the production alternatives are more complicated. For example, there may be other pieces of plant besides Z and machinery cannot be used all the time or equally flexibly for alpha and beta. Also, very important, alpha and beta command money costs and prices and, moreover, the decision makers have targets related to these which are clear and quantifiable. Let us say that the decision makers are keen to minimise costs or maximise profits. Here mathematical solutions are ascertainable. Problems involving linear functions can be solved by linear programming, using graphical methods or algebraic techniques. For example, a more complex version of the alpha–beta production case already discussed would frequently be solved by such means. In certain cases the linearity assumption may also cease to apply. Here the more advanced dynamic programming techniques of operational research will tend to be used.[3] But from our point of view just now the important point is a different one. A moment's reflection will show that, in this first zone, mathematical solutions have the effect of resolving opportunity cost problems altogether. Given the still rigorously quantifiable framework, a concern about opportunity costs is able to call forth a solution. When both the relevant variables and the organisational targets are nicely measurable, type (*a*) opportunity costs are nicely measurable too. The 'greater cost' and/or 'lower profit' opportunities all fall away, yielding place to a clearly superior alternative. Moreover, this alternative is not merely the best of a visible bunch. Within the production frontier of the given technology, it is the 'best attainable' from the decision maker's point of view at the time.

As suggested in Chapter 3, the next zone of decision making is rather more difficult. Quantitative analysis is essential and useful, although mists are rapidly starting to appear. This second zone is broadly that of financial analysis, the zone in which money flow opportunity costs are compared. Typically, comparison is between varying costs of capital, returns on investment, cost savings or financial cost: benefit ratios. To a large extent the alternatives being compared are still quantifiable and commensurable, although subject to various reservations connected with the unquantifiable objectives of organisations and some other factors to be explored later (see Chapter 6 on time, risk and uncertainty and Chapter 8 on market knowledge). Subject to these reservations the expression of opportunity costs is still fairly straightforward. In this zone the opportunity cost of pursuing one alternative rather than another can be viewed as the difference between the monetary value of that alternative and the monetary value of its best rival. The difference can be expressed using a plus or minus sign. On financial grounds, if the sign is minus the alternative under consideration is inferior, if plus it is 'the best'. Here are some simplified examples:

(1) A business is trying to decide between three investment projects involving equal outlays but with net present values (discounted at 10 per cent and risk adjusted, see Chapter 6) of (*a*) £2·5 million, (*b*) £2·0 million and (*c*) £1·5 million. The opportunity cost of (*a*) will be plus £0·5 million, of (*b*) minus £0·5 million and of (*c*) minus £1 million.
(2) A hospital can rationalise its purchasing in two main ways, yielding estimated net annual cost savings of either (*a*) £100,000 or (*b*) £150,000. The opportunity cost of (*a*) will be minus £50,000, of (*b*) plus £50,000.

A problem often arises in estimating monetary values of alternatives. This is that some of the resources which are being priced for the estimates do not command current prices. These are things that the organisation already possesses but is unwilling or unable to lend or sell to others. Supposing a firm is thinking of using some of its

F

spare cash to rebuild an old warehouse. If it is applying opportunity cost reasoning, it will first do an important sum. It will compare the return on this particular investment with the other uses the cash could be put to either inside the firm (in terms of alternative improvements) or even outside it (in terms of, say, equity investment, government stock or bank deposits). The important point here is that with money such alternative uses can be estimated relatively easily. In particular, the external use can be easily derived because there is a continuous market in money. But with certain other things the firm already owns this hardly applies. For example, the firm may wish to use some currently available plant for purposes of making product X. Now the alternative uses to which the plant could be put may well include hiring it to outsiders or even selling it off. But there may be no current market prices to indicate what it would fetch. In such cases the organisation has to fall back on what are called imputed costs. In effect it has to use shadow prices.

UNUSED RESOURCES

Our next move on this rapid tour of opportunity costs involves one of the most economically important and socially complex problems, that of unused resources. The idea of maximum production (the production frontier) serves a useful purpose partly because it highlights the problem of slack, of unmobilised abilities. When related to engineering conditions and machines, as in the alpha–beta case above, slack is relatively precisely measurable. With unused human resources it hardly needs saying that the problems are more complex and sensitive. It is often assumed that people's normal financial rewards when they are fully employed can be taken as a reasonable measure of the 'slack' or 'loss to society' when they are unemployed or underemployed. But whether people's financial rewards necessarily measure their value either to organisations or society is often highly debatable (nurses? property speculators? poets?). Moreover, people's feelings and experiences must be considered. Apart from a minority, most unemployed people appear to suffer more than just wage losses when they are consistently on the dole. Therefore, to measure the opportunity cost of human unemployment by lost wages or lost production at current market values can be somewhat crude. Nonetheless, the opportunity cost principle insists that the sacrifice of unemployed people's contributions must be properly focused and taken into account.

Seriously under-used resources, physical or human, are not only a reproach to society, particularly to one under pressure, they also pose certain practical problems for organisations. For example, physical plant may be under-utilised because of a seasonal downswing, a temporary drop in demand, the existence of indivisibilities or fixed working hours (electrical plants, railways and buses, hay making machinery, school and university buildings, etc.). As a result people employed by the concern may be in a state of idleness. The organisation is reluctant to fire them, partly for financial reasons – they would be difficult and expensive to replace – and partly because of humanity. Assuming that organisations are constantly on the lookout for chances of bringing such unemployed resources into action, how then does opportunity cost reasoning apply?

Supposing an opportunity exists for using some unemployed plant, X, as a result of a new activity, Y. In estimating the cost of Y, the decision maker must be wary of allocating to it the existing costs of X. If he sees no alternative use for X the opportunity cost of employing it on Y may well be virtually nil. Strictly speaking, the opportunity cost may relate to the more radical alternatives of selling X or even disposing of it for scrap. But, on the assumption that the decision maker does not want to do this, he will certainly be justified in regarding the opportunity costs of employing X on Y as virtually nil. It follows that he should emphatically *not* pile the existing costs of X onto the costs of Y. If he does so, the advantage of Y in bringing X into use will be understated. A valuable contract may even be turned down, an excessively high price quoted, a useful mobilisation chance missed.

Transposing this reasoning onto the more sensitive plane of human resources, supposing the organisation has some temporarily idle employees whom it is considering using full time on an activity, A. So long as the only alternative to using them on A is complete idleness, then their entire employment costs should be disregarded for purposes of estimating the costs of A. In the case of another alternative, B, which would occupy 25 per cent of their working hours, 25 per cent of their employment costs should be disregarded, and so on. Here again, to do otherwise would be to load the dice against employing human resources more fully. In this case the organisation may well feel that the intangible benefits to employee morale should be considered, too. But whatever the nuances, opportunity cost reasoning should be followed in this critical matter of mobilising otherwise idle resources in the face of new opportunities.

STRATEGIC DECISIONS

We now turn to the most difficult zone of all, that of strategic decision making. Here all sorts of elements – measurable, partially measurable or plain elusive – jostle together. Decision makers are faced with boldly assorted packages of alternatives, each including, so to say, apples, oranges, elephants or perhaps mermaids. In this zone it is a caricature to imagine that a mere plus or minus sign followed by a figure can measure the opportunity cost of one alternative against another. Instead, entirely non-quantified approaches may have to be used. Alternatively, more elaborate methods of marshalling the relevant data must be applied. Nonetheless, as we finally reach the boardroom, executive committee or council chamber – or in many cases simply the mind of a single boss – the packages do take some recognisable forms. One form is that of the purely verbal sort of balance sheet of advantages and disadvantages of alternatives A, B. C, etc. Another is where A is partially or wholly measurable, but B and C not so. Again, A, B and C are all measurable on the same scale, that of money, but only partially so. Or again, A, B and C are all partially measurable, but incommensurably.

In the case of such complex alternatives opportunity costs may have to be expressed in plural form. For example, suppose that the board of directors of a company are considering three alternative investment projects. They are concerned not only with the quantifiable financial flows but also with less quantifiable factors bearing on the company's long-term profitability and growth. Drastically simplified here for presentation purposes, the final package coming before the directors might look something like Table 4. Here the opportunity cost of B will be minus £2 million and a higher risk than with one alternative. The opportunity cost of C will be minus £5 million and a considerable loss of potential unquantifiable benefit. The opportunity cost of A will be a higher risk than with both alternatives and a loss of some potential unquantifiable benefit. The

Table 4   *A business investment*

| | Alternative projects | | |
	A	B	C
Net present value	£18m	£16m	£13m
Risk	'High'	'Middling'	'Low'
Unquantifiable benefits for firm (public relations, morale) – ranking	(2)	(1)	(3)

plural opportunity costs having been marshalled to clarify their choice, the directors will have to exercise judgement in reaching a final decision.

In the social sector strategic decisions often involve still more diverse contours of opportunity cost. For example, suppose a local authority is considering two alternative town plans. A final 'planning balance sheet' sort of package (see Chapter 11), again drastically simplified, might look something like this.

Table 5   *Town improvement*

| Net benefits | Alternative plans | |
	A	B
Local authority	+£2·0m	+£0·5m
Local business	+£0·8m	+£0·3m
Car owners (20,000)	+	−
Pedestrians (60,000)	+	+ +
People in Area 1 (44,000)	Not affected	+
People in Area 2 (36,000)	+	Not affected
Appearance of town	+	+ +

Roughly speaking, compared with B, A denies potential benefit to 60,000 pedestrians, 44,000 people in Area 1 and the appearance of the town. Compared with A, B denies potential benefit to the council and local business financially and to 35,000 people in Area 2; and compared with the existing situation it also deprives 20,000 car owners of some benefit. Assuming that car owners and pedestrians are evenly distributed between Areas 1 and 2, a crude head count would suggest B as the potentially 'more popular' alternative, since it would benefit greater numbers of townspeople. The shape of public response to the proposals, though, would need to be gauged. An important point is the difference between hypothetical and real losses. Compared with the present situation most town-dwellers would gain under either plan, but the car owners would actually lose an existing advantage under B and they might shout particularly loudly. Another factor is that of external opportunity costs (see Table 2, column (*b*)) – perhaps the government would have views on the implications for people *outside* the town. Presumably the local authority's decision will finally depend on the attitudes of the elected representatives to (*a*) financial economy, (*b*) aesthetics, (*c*) equity criteria and (*d*) their electoral interests. In this final zone opportunity cost reasoning is still applied – often most intensely of all.

FAILURES AND PROBLEMS

Although much of this is rather obvious, opportunity costs are frequently ignored or mishandled in practice. As a result organisations are less efficient than they could be according to either their own standards or those of market performance or society. At worst, miscalculations are made and opportunities missed. At best, subtle and invisible elements of slack tend to accrete. The existing production frontier, using this idea in a very general sense, will be unwittingly missed by a long chalk or perhaps chances of actually pushing it forward will be passed up. Of the managerial failures over opportunity costs some of the most frequent are merely perceptual insofar as decision makers are averse to change and fail to see that the 'no change' option itself has costs. Failures may arise because of the baneful influence of antiquated accounting notions (sometimes as bad as antiquated economic ones). More subtly, perhaps, the resources to which opportunity cost reasoning should be applied are too near at hand. Perhaps they are resources actually 'owned' by the decision maker which he finds it hard to see all that clearly, not excluding that nearest resource of all, his own skills and time. Consider the following:

(1) A firm with essential but spare capacity costing £1,000 per annum to maintain gets the unique chance of an order which would use the capacity for six months. Its accountants insist that unless the quoted price of the order includes £500 maintenance costs relating to the capacity, the order would be 'uneconomic' or 'not fairly contributing to overheads'.

(2) A local authority is considering the purchase of two possible sites for a swimming pool. It compares their physical attributes and purchase prices but fails to consider other social uses to which they might be put.

(3) The same thing happens but perhaps the authority already owns one of the sites, which is currently used as a football ground. In discussing the swimming pool project the authority's officers include the problem of losing the football ground as an opportunity cost – and also the problem of obtaining another football ground – but again ignore the alternative uses of the site.

(4) A company contemplating a major investment is wondering whether to borrow or use a major accretion of internal funds. It carefully calculates the cost of borrowing but sees no costs applying to the internal funds 'because they are just lying idle'.

(5) A young man, who recently earned £6,000 a year in a large organisation, starts up a company where he uses the same skills as before. He currently takes a salary of £3,000 from the business which he reckons is making a pre-tax profit of £2,000. When an economist friend points out to him, not altogether tactfully, that the 'true profit' is probably nearer a loss of about £1,000, he is irritated and confounded.

These are basically failures of perception within an existing band of relationships and possibilities. At the other extreme there is the inability of many organisations to perceive new or unusual resource–use alternatives or, indeed, to create new resources altogether – a failure which is set into relief by the small minority of social and business innovators who do succeed in this. Not least, there are differences of perspective on opportunity costs – between the decision makers on the one hand and others in their sector or in the wider markets in which they operate, or in society as a whole. Such differences may be about internal or external opportunity costs, sometimes both. Moreover, it is not always easy to decide who is right. We may be confident that the directors of a large corporation who install marble wash basins in their top executive washrooms are sub-optimising the use of resources. We may criticise a charitable organisation set up in 1850 to aid British sufferers from jemillitis because, although there are hardly any of such people still alive today, this charity has £10 million investments and refuses to assist jemillitis sufferers in Biafra or to seek legal changes in its status so as to pursue other charitable activities.[4] We may puzzle over the activities of a charismatic bishop who has such success in channelling diocesan resources into children's homes or theological libraries that other possible uses of church money for diocesan purposes are not even considered.[5] Such cases certainly appear to involve defective opportunity cost reasoning. But what are we to make of the small firm boss who refuses to borrow from a bank for urgently needed capital re-equipment because he has 'conscientious objections to borrowing'? Or of an organisation which has used a valuable city site for half a century and, although offered the chance of a large capital gain, refuses to sell? Or of a local authority which demolishes an historic town centre and builds a vast new shopping centre in the interests of 'a more economic use of wasted resources'? Or of a squatters' group which moves homeless families into properties that have remained empty for over two years?

OPPORTUNITY COST REASONING IN PRACTICE

The best way of drawing the threads of this chapter together is to give some examples of opportunity cost reasoning in practice. Comments on these are restricted to a minimum and to a large extent the reader must draw his own conclusions. In our discussion of management problems we have moved from the more tractable, if often complex problems towards increasingly intractable ones. This has meant successively relaxing the conditions of quantifiability and determinateness. But the time has now come also to relax some further assumptions that have been made, usually implicitly. These are that single decision makers face explicit choices which are neatly lined up at a single moment of time. Although such assumptions help to clarify discussion of rational approaches to management, they are for the most part hopelessly unrealistic. The following examples remind us of the messiness in which opportunity cost reasoning can and must still be pursued. Split decision making, fuzzy or merely implicit choices, decisions that cannot be attributed to particular points of time or that were rushed in response to crisis or emergency – all these will be found. Returning to our earlier distinctions, the reader should also find examples of both internal and external opportunity costs, monetary or non-monetary, *ex ante* or *ex post*, and internally or externally perceived.

(1) In the 1960s and early 1970s financial operators like Jim Slater, Max Joseph and John Bentley made big profits by buying up sleepy companies which were merely sitting on potentially lucrative assets. Sometimes the financial operators reactivated the companies they bought, sometimes they stripped their assets for cash. They were continually scanning the horizon for vulnerable firms, smelling out under-valued items in balance sheets, comparing the profits they themselves could make between one takeover situation and another. For example, an important consideration was whether a company was using a currently, or potentially, valuable bit of land. Perhaps they could be renting a site instead, or locate somewhere else altogether – in which case the land could be sold at a handsome profit.

Comment: A straightforward case of financial opportunity cost reasoning by the takeover tycoons, with probably complex management situations in the sleepy 'victim' firms and with conflicting views on the opportunity costs of present resource uses being held by insiders and outsiders.

(2) Many older family firms stagnate and decline. They become not

only inefficient and tradition-bound, but also caught in a position where, even with the best of intentions, reform is exceedingly difficult. Their bosses may perceive the desirability of rationalisation or diversification. But they may be held back by outdated buildings, obstructive employees to whom the firm owes loyalty or managerial limitations. Moreover, a takeover by another company may be difficult on account of the firm's unattractive assets. But nor do the bosses wish to liquidate, partly because they would find it hard to get other jobs offering comparable status and rewards.[6]

Comment: Probably these men have already weighed up, among other things, the personal opportunity costs of staying where they are compared with liquidating or selling out and seeking other employment – and they have felt better off battling on.

(3) A medium-sized engineering firm, the Adeco Company, faced some crucial decisions about its future. Basically, there seemed to be three alternative courses of action. Mr Newman, the managing director, a hard-working and dedicated man who had built up the firm from humble beginnings, favoured a vigorous, long-term policy of expansion and diversification. His colleague, Mr Fullslow, a conservative-minded man, took little interest in the business and wanted things to stay pretty much as they were. Mr Sharp, an accountant and outside director, wanted the company to take advantage of the rocketing value of its city centre premises by selling this property and moving elsewhere – or better, selling out altogether. Both Newman and Sharp maintained that his alternative was the most profitable, Sharp in a highly quantified way.

Comment: A case of conflicting internal objectives and almost completely incommensurable alternatives.

(4) An important social consideration for the nationalised industries is the effect of their major decisions on local employment. Their new investment plans may involve external benefits insofar as they provide jobs in less prosperous areas for people who might otherwise be unemployed. This aspect was covered in a cost–benefit assessment of the Seaton Carew Power Station carried out for the Central Electricity Generating Board in 1968. This first appraised, in a conventional manner, the relative merits of a nuclear or coal-fired station, purely from the CEGB's point of view. But the labour costs were then reduced in the light of estimates of the number of people taken on who would otherwise be unemployed and of how long they would be otherwise unemployed. In effect this meant virtually excluding from the anticipated costs the potential power station earnings of these otherwise-to-be-unemployed people. The

result of this adjustment was to swing the balance towards having a coal-fired station.[7]

Comment: The decision makers considered the external opportunity costs of their alternatives in relation to unemployed people and took these into account specifically and quantifiably.

(5) The Board of Directors of a large international company were faced with a difficult decision over senior management promotion. They had to appoint a new managing director for an important overseas division – a job requiring great ability and knowledge of the business. The choice had narrowed down to two men, James Worthy, the existing number two of the division, and Frank Brilliant, one of the company's most outstanding managers who was strongly tipped as an eventual member of the board. On balance the directors favoured Brilliant as the man most likely to put the division into a proper shape. One problem, though, was whether Worthy, who would need to be kept on as number two, would agree to work for Brilliant. Another was whether Brilliant could be spared from his present job, where it would be very hard to find a replacement. There were also at least two other assignments coming up where Brilliant's exceptional abilities might be needed.

Comment: An example of keen-edged opportunity cost reasoning in the critical but almost completely unquantifiable area of personnel decisions.

(6) Public authorities provide extensive grants to voluntary organisations in the fields of sport, the arts and social welfare. Sometimes the grants are provided for voluntary services which overlap with those provided by local authorities, for example certain welfare services for the blind or deaf, children or the very old. An authoritative report considered that 'such arrangements can present problems both to the local authority, which may be led to neglect its own responsibilities, and to the voluntary organisation, which may be prevented from developing its critical and pioneer role'.[8] However, local authorities which want to tackle what they regard as urgent social problems, but which are faced with critical shortages of staff and money, may feel they have no alternative but to subsidise such 'parallel' or 'overlapping' voluntary activities. In these cases they may figure out how much less this costs them than they would have to pay for the services themselves – even though the question of whether they *could* provide such services may be academic for the time being.

Comment: Opportunity costs of concluding agency arrangements apply to both the voluntary organisations and the local authorities.

But they do so in differing forms. Moreover, in both cases, cross-currents in opportunity cost reasoning apply.

(7) A large business, occupying a valuable urban site, applied to the local authority for planning permission to develop the site for an office block and hotel. The application was controversial because there was an acute shortage of land in the borough for housing and other social purposes which many borough council members considered to be very pressing. The council's officers reported that the proposed office and hotel development was technically sound from a planning point of view and also that it would provide a sizeable and welcome addition to the borough's rate income. However, many councillors were averse to a commercial development on the site and wanted the council to buy it for housing and children's play space. They argued that a commercial development would pre-empt the land from social needs for many generations. The owners had already refused an offer to purchase from the council. There was then a vigorous debate between (*a*) elected members who were prepared to accept the commercial development, mainly for financial reasons, (*b*) those who wanted the council to increase its offer, and (*c*) those who wanted the council to refuse the planning application, in which case there would be an appeal to the minister, who would have to decide finally what should happen to the land.

Comment: The biggest mixture of opportunity cost evaluators, the most heterogeneous collection of quantifiable and unquantifiable factors, and the biggest actual or potential conflicts.

(8) In his empirical study, *The Nature of Managerial Work*, Henry Mintzberg discusses a vital but often neglected issue, the opportunity cost of the time of senior managers.

'Throughout each working day, the manager is faced with a myriad of decisions involving the allocation of his own time.

Should I make an appointment to see this salesman? Can I afford the time for a tour? Should I call him back or ask my assistant to do so? Is half an hour long enough for our PR man to explain his problem? Is this trip abroad sufficiently important or should I delay it? Should I represent us at the dinner for the trade mission?

Most important, these decisions have effect well beyond the manager and his own schedule. In scheduling his own time, the manager is in fact determining the interests of his organization and setting its priorities for action. In effect the manager announces by his schedule that certain issues are important to the organization and that others, because they receive little or none of his time, are inconsequential. Those issues that receive low priority do not reach the formal authority of the organization and are blocked for want of resources. Subordinates, it would appear, react strongly to these priorities set implicitly by the manager. They will learn, by their inability to interest him, that certain issues are to be avoided in favor of others . . . The results of his scheduling decisions indicate how powerful the manager of an organization really is, how much influence he can exert in simple ways over the diverse affairs of his organization. They also indicate the enormous opportunity cost of the manager's time to his organization.'[9]

Comment: Opportunity costs here are diffuse, widespread, likely to be implicit and possibly even veiled from the top decision makers concerned. Here again there is the key problem with which this chapter began: how far are decision makers aware of the opportunity costs of their actions – and both able and willing to make these explicit?

Chapter 6

Time, Risk and Uncertainty

Among the challenges facing decision makers there are none so inescapable and baffling as those presented by time, risk and uncertainty. Over the past fifty years economic discussion of these issues
has greatly increased. Two main themes have dominated, the idea
of time discounting and the possibilities of confronting risk and
uncertainty in a rational manner. On both of these fronts certain
clear intellectual formulas have emerged with both descriptive and
normative uses. The formulas can help us to understand what
decision makers actually do, usually implicitly, about the problems
of time, risk and uncertainty. Properly used, the formulas can also
help decision makers in organisations to think about time, risk and
uncertainty more consistently and clearly. The formulas cannot
substitute for creative, imaginative and courageous decisions about
the future but they can prepare the ground.

TIME PREFERENCE, RISK AND DISCOUNTING

Consider first of all the varying time scales of decision makers and
organisations. The owner-manager of a small firm may be in the
saddle for thirty or forty years. The director of a large corporation
probably sits on the board for only a few years but may identify
with corporate time horizons extending over several decades. Local
politicians can be thrown out of office at the next elections, but
they too may identify with party or municipal aspirations stretching
to great chunks of a century or even beyond. A welfare pressure
group may be ephemeral, a religious organisation millennial. Consider also the varying physical time scales of productive factors. It
takes three or four years to plan and build a new housing estate,
perhaps more than a decade to develop a sophisticated new chemical
product. A cinema set may be discarded after a single production,
a car assembly line after a decade, a dam after a century. To these
categories of organisational time economics applies certain familiar
decision-related concepts, notably the *short run* (in which an organisation's productive capacity, plant, land, artists' materials, muni-

cipal buildings or whatever are fixed); the *long run* (in which the productive capacity is variable); a project's *economic life* (the period during which its benefits exceed its costs); and *investment decisions* (spending on new physical capacity, research, development, training and social capital, from which long run rather than short run benefits are anticipated).

The most important decision-related concepts of time discussed by economics, however, have to do with expectations about and attitudes towards, the future. Organisations are constantly deciding, for themselves or others, how far to favour one period of future time, immediate or distant, over another. For example, a business or local authority which fails to modernise its capital is effectively relieving the present of the burden of paying for the future. Conversely, expenditures on new synthetic materials, advanced medical research, the building of new universities or the planning of forests imply massive assumptions about people's desires or needs in the distant future. Such long-term expenditures may also express a sense of moral responsibility for the continuity of communities or corporations – or indeed towards future generations. On the whole organisations tend to discount the future. They see far distant horizons as too blurred for sensible planning – and the human pressures and responsibilities of the immediate future are strong. But whether decision makers sacrifice the future to the present or vice versa, their effective choices on such issues of time are frequently blurred. The allocative choices between time periods – together with the underlying reasons for preferring benefits in one period rather than another – are often implicit, unconscious and confused.

At this point economics proclaims an important, although sometimes unwelcome doctrine. It declares that present-versus-future allocative choices should be brought into the open. It affirms that decision makers should (a) make certain distinctions on why they discount the future if this is what they are doing, (b) seek to measure the extent to which they discount the future and (c) make such choices fully explicit so that they can be tested and, if necessary, debated.

With regard to (a), clearly there are many reasons, psychological, sociological, cultural and ethical, why decision makers should, colloquially speaking, take the view that 'a bird in the hand is worth two in the bush'. The question posed by economics is, do they discount the future because they prefer near benefits to far-away benefits, whether for themselves or others now living, and both of these to ultra-distant benefits which will affect only future generations? Alternatively, do decision makers discount the future because they perceive it as full of risks and uncertainties which they simply dislike – and the further ahead, the greater these risks and uncertainties? Although these reasons for preferring near horizons and discounting distant ones tend to interrelate, they are distinct. For example, a mining company possesses some potentially highly profitable mines which it has no need or possibility of exploiting in the near future. Nonetheless, the company may decide to borrow heavily on the security of the future earnings. Effectively, it prefers money now to money later. That is on the assumption, of course, that the mines will in fact turn out to be profitable. But if the company sees a strong risk that they will not be – perhaps as a result of potentially adverse shifts in supply and demand – it will have even more reason to discount the future earnings. The reader, faced with a clear choice between jam in 1980, jam in 1990 or jam in 2000, other things remaining equal, should ask himself which he would prefer. He should then ask himself how his preference would change if the probability of jam being available in 1990 or 2000 increases or decreases as opposed to, say, honey, or even perhaps a new type of synthetic sandwich spread. Clearly, there is a distinction between the two sorts of problem. The first problem, which economics labels *time preference*, concentrates on attitudes towards present versus future benefits in themselves, other people's or one's own, and has the advantage of highlighting certain questions of largely moral choice. The second problem, that of *anticipating risks and uncertainties* concentrates on how we actually perceive future events and on how we react to these perceptions.

Next, (*b*), economics suggests that the precise extent to which we discount the future, if that is what we are doing, should, as far as possible, be measured. Where the source of benefit is readily quantifiable (money, jam, days on the beach), measurement involves using a *discount rate*. To take a simple example, if immediate expenditure of £100 on a project is estimated to yield net returns of £50 in year 1, £50 in year 2 and £50 in year 3, the best measure of the expected total return is most emphatically not a crude £150, since this implies that an equal weight is attached to receiving £1 in any of the three future years. Such a point of view is unlikely. More probably, earlier money returns will be preferred to later ones, either because this simply gives more satisfaction (positive time preference) or because of fear that later returns are more liable to risk (uncertainty discount) or very likely both. Suppose that we decide that the extent to which we prefer one year's money to the next year's money applies evenly all the way through. Such a constant or linear discount rate, although not always applicable, is normally a convenient assumption. Now suppose, finally, that the extent to which we prefer one year's money to the next is 6 per cent. All that discounting does is then to take our estimated returns over the three years and, using the selected discount rate of 6 per cent, compress these into a single figure, the *net present value* of the project. This simply reverses the familiar process of compound interest. With compound interest we work forwards from an existing sum, say £100, and apply an interest rate to see how much more the £100 will be worth in so many years time. With discounting, however, we work backwards from estimated future sums and apply a discount rate to see how much less these sums would be worth now. An alternative method is to compare the expected outlays on a project with its expected benefits and then to apply an algebraic equation so as to find a rate of discount that equates the two. This mathematically derived rate, described as the *internal rate of return*, is then compared with a target or standard discount rate, say 6 per cent as above, to see how the project shapes up. Both methods have their technical advantages and disadvantages. In both cases the mathematics are straightforward. The net present value method uses simple discount tables, the internal rate of return method an algebraic formula. The intricacies of these formulas do not matter for our purposes and the interested reader is referred to the literature if he wants more detail (see the Note on Further Reading at the end of the chapter).

What is important in the economic sense is that discount rates can precisely express the degree to which near benefits are, in practice, preferred to more distant ones. They provide decision makers with useful benchmarks for deciding between future projects. Armed with the discount rates or rates of return which the market, the government or they themselves think appropriate, decision makers simply apply these to the estimated cash flows from alternative investment projects. Discounting represents a fairer and more consistent method of screening potential investments than more old-fashioned methods of investment appraisal. Unlike them, it takes three very important things into account: (*a*) the complete stream of quantifiable benefits estimated to result from an investment, (*b*) the shape of this stream over time and (*c*) the opportunity cost of the funds invested. Hence the increasing use of DCF techniques over recent years, particularly in large companies and nationalised industries. But there are many problems about discounting in practice.

DISCOUNTING IN PRACTICE

The first major problem is that of deciding what discount rate should be applied. Obviously the mere mechanics of DCF as applied to serried rows of estimates are unimportant compared with the choice of discount rate. To start with, how much freedom do organisations have in deciding what discount rate to use? Planners in private sector businesses have their hands partly forced by the money markets. It is through the capital markets that time preferences – and attitudes towards future risks as perceived by a myriad interacting business opinions – are collectively evolved. The resulting costs of capital, both rates of interest on loans and equity returns expected by shareholders, *already* discount the future. These costs of capital in turn help to determine the discount rates employed by business planners in their investment decisions. A profit-anxious business cannot afford to invest in too many projects whose discounted rates of return appear to fall below market rates. Indeed, some companies estimate the long-term market costs of capital – a complicated calculation involving past experience and assessments of lenders' and investors' future expectations. These companies then regard this rate as an opportunity cost of capital, measuring not only what investors but also what they themselves might receive by investing outside the firm. This market rate is then used as a 'cut-off', minimum or 'test rate of discount' when considering whether to back particular investment projects with widely varying net present values or internal rates of return.

In nationalised industry it is the government that decides what test discount rates or financial benchmarks are appropriate. Generally, long-term market rates are used for this purpose with various modifications mainly for risk. The application of market-related rates to nationalised industries is another example of opportunity cost reasoning. Since money required for public sector investment, so it is said, would otherwise be employed for private sector investments, it should be subjected to a comparable test in the interests of both equity and efficiency. Against this it is sometimes said that, as articulator of the long-term national interest, government should be prepared to apply a discount rate considerably lower than the market's, in order to allow for social benefits in excess of internal ones. It is certainly arguable that any market-related discounts applied to the public sector should be adjusted to take account of social costs and benefits. For example, if a nationalised industry investment would provide much needed local

G

employment or strategic value to the country, then the market-related opportunity cost discount rate should arguably be adjusted to take account of this. In fact, such an adjustment is frequently attempted.

A very important point is that discount rates are often applied implicitly rather than explicitly. This is particularly the case where management is unsophisticated or where the benefits from investments are hard to quantify. In the business sector decision makers often look at the estimated costs and benefits of a project and apply a subjective or informal discount. For example, perhaps a businessman 'doesn't want to know' about any investment with a longer economic life than, say, 10 or 15 years. Such cut-off points or rules of thumb are ubiquitous. Many businesses pare down their reserves and borrow to the hilt whereas others accumulate fat balances and may even refuse to borrow. The same contrasts are to be found among charitable organisations. In all such cases discounting is implicit.

But it is in the social sector that implicit discounting is most prevalent. In considering long-term expenditures on health and education, housing, social services and the environment, social decision makers are bound to attach weights to estimated social benefits at different points of future time. To quantify such weights is extremely difficult for the obvious reason that the benefits from social investments are themselves hard to quantify (see Chapter 11). But although precise discount rates are often inapplicable, this does not mean that nothing can be done. The economic principle is still the same as elsewhere – that the implied discounts of the future, the time preferences and risk evaluations underlying them should all be laid bare, properly justified and if necessary debated. Indeed, in the social sector such openness and explicitness are demanded not only by economic rationality but democracy itself. It is often essential to raise such questions as, how many people are likely to benefit from the social investment at various times in the future? Should benefits for those now living and future generations be equally weighted? Are the social resources invested in likely to become obsolescent because of advances in technology or wealth, or changes in social attitudes? Alternatively, are the resources likely to produce new benefits which can only be dimly glimpsed at present? In other words, what is their economic life? For example, consider the following:

(1) A large hospital is considering major expenditures on kidney machines. Is it possible to quantify the estimated benefits from

the machines in terms of estimated years of life saved for present and future kidney sufferers? If so, should the estimated life savings be valued equally for all concerned? (Presumably the answer to this question would be 'yes'.) How likely are the kidney machines to be superseded by new medical break throughs by, say, 2010 or 2020? How far, therefore, should the future benefits be written down to allow for this factor? Preferably, all this should be done in such a manner as to produce an estimate of the total return (years of life saved) relative to the money expenditure – or perhaps a range of such estimates linked with varying assumptions about risk (and incidentally this estimated return on kidney machines could be compared with that on other medical investments, see Chapter 4).

(2) Local authority housing schemes exemplify difficult problems of time preference and risk. For example, what are the risks of later generations disliking the housing, being able to afford better or at least wanting modifications? How can such risks be taken into account? Is it right to spend so much on durable buildings for future generations when so many people today urgently need housing? If lower-cost, shorter-life housing could be erected or improved to an acceptable standard – letting the far distant future take care of itself – would this time preference not be fairer by housing more people more quickly? Such questions should at least be debated.

(3) Public and voluntary money is used to preserve cathedrals, stately homes, stretches of beautiful coastline or national parks, often applying time horizons of several centuries. Whereas in (2) there may be a risk of foisting something onto future generations to the detriment of existing ones, here there is a risk that if something is not done, various options may be closed to future generations altogether. The assumption behind preservation is that if a building or environment has been revered and enjoyed for centuries then, if still available, it will continue to be so. The implied discount rate, based on probabilistic reasoning is virtually nil. But should this not be made explicit?

(4) Haunting dilemmas in social time preference arise over the so called 'cycle of deprivation', in which the children of poor and deprived parents grow up to become poor and deprived themselves and then hand on the same legacy to their own children. What should be the balance between spending to alleviate the immediate symptoms of such deprivation – basically for the sake of the near future – and more radical expenditures aimed at

'breaking into the cycle' in the longer term? For example, what should be the priority between emergency aid for, on the one hand, helpless old people and 'problem families', and, on the other hand, long-term investments for infant children, community life or family education?

(5) Overseas aid agencies like Oxfam face an even starker dilemma. Is it better to concentrate resources on urgent famine relief in poor countries or on community projects designed to increase self-help and food-growing capacity in the longer term? The agency may try to get round the dilemma by mounting special appeals to help in the worst emergencies whilst using its regular funds for longer-term development projects. But given the relatively infinitesimal funds available for overseas aid, the dilemma is inescapable and also particularly morally difficult. At this point economics probably has no need to urge the need for explicitness and debate. Decision makers on the grim frontiers of starvation and poverty are likely to be acutely aware of the problem of time preference.

RATIONAL METHODS OF DEALING WITH RISK AND UNCERTAINTY

So far we have talked about risk in general terms. The time has come to be more precise. What is meant by 'risk' anyway and how do we distinguish it from 'uncertainty'? The basic distinction here was clearly expressed by, among others, Frank Knight over fifty years ago.[1] Knight identified the key concept as that of probability. When decision makers lack certain knowledge of future events but can estimate statistical probabilities fairly reliably on the basis of past experience, then we have situations of *risk*. When past experience cannot be mobilised in this way and future probabilities can only be subjectively assessed, if at all, then we have situations of *uncertainty*. Many situations of risk, where past experience is used statistically to generate objective probabilities, are handled by the insurance industry, for example, fire, accident, theft, natural disasters, early death. Although Knight and others who followed in the debate often differed on the underlying meaning of probability in itself, they tended to agree that the most important and difficult management problems involve uninsurable uncertainty. In practice, the distinction between uncertainty and the more actuarial situations of risk is far from rigid. In ordinary language risk situations roughly correspond to those that can be 'calculated' or 'estimated', whereas uncertainty implies the 'guesstimate', the 'guess' or the 'hunch'. But the spectrum appears to be continuous, ranging from pure risk, where observations of past experience form a clear guide, across to deep uncertainty which may take the form of believing that any of an indeterminate number of future possibilities are equally probable, and even of mistrusting that belief in itself.

Let us now briefly outline the principal methods of thinking rationally about risk and uncertainty as recommended by economics and decision theory. There is no need for anything more than a brief glimpse of each. The interested reader should refer to the technical literature for more detail. The important thing is to have some idea of these methods as a guide to the sort of thinking required.

Probability distributions
Starting from the clearest situations of risk, let us assume that, in approaching a decision, the organisation possesses useful data (its own or other people's) on past experience. Let us also assume that the organisation intelligently mobilises this past experience in the form of statistical probability distributions. For example, the probability distributions shown in Figure 3 might represent estimates, based on past experience, of (*a*) expected rates of return on a business investment and (*b*) expected cost escalations on a local authority building project. (Another method of showing the same information would be a cumulative probability distribution. This would enable decision makers to see what are the probabilities of rates of return or excess costs being greater or less than certain amounts.) Obviously such probability distributions depend on the quantity and quality of past data, the competence of statistical

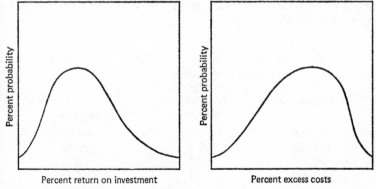

Figure 3 Probability distribution; returns on investment and excess costs

analysis and the reliability of inductive judgement as to the continuity of the future with the past. The important thing is that where past data exist probability distributions should be derived and used in decision making.

Expected values
Most methods of thinking rationally about risks and uncertainties are adaptations or developments of the basic theme of the probability distribution. For example, the second principal method, that of expected values, collapses a given probability distribution into a single figure. Suppose estimates of the financial outcomes of a decision are concentrated around five figures – minus £1,000, +£1,000, +£2,000, +£3,000 and +£4,000. The chances of an outcome outside these limits are considered to be derisory. Suppose, too, that the probabilities of each outcome occurring are estimated as shown in Table 6. Note that the probabilities must sum to unity because, for practical purposes, the listed outcomes are considered to be collectively exhaustive. What then happens is simple. Each outcome is weighted by the estimated probability of its occurrence and the weighted outcomes are added up to a single figure, the expected value resulting from a decision. As a weighted average derived from a probability distribution, the expected value is much better than a simple arithmetical average. Whether it is best for a particular decision depends on the nature of the problem. Expected value may be fairly used to portray a sub-element of risk within an overall risk profile for a major decision – for example, the estimated costs of certain materials required for a big project. However, if the sub-element is particularly important – and also if the dispersion of outcomes is particularly wide – it may be better to show the full probability distribution.

Table 6 *Derivation of expected value from estimated probability of outcomes*

Values of outcomes	Probability of occurrence	Weighted values of outcomes
−1,000	0·1	−100
+1,000	0·3	+300
+2,000	0·4	+800
+3,000	0·2	+600
	Expected value	+1,600

Focus values

As developed by the economist Shackle, this third idea echoes and crystallises a common experience in confronting uncertainty. Suppose a decision maker is faced with a wide array of possible outcomes and lacks the confidence to say anything objective about their relative probability. Specific experience is so lacking that there is true uncertainty. Nonetheless the decision maker is still able to summon up his general experience and powers of judgement. What he should do, according to Shackle, is to concentrate on just two outcomes, namely those which seem 'most interesting' to him – one of these outcomes being 'desirable', the other 'undesirable'. In this way, 'the individual reduces any uncertainty situation to the simplicity of an ordinary bet, in which only two possible outcomes are considered, one of which is a definite amount of gain, the other a definite amount of loss'.[2] Note that according to Shackle's concept the two values selected would not be the extreme values or wing boundaries, the 'very best' or 'very worst' outcomes. Instead, they would be the outcomes which the decision maker subjectively sees as the most realistic, interesting and worthy of attention, respectively for good or ill. In Shackle's theory the decision maker also envisages these outcomes as potentially the 'least surprising', at least to himself, if they were actually to happen.

There are, of course, several variations on the focus values idea. Investors approximate closely to it when making a 'best guess' about 'things turning out well' or 'badly'. Decision makers may well concentrate not on two outcomes but rather three – the 'worst likely', the 'best likely' and the 'most likely'. If they feel that the extreme values should not be forgotten, they chip in two more as well, the 'worst possible' and 'best possible'. The essence of the approach is that even where subjective judgement is essential, single figures are avoided and the decision maker still thinks probabilistically. Indeed, he is generating a subjective probability distribution, conceiving a rough and ready curve of risk, in his own mind, and, it is hoped, making this explicit. This makes for clearer decision making. Whether it actually makes for *better* decisions obviously depends on the decision maker's experience, judgement and skill.

Decision trees

In many cases decisions are not taken once for all at particular points of time. On the contrary, a set of decisions is taken which produces results A or B. If A happens, further decisions have to be taken, leading in turn to results A.1 or A.2. If B happens, further decisions have to be made, leading to results B.1 and B.2; and so on.

A number of theorists have discussed the decision making process from this dynamic, 'real time' point of view. They have seen decision making as an iterative, 'learning' or cybernetic process in which the organisation continually gets 'feedback' from the environment and adjusts accordingly, but with each decision also limiting the possibilities of later choice.

How best can estimated risks and uncertainties be clarified in advance when they fit into such a sequence of decisions and events? The answer is, through the device of a decision tree. This takes probability distributions, expected values or focus values, as outlined above, and depicts them as part of an unfolding sequence of anticipated future decisions and events. To illustrate, take a very simple example, that of a small building firm which is faced with a choice between two contracts. Contract A is potentially more profitable but since it involves outside work bad weather could severely affect the return. Contract B involves mostly indoor work and is relatively safe but less profitable. The situation could be portrayed in decision tree fashion as shown in Table 7. The reader can work out

Table 7   *A choice of building contracts*

Initial decision	Chance events	Estimated probability	Value of outcome
Accept contract A	Good weather	0·2	£5,500
	Middling weather	0·4	£4,000
	Bad weather	0·4	£2,500
Accept contract B	Good weather	0·2	£4,000
	Middling weather	0·4	£3,900
	Bad weather	0·4	£3,800

for himself, using the expected value criterion, that on these estimates contract B looks the better bet. But there may be disagreement within the firm about the probabilities of good, middling or bad weather. Moreover, the management may prefer to take a greater risk with contract A. For example, they may consider that even if the weather is bad, there is a chance of another indoor contract appearing, C, which would enable them to transfer workers temporarily from A to C, thus swinging the balance more firmly in favour of accepting A. This further possible event could be incorporated into the tree, with or without a probability attached to it, and so on. In this manner a decision tree can help to clarify thinking about future patterns of decisions and risks that are (a) estimated as possible or probable, (b) interrelated and (c) sequential.

Sensitivity analysis

What can be done if the elements of the decision are quantifiable but the number of variables is very large? It does not require a very complex problem to generate many hundreds or even thousands of possible outcomes. Here a computer may well have to be used. A quantitative model of the situation is developed and various techniques are used to clarify further thinking about risk. One such technique deserves special mention, that of sensitivity analysis. This involves repeatedly running a model through its paces by altering the critical assumptions behind it one by one. The object is to see how sensitive the estimated outcomes are to changes in the key variables. Simpler forms of sensitivity analysis are used every day without recourse to computers. For example, having constructed a simple model of a problem, as in the building contract example above, we use sensitivity analysis whenever we subject the estimated values of outcomes to systematic scrutiny by asking ourselves what would happen if X, Y or Z were to turn out differently. More complex forms of sensitivity analysis, though, involve a computer based technique called simulation.[3]

RISK AND UNCERTAINTY IN PRACTICE

Many of these approaches to risk and uncertainty may seem obvious. Many of them can be used simply and informally. Yet it is surprising how often they are ignored or transgressed. To point up the problems of application let us take an organisation to which the sort of thinking we have just outlined is completely foreign. How would such an organisation plan?

First of all, let us suppose that past data which could be used to generate probability distributions for future events are available to the organisation, perhaps in terms of other people's experience, perhaps lying fallow in its own records in the form of undigested statistics, sales vouchers, cost figures. But these data are ignored or, more subtly, misapplied. In the latter case, insofar as past data are used, there is a strong tendency to use crude averages and single figure estimates, sometimes also extreme values, rather than probability distributions. Second, in this non-risk-minded organisation statistical crudities are often compounded by various kinds of behavioural bias. Professional biases among the junior accountants and engineers propel them towards the spurious precision of single figure estimates; and these biases are unchecked. Moreover, people lower down the line tend to 'play safe' by producing consistently pessimistic estimates. They seek to minimise the risks to themselves by overestimating costs, underestimating benefits and producing low figures when asked for single value net benefit estimates. This reduces the risk of apparent personal failure if things turn out badly and makes subsequent performance look more impressive. Moreover, disagreements about the future which are sincerely held at junior levels are muffled or disguised in the interests of 'consensus' estimates and neat, agreed packages of recommendations for the higher-ups. Third, decision makers' preferences are not even consistently applied, for example DCF is not used in investment appraisal. Or again, more subtly, DCF is used but incorrectly. Thus, in the latter case, the discount rate may be varied as a means of allowing for varying risks, but such blanket provision for risk obscures underlying contours of uncertainty which may still need to be clarified and argued about.

But all is not over in this organisational chamber of horrors. On the one hand, the crudities and biases in assessing risk and uncertainties are not minor incidents on the way but actually become cumulative as they churn their way upwards through the organisation. Layer upon layer of implicit judgement is folded in without explanation or justification, statistical measures become cruder the further they move from the ill-digested or neglected raw data, pessimistic ploys are compounded, important differences smoothed over. Final estimates and recommendations to top management are correspondingly weak, crude or pusillanimous. But on the other hand, top management themselves are largely to blame for this situation. To a large degree the estimating weaknesses lower down reflect their inadequacies, it is their known attitudes that inspire anticipatory precautions, pessimistic biases or phoney agreements on the part of their juniors. For the top decision makers in this organisation are, and are known to be, risk averters and conservatives, or contemptuous of quantitative approaches, or, again more subtly, over fond of single figure estimates and extreme values, unaware of the massively greater merits of being 'vaguely right rather than precisely wrong'.

How can such problems be minimised? Ruth Mack, an economist who has written perceptively about 'planning on uncertainty' in business and government, suggests that the essential first step is to analyse the decision making situation in relation to various attributes before deciding what approaches to risk and uncertainty to use. For example, how much time is available for analysis? How many decision makers are there or people to be consulted? How much information is available bearing on possible outcomes? Are the objectives behind the decision sharp and quantifiable? Alternatively,

are the objectives complex, vague, conflicting, unstable and themselves even probabilistic? And not least, to what extent is the problem one of a series or apparently unique? Ruth Mack suggests that
an 'attributes profile' on these lines should be anticipated for the
decision making process. Only then should specific weaponry for
evaluating risks and uncertainties be selected.[4]

Most major investment decisions require complex mixtures of the
formulas. If elements of the problem are rich in data and precedents, these will cry out for probability distribution treatment. Once
these probability distributions have been obtained, they may be
carried forward as they stand to the next estimating stage. Alternatively, they may be wrapped up in neat parcels of expected values.
But other elements of risk will involve careful consultation with
experts – production or sales people, engineers, architects, foremen,
social workers. These people will be asked to provide personal judgements of ranges, 'best likely, worst likely' estimates, evaluations of
the odds in favour of A or B, or against Y or Z – all of these form-
ing mini-probability distributions or hillocks of focus values. In
other words the intuitive and subjective experience available will be
carefully husbanded and drawn out.

Then comes the stage of mapping all the estimates into top decision
making form. At this point, if the objectives are clear, say in terms
of profit maximising or cost minimising, relatively neat quantitative
bundles can be sewn up. Cash flows can be discounted, ranges or
likely variations shown, computer simulations of risks set up. If the
objectives and risks are more complex and many of the variables
incommensurable, however, as in most important social sector investments, several types of aid to final decision making will be needed.
These may well include decision trees, focus values and sensitivity
analysis. But it is important to realise that many of these approaches
can be applied in miniature and informally. Although sophisticated
thinking about risk and uncertainty may reach its apogee in large
concerns, it can be no less real in small ones. The fact that the risk
taker is a small businessman, a theatre manager or welfare organiser
– or that decision trees or focus values are crystallised inside a
single mind or on the back of an envelope – does not destroy their
clarifying power.

One theme should be clear. A rational approach to risk and uncertainty cannot remove the need for creative choice. There is
evidence to suggest that outright innovation and creativity inside
organisations may require approaches different from those outlined
above. The forecasting of long-term futures, the use of 'scenarios'
and heuristics, now has a literature of its own. So does the problem

of planning for conditions within and around organisations which appear to favour technological innovation, the development of new ideas in small, informal, unstructured groups, and the proper drawing-out of creative personnel. In this area economists have studied, for example, aspects of new entrepreneurship, inventions and artistic endeavour, the economics of research and development, and the apparent influence on innovation of such factors as market structure, size of organisation and managerial turnover. Better knowledge of these approaches may well be needed if the future is to be confronted creatively and imaginatively as well as rationally.

But in a wider sense, too, the rational approaches to time, risk and uncertainty discussed in this chapter have limitations. They are clarifying and preparatory rather than decisive. Economic rationality cannot remove the challenge of risk and uncertainty. Its task, still an immensely useful one, is rather to pinpoint where the real challenge lies.

SOME EXAMPLES

(1) A chemical company was considering a large extension to its plant. According to the company's 'one best estimate' approach, the project seemed likely to involve capital expenditure of $9·5 million, a sales tonnage of 250,000, a market share of 12 per cent and an economic life of 10 years. Consultants were called in to apply more sophisticated risk analysis. They asked company officials to produce ranges of estimates, for example in the case of a price they asked, 'What is the probability that the price will be higher than X? Is there any chance that it will exceed Y? How likely is it that it will drop below Z?' The experts were also asked to state what degree of confidence they had in their predictions. Subjective and/or objective probability curves were then produced for each factor. The results were incorporated in a computer simulation. The consultants finally suggested ranges for the items mentioned above – capital expenditure $7 million–10·5 million; sales tonnage 100,000–340,000; market share 3–17 per cent; economic life 5–15 years; and so on.[5]

(2) A Prices and Incomes Board enquiry into the gas industry, published in 1969, criticised the Area Gas Boards for 'basing their estimates of costs and revenues on unfavourable assumptions and taking no separate account of risk'. Boards were sometimes 'conservative' in assigning 'an unrealistically short life' for each project and in using DCF incorrectly (and also, sometimes, not even consistently) to deal with risk. The Report commented that 'where

conservatism is built into the estimates at various points and in various ways the decision maker has no quantitative measure of its cumulative effect'. The Report recommended the use of ranges rather than single value estimates; of focus values; of sensitivity analysis; and of subjective probabilities.[6]

(3) The directors of a multinational company were considering an investment in Bolazia. On the basis of production and market surveys cash flow estimates had been prepared and discounted at the company's test discount rate of 15 per cent (before tax). The project appeared to offer a high positive net present value on this basis. The estimated internal rate of return was between 25 per cent and 35 per cent, comparing very well with the test discount rate. However, there was a risk that a future radical government in Bolazia might later nationalise the investment, with or without compensation, or at least severely tax it. A further analysis therefore used decision trees, subjective probabilities and focus values in an effort to clarify (a) the political possibilities in Bolazia and (b) the company's ability to counteract these. The computerised model was successively re-run so as to simulate these possible combinations of events. Assuming a radical government, the probable range of internal rates of return was revised downwards to between 10 per cent and 20 per cent. Argument was then able to concentrate on how likely such a government might be, and the directors divided into 'optimists' and 'pessimists'. It was finally decided that the risks were at least serious enough to justify a much smaller investment until the political situation 'clarified'.

(4) A borough council were considering what sort of rate increase to levy in the coming year. Important considerations were (a) the need to maintain existing services, (b) likely government grants, (c) future inflation, (d) the council's plans to expand and improve its services, and (e) local elections due to take place in a year's time. Computer analyses were used to clarify (a), (b) and (c). These criteria suggested a rate increase of between 15 per cent and 20 per cent, depending on difficulties of defining 'maintenance of existing services' and also, more important, on some uncertainty over the level of government support. Criterion (d), on the assumption of no cuts whatever in existing plans, implied a rate increase of about 80 per cent. Criterion (e) cut two ways. On the one hand, it was felt by the senior politicians that an increase of more than 80 per cent would be 'too electorally risky' at any time and that anything more than, say 20 per cent would be politically damaging in the next (election) year. But to secure such an electorally tolerable increase in the following year would require a *bigger* increase in the current

year. If (*d*) were unchanged, something over 100 per cent might even be needed. On the other hand, severe cuts in projects could also be electorally damaging as well as internally painful and divisive.

In clarifying the problem for final decision making, the council's top politicians and officers applied focus values, subjective probabilities and sequential analysis (although not using these names). Attention was focused on three possible levels of rate increase. At each level attention was also concentrated on alternative mixtures of risks as between cuts in services or excessive rate increases in the following year. As a result six rough-and-ready bundles or packages were identified (see Table 8). Debate was then able to concentrate, in a reasonably clear-cut way, on trade-offs between politically sensitive risks.

Table 8

Possible rate increases this year %		*Implied increases next year*	
		Slight	*Large*
80	Expansion plan implications	Minor cuts	No cuts
60		Substantial cuts	Minor cuts
40		Draconian cuts	Substantial cuts

(5) In the giant computer company IBM a committee of enquiry proposed a radical new line of computers in 1961. These would completely replace IBM's existing computer line, incorporating vast technical improvements and offering many new business and scientific applications. Most of the top management thought the idea over-ambitious. There was no quantitative evaluation of risks and pay-offs. This was the only alternative sufficiently formulated to challenge the status quo. The decision to start was made: 'Everybody recognised that it was a gigantic task that would mean all our resources were tied up in one project – and we knew that for a long time we would not be getting anything out of it.' Over the ensuing four years about $5 billion was spent on the programme (equivalent to over 0·5 per cent of the United States GNP). The risk finally paid off in the shape of the IBM System 360. One enthusiastic comment was that 'the programme has pushed IBM itself into feats of performance in maufacturing, technology and communications that its own staff did not believe were possible when the project was undertaken'. One of IBM's managers was quoted as saying, 'We called this project "you bet your company",

but it was a damn good risk, and a lot less risk than it would have been to do anything else, or to do nothing at all'.[7]

Note on Further Reading

For a clear basic explanation of discounting see D. C. Hague, *Managerial Economics*, London, Longmans, 1971, Ch. 15. For a detailed discussion of the techniques and their role in capital budgeting see A. J. Merrett and Allen Sykes, *Capital Budgeting and Company Finance*, 2nd edition, London, Longmans, 1966,

For a discussion of discounting in public sector decision making see E. J. Mishan, *Cost–Benefit Analysis: An informal introduction*, 2nd edition, London, Allen & Unwin, 1975. See also relevant sections in other texts on cost–benefit analysis recommended at the end of Chapter 11.

For the treatment of risk and uncertainty, see relevant chapters in W. W. Haynes, *Managerial Economics, Analysis and Cases*, revised edition, Dallas, Business Publications, 1969; and H. Theil, J. C. G. Boot and T. Kloek, *Operations Research and Quantitative Economics: An Elementary Introduction*, New York, McGraw-Hill, 1965. For an extended non-mathematical treatment see Ruth Mack, *Planning on Uncertainty: Decision-Making in Business and Government Administration*, New York, Wiley, 1971.

Chapter 7

Size and Efficiency

We live in a world of large organisations. There is a lot of evidence to suggest that industrial concentration is increasing.[1] Many social organisations, too, appear to be getting bigger. So perennial questions about size have become more urgent. Can organisations grow too large to be efficient? Can they get too big to be effectively controlled by their managers? Even if they are internally manageable, what problems do giant organisations pose for society? Do giant businesses in particular imperil democracy and wider social interests? Is the apparent trend towards bigness inevitable? Or is it reversible, but if so at what cost? Economics helps to quantify many of these issues. Economics also provides a stimulating and necessary framework within which the debate on size and efficiency can be illuminated.

In this chapter, as before, we take efficiency to be the attainment of socially desired outputs at minimum opportunity cost. Efficiency in this sense can be looked at in three main ways. A first viewpoint concentrates on internal organisational efficiency, mainly measured by productivity ratios and average costs. Here the efficiency of a chemical plant, a printing works or a hospital, for example, is related to physical and/or money measures pertaining to inputs and outputs. A second perspective on efficiency considers wider issues. For example does the organisation produce large spillovers, good or bad? Does it control markets to such a degree that consumers are unduly manipulated or exploited? Does it defy society's desires as interpreted by constitutions and elected authorities? Obviously, an organisation may be highly efficient internally yet defective on such wider criteria. The third and final perspective on efficiency is socially comprehensive in the sense that it brings together the internal measures and the wider criteria. For obvious reasons a final judgement of social efficiency must take account of both organisational productivity and any wider social effects related to spillovers and organisational uses of economic power.

Economic analysis of the 'size effect' has revolved around one central and absorbing theme. That this theme has many intricate and even sometimes conflicting variations must not be allowed to obscure its underlying unity. The theme is that as organisations grow in size, so they become more efficient first at an increasing rate but then at a decreasing rate, and that there is a size beyond which they may actually become *less* efficient. In other words, as size increases efficiency is predicted as being likely first to accelerate, then to decelerate and eventually to go into reverse. The variations on this theme essentially play on the different aspects of efficiency just outlined. Thus some propositions concentrate on the internal efficiency of organisations. Here it is the curves of productivity and average costs that are assumed to reflect a sequence of accelerating, decelerating and eventually reversing progress as the activity or organisation grows bigger. Other economic propositions add the perspectives of externality and economic power. As organisations grow ever larger, so their impacts on society are assumed to follow the same sequence. Thus some organisations are felt to be 'too small', others 'too large', to be properly responsive to consumers and society. There are minor controversies: for example, on the rates at which increasing, decreasing and reversing economies occur, on their application to particular types of enterprise, and on whether 'optimum' sizes or ranges of sizes can be realistically discerned. But to repeat: basically, these are all variations on the central economic theme which links first increasing progress, then decreasing progress and finally outright inefficiency with increasing size.

SINGLE ACTIVITIES: ECONOMIES AND DISECONOMIES OF SCALE

Let us start with the simplest case: that of a single activity, pursued within some organisational framework as defined in this book. The activity may be anything from shops and shoes to sealing wax, from cabbages to swimming pools, from meals on wheels to symphony concerts. Although the activity may be synonymous with an organisation, as with small, single product firms or specialised voluntary groups, it is more likely to belong to a wider organisation which does other things, for example a product division of a multi-product business or a functional department of a local authority. It is in relation to such single activities that economic assertions on size-efficiency links have been most unequivocal. Analysis starts by assuming finite human and physical resources, both in the short run and the long run, and also the principle of diminishing returns. The principle of diminishing returns, as every elementary economics

H

student knows, simply states that 'as we increase the quantity of any one input which is combined with a fixed quantity of the other inputs, the marginal physical productivity of the variable input must eventually decline'.[2]

On the basis of these elementary assumptions economics first of all concentrates on the short run. In the short run physical production capacity is fixed. Typically, there is a given set of resources of buildings, land and equipment, although other factors, notably manpower, materials and money, tend to be variable. In this short run situation standard economics predicts that as production rises average costs will first fall rapidly, then fall more slowly and eventually increase. The theoretical short-run cost curve in Figure 4,

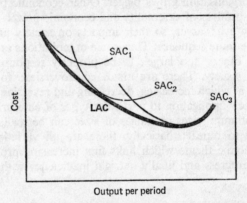

Figure 4   Theoretical short-run and long-run average costs

SAC_1, illustrates this idea. With increasing output average costs initially decline rapidly as fixed costs are spread wider. Then the rate of cost decrease tapers off as these advantages are successively used up. Finally, beyond a certain point it is assumed that average costs would actually start to increase because of diminishing returns. Piling extra manpower and materials onto a fixed scale of production unit would eventually overload capacity and create sheer mess. So assuming that the organisation wishes to expand the activity, it responds to this bottleneck situation by investing in more physical capacity. Now suppose that the technology of the activity, whether this be making widgets, collecting sewage or distributing food parcels, remains unchanged. The activity will then move onto another short-run cost curve, SAC_2. Here the same process is assumed to recur, leading to yet another short-run cost curve, SAC_3, and so on. Within each scale of operation the short-run cost curve is supposed to reflect the same sequence of accelerating and then decelerating economies, followed by outright diseconomies unless the scale of operation is once again increased.

This seems straightforward enough but what does theory predict about the long run? Figure 4 outlines the answer. First, if the state of technology still remains unchanged, the whole sequence of short-run cost curves is held to underlie an 'envelope' long-run cost curve, LAC. But this curve eventually shows the same pattern. The long-run cost curve eventually turns upward too, so it is predicted, in this case because of the limitations of the whole technology. This time it is the general ceiling of given technical skills and knowledge that causes diminishing returns to appear. On the other hand, the technology may change, opening up a whole new vista of further productivity increases, but only at much higher levels of size. In that case an entirely new LAC curve emerges. Frequently, of course, as organisations move their activities from one short run to the next, the technology is itself moving as well. The obvious analogy would be that of running down a descending escalator in terms of costs (or in terms of productivity, running up an ascending one). This may tempt one to imagine that the long-run cost curve can be kept moving persistently downwards with ever-increasing size so that the dread reappearance of diminishing returns can be indefinitely postponed. Economic theory, however, denies this. Sooner or later, it predicts, a final set of constraints would operate, this time related to the limitations of physical resources in a finite world. The activity would get so big that such resources would dry up (the human types of constraint will be discussed below). Alternatively technological change may effectively alter the nature of the product. But this would take us onto a new diagram by generating a whole new dynasty of LACs and SACs, possibly once again (although not necessarily always) at higher levels of size.

SINGLE ACTIVITY COSTS: THE EVIDENCE

So much for the theory of single activity size–efficiency relationships. What about the facts? Various studies have been made of relationships between physical inputs and outputs (called production functions) and also of relationships between accounting costs and outputs (statistical cost functions).[3] The empirical difficulties of such studies should not be underestimated but cannot detain us here. The studies broadly confirm that, within a given capacity, as very low outputs give way to higher outputs, average costs do indeed first fall rapidly and then more slowly. Intriguingly, the evidence suggests a frequent tendency for short-run cost curves then to become L-shaped, with average costs remaining constant over a considerable part of the output range, as illustrated in Figure 5. Insofar as this happens, average costs and marginal costs will coincide (which incidentally means that managers may accidentally avoid some of the pitfalls of using average costs for decision making which were mentioned in Chapter 4).

In tracing through average costs at different outputs as experienced by organisations, though, the studies fail to disclose an eventual upward tilt as predicted by the theory. Perhaps the reason is obvious. Within a given capacity the risk of excessive output levels may be so daunting as to be an effective deterrent in normal circum-

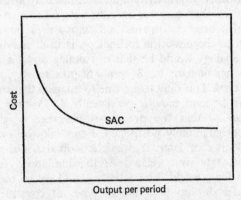

Figure 5   L-shaped average cost curve

stances. The evidence suggests that decision makers aim for production at somewhat less than full capacity, itself often a difficult concept, precisely because even full-capacity working, let alone higher levels, would create wasteful bottlenecks. Sometimes such bottlenecks are all too obvious, as where a firm is compelled for goodwill reasons to take on extra orders which it cannot contract out. In the same way a hospital's resources may be overstrained by a sudden epidemic. The fact that no economist observer is present to measure such (normally irregular) spasms of actually increasing average costs hardly implies that they do not occur.

Short-run cost curves are often essential for decision making purposes. But more significant for the basic issue of size and efficiency are studies comparing productivities and average costs at widely varying levels of size of operation across whole sectors.

Such studies confirm, as one might expect, that economies and diseconomies of scale strikingly differ from one sector to another. Cost efficiency demands elephant-size operations in some sectors, but mere mice or even insects in others. For example, a minimum efficient scale in the steel, motor and oil industries involves very large plants. In a few cases like the aircraft industry minimum efficiency demands operations which are now too large for most nation states. But in sectors like footwear, specialist engineering and electronics, efficient units need employ only a few hundred or even substantially less. In the United Kingdom, some years ago, to be cost efficient a sheet steel factory needed to represent about 50 per cent of the entire capacity of the industry, whereas a printing works only required 1 per cent or 2 per cent.[4]

In public and social enterprises similar contrasts emerge. In water supply, in order to be able to minimise working expenses, an undertaking probably needs to serve a population of over 100,000.[5] Social services, though, tend to be both technologically stable and labour intensive. Their most economic size is also strongly influenced by factors related to intensity and quality of care and by redistributive objectives. But here again there are striking variations. For example, it is widely assumed that hospitals should be bigger than schools and that services for certain specially disadvantaged

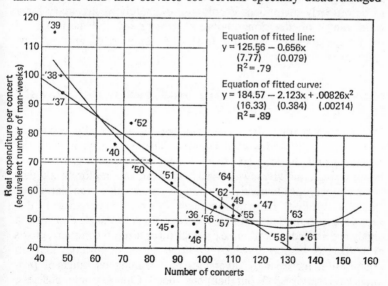

Figure 6 Real expenditure per concert and number of concerts for a major orchestra, 1936–1964

minority groups need to be organised on a wider geographical basis than, say, those for the housebound elderly.

Typical cost and production functions show that as the size of productive unit increases, once again the average cost curves tend to fall rapidly at first and then to bottom out, as the theory would predict. A shallow, saucer-type levelling-out implies, of course, that minimum cost efficiency is consistent with a wide range of unit sizes. Once again the alleged upward tilt of the curve is not evident from studies of actual operations. But once again, this is not inconsistent with the theory. Organisations may decide that to increase the size of productive unit beyond a certain level would be self-defeating. Another point to note is that cross-sectional cost functions of this kind only roughly approximate to the theoretical long-run average cost curve for a single unit. They show the size vistas available to, say, a shoe firm, an oil company or an orchestra if it wishes to grow larger (or perhaps smaller) consistently with efficiency, within the ambit of an existing technology. Evidence on average costs of single activities over long periods is still scanty. But, from the decision maker's point of view, it is the cross-sectional cost and production functions that are useful. Every efficient manager has *some* idea of the cost and production functions pertaining to his activity across its whole sector. For these functions to be properly quantified, if only approximately, is necessary for a wide range of decisions, notably on pricing, the best use of resources generally and, not least, the planning of entirely new operations.

CAN BUSINESSES GET TOO BIG? THE ECONOMISTS' DEBATE

On single activities, then, the evidence seems broadly consistent with the economic idea of a U-curve. That is to say, in both the short run and the long run there appear to be scales of operation for any single activity – widely varying from one sector to another – which are, productively speaking, 'too small', 'too large' or 'roughly optimal' (for the moment ignoring externalities). But supposing production and demand conditions are such that even a highly specialised operation, say a steel, oil or aircraft company, grows ever bigger? Suppose, which is often more important, that an organisation increasingly diversifies by widening its range of products and services? What happens then? Can a whole business, highly complex and diversified as it may be, also be regarded as 'too small', 'too large' or 'just about right'? To this more sweeping and difficult question economists have tended, on the whole, to answer 'yes', although in differing ways. Contrary to what is sometimes thought, economists have tended to be particularly suspicious of very large organisations, although once again for varying reasons. We need to glance briefly at their hypotheses before considering the evidence.

The first hypothesis derives from classical economic theory. It suggests that as organisations grow bigger a U-curve of long-run costs will still probably apply. To begin with, so the argument goes, as the organisation grows in size, it may be able to exert a bigger leverage on suppliers, to raise bigger sums of money on more favourable terms, to share common facilities over widening activities, to use marketing resources more fully. These internal economies of scale may take the organisation well beyond pure economies of production, with average costs still falling. But sooner or later, so the hypothesis asserts, these economies will also prove to be finite and exhaustible. Beyond a certain size internal diseconomies are assumed to set in, this time related to the managerial and human factor. It becomes more difficult for the controllers to oversee and direct an increasingly complex system. The organisation becomes managerially top-heavy and socially conflict-ridden. These forces would eventually be reflected in average costs. Once again these would taper off in their improvement and eventually deteriorate. This hypothesis of a generalised U-curve – applied to whole organisations and primarily derived from a notion of managerial constraints – has considerable intuitive appeal.

A second hypothesis, also derived from classical theory, was somewhat breathtaking. This was the assertion that in the business sector at any rate the process might actually be self-correcting. The classical and neo-classical economists tended to assume single-product firms. Given this assumption, even if productive efficiency were still rising as the firm grew in size, its growth would eventually be checked on the side of demand. Diminishing marginal utility would set in. People would grow tired of more and more of the same product. If you were too dependent on this product, your firm would eventually decline and even disappear. More important, these earlier economists were influenced by their wider theories of competition. They supposed that competition would (or could) be so dominant that any firm which exceeded an efficient scale of operation would be compelled to adjust. If the firm did not reduce its costs to the minimum, its competitors would assuredly do so, forcing it to follow suit or else to suffer. From this a further crashingly important implication followed. This was a neglect of considerations of market and social power. Although the classical and neo-classical economists were well aware of one possible threat from massive organisational size, that of monopoly power, they had great confidence in the power of competition. Other types of external effect, at least until the time of Pigou, they tended to ignore. Overall, therefore, given these wider assumptions, the implications these earlier economists drew for size and efficiency were radiantly optimistic, at least for society (if not for sloppier firms). In practice, so they thought, demand limitations, fear of excessive costs and, above all, the pressures of competition, would act together to prevent excessive size. The system would adjust itself well before businesses could grow large enough seriously to undermine efficiency and social interests.

A third and more recent economic hypothesis basically contradicts the U-curve or at least relegates it to a far-distant horizon. This is the hypothesis which sees the growth and size of firms as indefinite. For example, in her *Theory of the Growth of the Firm*, Edith Penrose suggested that firms could go on achieving important internal economies regardless of their size and simply as a result of growth.[6] She argued that managerial and other human resources available inside the firm could be more fully exploited as it expanded. Far from being given and fixed, the firm's human resources could be highly flexible and dynamic, at any point of time, in each firm. Such human resources married with physical resources so as to create a unique combination of factors which, if properly drawn out, would provide an economy of growth. Edith Penrose suggested that, unlike economies of scale, such economies of growth were essentially 'one-off' and transient but that they were constantly available to a progressive firm at any level of size. Indeed, the economies of growth offered the opportunity of what she eloquently termed a 'receding managerial limit'. Combined with the great possibilities of innovation and diversification in modern conditions, this meant that although there were optimal rates of growth, there was no such thing as an 'optimum size of firm' (as distinct from plant). Instead, there was 'nothing to prevent the indefinite expansion of firms as time passes'. This theme has many variations. Essentially it sees managerial dynamism, diversification processes and changing technology as providing escape routes from any threatened upturn of the average cost curve, at least for the most capable firms.

Many economists suggest more sombre perspectives for overall social efficiency. They agree that under modern conditions there are no built-in checks to giant size, partly because competition does not operate according to the classical model, partly because of managerial ingenuity and partly because of the possibilities of technology and diversification. But many (probably most) economists tend to be worried about the *social* diseconomies created or threatened by giant size.

This worry takes several forms. First, there is the traditional concern about monopoly power. The economic theory of monopoly and oligopoly broadly states that the more concentrated the ownership, control and knowledge within a particular sector, the more homogeneous that sector, the more differentiated from neighbouring sectors, the higher the barriers to new competition and entry into the sector and the greater the size of its leading members relative to suppliers and/or users in other sectors, the greater the degree of potential organisational power. On the assumption that organisations pursue their own interests, the theory goes on to predict that they will tend to show higher prices, profits or wages, greater security and political influence and also, very important, higher costs, than if the degrees of 'market imperfection' were less. In modern times this economic theory of power has been applied primarily to business corporations, but also to such diverse fields as labour and trade unions, communications and the mass media, the professions, even crime, sport, charity and the arts.

Other economic worries about giant size go wider. Theorists like Baumol and Marris have suggested that large corporations do not primarily hunger for optimum efficiency and profitability but rather for increased stability of profit, together with greater market shares, size and power, often as ends in themselves.[7] If true, this would weaken any 'built-in' checks to increased size which an obsessive concentration on productivity might promote. Again, a long line of economists have focused attention on the ability of large firms to manipulate markets by product differentiation, innovation and mass advertising. Although some, notably Schumpeter, have tended to welcome aspects of this process as conducive to social advance, others have been more astringent. In particular, Galbraith's theory, mentioned in Chapter 2, is that the large corporation secures striking internal advantages through size and growth, mainly because of increased stability, rewards and opportunities for people in the 'technostructure'. But, in Galbraith's view, this entails severe social costs. For the benefits to the corporation and its élites do not necessarily correspond to falling average costs. There is no guarantee that in its pursuit of growth the large corporation will approximate to optimal efficiency and minimum costs. Indeed, its very size makes this hard to discern. For Galbraith, though, the social costs of increased corporate size primarily relate to the alleged ability of giant corporations to manipulate consumers in a wider sense, to influence elected governments and subtly and pervasively to bend social priorities and the entire growth process towards their own ends.[8] Thus the central theme of economic analysis of size and efficiency with which this chapter began is restated. In Galbraithian and related theories business giantism eventually becomes damaging primarily because of its socially excessive power. With mammoth size, it is external costs, often of a subtly diffuse kind, that are held to threaten social efficiency.

ARE LARGE BUSINESSES INEFFICIENT? THE EVIDENCE

The efficiency of a whole organisation is an elusive idea. Its overall productivity is hardly susceptible to physical measurement. Cost data are difficult to use insofar as overheads are (inevitably) arbitrarily allocated and also insofar as activities genuinely interconnect and overlap. In the case of business firms reliance may have to be placed on profit measures, which are notoriously hazardous (see Chapter 8). Where giant-size organisations are unique to nation states – as in telecommunications and railway systems, and in many national motor, oil and chemical industries – international comparisons have to be employed; and these pose distinctive problems. Not least, it is hard to separate out any 'size effect' from other important factors, notably the quality of management.

There is some evidence that the internal efficiency of large firms may not be very different from that of small firms. Although only proxy measures are available, these are interesting. For example, Singh and Whittington studied the 6–12 year financial records of nearly 500 quoted companies in the United Kingdom. Among other things they looked at the relationships between size of firm and profitability. But, in each of the industries they studied, average profitability seemed to be pretty independent of the size of firm. In other words, large firms did not appear, on average, to have higher profit rates (although incidentally their profit rates were more stable).[9] Not long afterwards a major official study in the United Kingdom also looked at large versus small firm efficiency. It found that large companies tended to have a higher net output per person than did small firms, but a slightly lower return on capital. This enquiry took account of productivity and technical innovation as well as profitability. It ended agnostically: 'All we can conclude is that our analysis so far provides no evidence for assuming that small firms are, in general, any less efficient than large, or vice versa'.[10] Inter-firm efficiency comparisons, particularly on profit rates, are very hazardous and the evidence so far is inconclusive. But, for what it is worth, it does not suggest any massive or general superiority for giant size.

Another test of whether large firms are efficient is more indirect. It focuses on the extent to which potential internal economies may exist, whether or not these are actually seized. Here one looks at the degree to which the activities of a large business genuinely interrelate in such a manner as to offer scope for cost reductions and production efficiency. Examples are when a firm has joint or complementary products or a high degree of internal product flow. Such factors at least suggest potential efficiency gains. But the way in which many large firms group together activities in a much looser fashion offers scope for something rather different: reduced risks, more stable supplies or markets, steadier profits or financial 'optimisation' across national frontiers. In Chapter 9 we consider this diversification phenomenon more fully. For the moment the essential point is that, from the viewpoint of economic efficiency, it is debatable.

Another test is simpler, although again circumstantial rather than direct. Why, anyway, do big company bosses seek to expand their organisations? A difficult field, this, in view of the problems of researching managers' motives and policies, let alone the outcomes of their actions. However, several studies have made the attempt. For example, a study of United Kingdom mergers asked a sample of companies why they had taken over other companies. A desire to increase market shares and eliminate competitors appeared to account for 27 per cent of the rationale behind such acquisitions, a desire to preserve the firm's existing position from competitor moves or possible take-overs for a further 21 per cent. Financial motives, connected with asset structure, cash flow, taxation etc., were quite frequent. A desire to get hold of assets which could be more profitably employed accounted for 16 per cent of the take-over rationale, a related feeling that spare cash might be well used on acquisitions for a further 9 per cent. Other motives trailed behind. In particular, technological and economic criteria, related to a feeling that the firm was not big enough to be properly efficient, accounted for only 9 per cent of the takeover rationale. Analysis of what happened afterwards, incidentally, showed that about half the sample had engaged in some merger-related rationalisation of production and other facilities, in varying degrees.[11] The general flavour of these findings was echoed in another study, this time of the reasons why some 80 manufacturing companies and 30 banks had decided to go in for multi-national operations. The most important reasons for extending overseas appeared to be defensive: worries over new tariff barriers and transport costs and delays; overseas nationalist pressures for local manufacturing operations; difficulties with agents and licensees; a need to protect supply lines or to match competitor moves overseas; or simply a desire to spread shareholders' risks over a wider geographical area. Economically ambitious and 'aggressive' motives related to a better use of resources and opportunities seemed less important. Criteria of product diversification, better use of personnel and access to foreign 'know-how' appeared to play only a minor role.[12]

What emerges from such admittedly imperfect indications is an apparently widespread managerial thrust towards greater corporate security and power. Businesses which are already large appear to want still greater size in order to defend their existing positions, to increase market shares and generally to reduce or avoid risks. This is consistent with the evidence that larger size genuinely appears to ensure more stable profits (see above). It is true that a desire to get hold of assets which could be more profitably employed appears to be a frequent motive. For example, purely financially orientated takeovers played a strong part in concentration phases in both the United States and the United Kingdom in the 1960s and early 1970s. On the other hand, by their nature, such financial gains, once achieved, are often once-and-for-all affairs and sometimes even unstable. In any case quick cash motives appear to be rather less prevalent than the managerial orientation towards long-term growth, security and risk reduction. As far as managerial motivations towards greater size are concerned, then, the implications for economic criteria of efficiency are not very reassuring. Social efficiency does not appear to be the dominant rationale.

Another approach, more frequently used by economists, is to examine whether increased business size reduces the effectiveness of competition. Clearly, if it does, the implications might be serious. Some big businesses do enjoy monopoly in many fields (although not all monopolies are large). There is little doubt that monopoly does itself have certain bad effects on efficiency. For one thing, monopoly tends to involve higher prices and profits, and lower outputs, than would apply under more competitive conditions. Therefore, society gets less of certain goods than it wants and consumers are to some degree 'exploited'. These are generally labelled as the 'allocative/distributional inefficiencies' resulting from monopoly. But monopoly may also increase cost inefficiency or productive slack: what is often called 'X-inefficiency'. This is because the absence of competition probably lessens the incentive or pressure on businesses to reduce costs and struggle for improvements. Economists disagree on the extent to which allocative and/or 'X-inefficiencies' actually result from monopoly. There is some evidence that monopoly-related allocative inefficiencies are small, certainly smaller than is often thought, perhaps representing much less than 1 per cent of national income. There is also some evidence for thinking that the 'X-inefficiencies' resulting from monopoly may well be larger. There is certainly evidence that such frequent concomitants of monopoly as restrictive practices and barriers to entry are generally economically undesirable. Thus, whatever the precise mixture and extent of monopoly damage, it undoubtedly exists. To the extent that it combines with a large scale of business, any problems inherent in the latter are probably compounded.[13]

But many large firms are monopolistic in some fields, competitive in others. Diversification often means that giant firms poach in the fields of other giants. Perhaps most important, market frontiers frequently shift as a result of technological change, the introduction of new processes and materials, widening trade and communications, and international competition. In this situation, stable and obvious monopolies are often hard to pin down. So a more pertinent question may well be, how genuine is competition between the highly diversified large companies that are increasingly emerging? How far can competition be relied upon to keep the giant conglomerates both on their toes ('X-efficient') and price–output responsive (allocatively efficient)?

The issues here are more difficult. On the one hand, it is argued that in place of product competition there now exists a new spur towards efficiency and profitability in managerially-controlled giant companies: the fear of take-over. In this view, if the capital market is working effectively, dissatisfied shareholders will exert pressure on inefficient companies and may even sell out to new owners. Even such a threat is seen as a possibly effective deterrent to sloppiness. It is said, moreover, that the large financial institutions which own a major and increasing share of the equity of large companies will intervene more actively to ensure that they are profitable. But there are strong arguments on the other side. For capital markets to act as an effective discipline requires high levels of disclosure, penetrating investor knowledge and free capital movements. It is debatable whether capital markets can work that effectively – and also whether public authorities are going to be able to allow unhampered capital movements. If giant financial institutions discipline giant industrial firms, this merely exchanges one form of elephantine power for another. More important, a capital market pressure on firms might have 'X-efficiency' effects but if these are merely siphoned off into higher profits to the advantage of shareholders, consumers would hardly benefit. Moreover, supposing a very few conglomerate companies did eventually control most of business activity, it is an interesting question whether they would effectively compete. The industrial economist Corwin Edwards suggests that a handful of conglomerates, facing each other in a web of markets, might be likely to pursue live-and-let-live, empire sharing policies – a hypothesis described by another major authority in this field, F. M. Scherer, as 'provocative and plausible'.[14]

HUMAN AND MANAGERIAL FACTORS

Some final criteria on bigness still remain. Not the least are the human implications. The notion that people are in some sense more fulfilled in small units goes back for many centuries. A number of modern studies lend some support to the view that smallness is good for worker morale. Various findings have suggested negative correlations between bigger units and such factors as strikes, absence from work, job satisfaction, quality of work, understanding of payment systems, social interactions (both vertical and horizontal), variety and automony of work tasks, and even mental health.[15]

How to interpret such findings is more difficult. Some critics proceed to argue a blanket 'human' case for smallness, often with passion; others are more circumspect. One reason for caution, urged by some, is that small firms tend to pay their employees less. It has been argued that many workers may well positively prefer the higher wage/lower social satisfaction syndrome, associated with the big unit. More cogently, perhaps, it is claimed that the effects of industrial jobs on people should not be exaggerated. Correlations are one thing, actual causation quite another. If workers are alienated, dispute-prone or foot-loose, so it is said, this may have more to do with increased privatisation, mobility and lack of community feelings in society at large.[16] More important still, caution arises over the possible remedies. Systematically to break up existing large concerns simply for the sake of improving their internal morale would hardly be feasible nor even perhaps desirable. For example, if greater fulfilment at the place of work involves sub-

stantially higher production costs, the price might well be unacceptable to society.

On the other hand, the worker morale case for smallness is more
powerful when it clearly goes with the grain of wider social economies. The case for workplace decentralisation within large organisations largely rests on such wider linkages. For example, some
experiments in worker participation like those of Saab Scania in
Sweden appear to suggest an encouraging alliance between human
fulfilment and cost savings. Plants planned around small groups
which offer the workers greater job variety, participation and social
contact may well increase productivity. On certain assumptions this
should benefit consumers. At the very least crude arguments for
technical economies of giant-size plants, which fail to take careful
account of the risks of human discontents, should be scrapped.
On the contrary, such risks should always be incorporated in average
cost estimates, even if these become less apparently precise and
more probabilistic (see Chapter 6). If the eventual result is smaller
and more balanced productive units, less vulnerable to sudden
paralysis because of managerial ineptitude or minority strikes, more
humanly fulfilling to work in and so more cost efficient and productive, so much the better for society. And still better if proper social
cost–benefit analysis suggests favourable external effects on local
communities and family life as well.

The human viability of large organisations can be tested in further
ways. One fascinating question, for example, is whether giant concerns actually require a bigger proportion of managers. The evidence so far suggests they don't. Thus a major study on the relationship between size and organisational structure was carried out by
two American sociologists, Blau and Schoenherr. Blau and Schoenherr analysed 53 employment agencies, with nearly 400 functional
divisions and some 1,200 local employment offices – organisations
with very homogeneous activities but widely varying in size. Their
study found two forces at work. As a result of spreading managerial
overheads, an increased size of organisation had the effect of reducing the ratio of administrators. At the same time greater size meant
greater complexity and this demanded *more* administrators. On
balance, the (managerial) economies of scale tended to exceed the
(managerial) diseconomies of complexity over the observed size
ranges. Therefore, the overall administrative ratio declined with
increasing size. Significantly, though, the decline in the administrative
ratio occurred at a decreasing rate. Thus, as Blau and Schoenherr
pointed out, support could be found here for the inescapable economics of diminishing returns. Their study incidentally found the

same relationships repeated in the major finance departments of 416 state and local governments in the United States. And similar findings have been reported for industrial firms, hospitals and universities.[17]

But there is one argument that finally brings us back sharply to the central economic thesis of an eventual U-curve – at least in the long run – if organisations continue to increase in size. This is the fundamental question mark that hangs over the continuity of good management in large concerns. Where opportunities for more efficient operation exist as a result of massive size and diversification, whether these are actually seized or not seems critically to depend on the quality of management. Even the most gargantuan combinations can be made to work, it seems, by top grade managers (a possible example being the UK electrical engineering giant, GEC, under Sir Arnold Weinstock). But if the biggest business empires are created – or rationalised and reformed – by brilliant managers, there is no guarantee that such qualities will indefinitely survive their departure. Millennia of organisational experience – including that of armies, churches and religious orders, republics, provinces and nation states – suggests that even non-hereditary organisations tend to go through successive phases of good, bad and mediocre leadership. It seems unlikely that the modern giant businesses will be able to outsmart the lessons of history. A number of theories suggest that cross-sectional studies of the 'size effect' are inadequate: the extra dimension of *age* of organisation needs to be added. One hypothesis is that as organisations get older they tend as a general rule to perform less well. But if older organisations often appear to deteriorate, they do not necessarily disappear. It is possible to hypothesise a twofold 'age effect' such that, broadly, the older the organisation, the slacker the performance but also the greater the ability to survive for long periods as a result of respectability, articulacy and entrenched power. Obsolescence and resilience may well go together. The American economist Anthony Downs has interestingly developed this idea in relation to public bureaucratic agencies.[18] And the author has applied the label 'congealment' to the notion of a dual tendency towards conservatism and survival power in mature enterprises.[19] Nor is this idea very novel. It was the great economist Alfred Marshall, writing in 1911, who referred to 'the great recent development of vast joint stock companies, which often stagnate but do not readily die'.[20]

If such worries about the risks of corporate congealment are added to those about sprawling growth, monopoly, social power and worker morale already referred to, the case for suspicion of giantism grows formidable. And so, correspondingly, do the socio-economic arguments for checking, searchlighting and sometimes even splitting up the monoliths.

Chapter 8

Profits and Market Knowledge

In 1947 two ex-servicemen John W. Odell and Leslie C. Smith, put their war gratuities together and started to produce pressure die castings for industry in an old pub in Tottenham, North London. By the early 1950s they were producing die-cast toys. Their success in selling over one million miniature Royal Coaches in Coronation Year, 1952, was followed by the introduction of their cheap 'Matchbox' miniature vehicles. These did so well that the company had to move to larger premises in 1955 and again in 1957. In 1960 Lesney Products became a public company. Further plant was built in 1962 and again in 1968. By 1970 Lesney employed nearly 7,000 people and had the capacity to produce about $5\frac{1}{2}$ million 'Matchbox' models per week. About 80 per cent of the products were exported and the company had received the Queen's Award for Industry for Exports in four separate years. Annual sales in 1970 were over £19 million, pre-tax profits about £5½ million. The company's stock market valuation was then an astounding £120 million, its price–earnings ratio over 50:1. Lesney had grown much faster than any of its direct United Kingdom competitors. However, by the early 1970s the firm was experiencing tougher competition from overseas companies, particularly from Mattel Incorporated of America (producers of the famous 'Barbie doll') with their die-cast model cars. By then, too, the United Kingdom toy industry was going through major upheavals and takeovers.

ECONOMIC ANALYSIS OF PROFITS

Let us suppose that an economist sought to evaluate the performance of Lesney. Almost certainly, his first step would be to try to interpret the company's profit figures. This would mean getting behind the purely accounting data, which were designed for historical and legal and reporting purposes, not economic ones. The economist would use the basic definition of *profit* as total income minus total costs, subject to keeping capital intact – all of which terms, needless to say, bristle with problems. But the economist would be initially concerned with Lesney's *profitability*, that is, the relationship between their profits and other relevant variables. Here his main concern would probably be with their *return on capital* as measured by the ratio between (*a*) profits, defined in various ways, and (*b*) capital employed, also measured in various ways. The reason why this ratio is of particular economic interest is obvious. As an indicator of the productivity of capital, it represents an important approximation to overall efficiency (although not, of course, the only one). The return on capital usefully stands at the apex of a pyramid of financial ratios. In particular, it is mathematically related to two other important ratios, profit to sales and sales to capital employed, such that:

$$\frac{\text{Profits}}{\text{capital employed}} = \frac{\text{Profit}}{\text{sales}} \times \frac{\text{Sales}}{\text{capital employed}}$$

Applying these definitions, our probing economist might first of all ask the question, *how profitable have Lesney really been?* For example, were profits overstated in the early years because of low rewards accepted by the founders, Odell and Smith, in the interests of building up the business? Note that this is an application of the opportunity cost principle. Again, was reported profitability temporarily depressed by each of the major increases in plant and equipment in the period? Note that these defined Lesney's short runs. The important point here is that major capital investment tends to depress immediate profitability partly because the benefits therefrom are delayed but partly also because the newly bought assets, by increasing the value of capital employed, have the effect of increasing the numerator of the return on capital ratio. The extent to which this latter effect occurs is linked in turn to the method of depreciation used. But whatever the depreciation method, the greater the proportion of newly bought assets, normally the lower the apparent return on capital. Again, in sorting out the 'true' position, a further question would be: what has been the real, inflation-adjusted increase in profits or profitability? Obviously a price deflator would suggest a less dramatic growth record for Lesney, but perhaps a real decline for some of its competitors. A vitally important question would be: how far have Lesney provided for replacement costs of capital equipment, particularly in face of the uprush of competition and technological change? On the basic definition of profit just outlined, any shortcomings here would be

serious. For the value of capital would not have been kept intact
and in that sense, too, profits might have been overstated. On the
other hand, the company might have valued their assets to take careful account of replacement costs and inflation, in which case this
particular worry would not necessarily apply.

Next, of course, our economist would be keenly interested in the
question, *were Lesney more efficient than their competitors?* This
question could be assessed on four levels. First, taking profitability
as an approximation to overall efficiency, the analysis just applied
to Lesney would be extended to their competitors. Second, though,
the economist would not be satisfied with profitability or the productivity of capital as the sole efficiency measure. He would also be
interested in other forms of productivity, particularly in relation to
inputs of labour and materials. For example, he would be anxious
to obtain data on average costs and input–output ratios, both in
Lesney and the other firms. Even with an inter-firm comparison
scheme in the industry, this would be difficult; but various approxi-
mations might well be possible. Third, the relative efficiency of
Lesney would involve non-financial factors. For example, competitors might have as good, or even better, labour relations. Fourth,
an economist would apply the criteria of market power and other
external effects. Degrees of monopoly and data on selling costs
would be relevant here. So would such factors as Lesney's apparently
bigger export ratio, possible technological spillovers and pollution
effects, if any. The question of how far 'Matchbox' toys were an
undiluted gain to the community in the wider sense would require
social and moral judgements. Possibly on most, if not all, of these
counts Lesney would emerge very well, relative to competitors.
Although many of these questions would be hard to answer, in
assessing economic efficiency all would need to be considered.

But our persistent economist would already be on the trail of
further issues. For example, an obviously critical question is, *were
Lesney as efficient as they could have been?* Note that this question
is particularly relevant if a firm enjoys a measure of market unique-
ness because of high product differentiation. For this means few,
if any, truly similar competitors to use as yardsticks. The element
of monopoly might even have produced some 'X-inefficient' slack
inside the firm (very unlikely with Lesney, perhaps, but with less
dynamically run firms possibly an important aspect). The question of
whether Lesney could have done even better than they did would
require careful analysis of their past managerial practices and
decisions. In particular, had the company been geared to consider
strategic alternatives rationally, thoroughly and imaginatively? What

was their approach to risk and uncertainty? Were any good opportunities likely to have been missed or actually turned down? Note that all this would involve considerations of *ex post* opportunity costs (see Chapter 5).

Our economist might pose yet a further question, *what was Lesney's actual market worth round about 1970?* In attempting to answer this question, the economist would probably make some wry comments on the dizzily high stock market valuation (an example of the sort of over-reaction of financial markets, in this case to success, commented on by J. M. Keynes many years ago). He would then get his teeth into a great mass of empirical data. He would begin to be involved, in fact, in a forecast of the toy industry into the 1970s and 1980s, including such factors as technological change, consumer attitudes (child and adult), the anti-car syndrome, the sociology and even anthropology of present-giving, etc., etc., together with potential competition, perhaps from Japan as well as the United States. All of this would be a guide to some sort of profit forecast for Lesney, suitably discounted and risk adjusted, on which a rational calculation of the company's net worth in the market would be based. But enough . . .

The Lesney case illustrates the complexities of evaluating business performance in general and business profits in particular. Both the strength and weaknesses of profit as an efficiency measure clearly emerge. Reported profits are influenced by tax considerations, by public and shareholder relations and by a host of accounting variations. These have to be cleared up first. More important are the economic criteria. Considerations of time perspective (the short run and the long run), inflation and capital replacement must be taken into account before we can accept stated profits as representing the true profits of the firm in any realistic sense. Even then profits and profitability do not fully measure efficiency. Labour and other forms of productivity, together with non-financial internal costs and benefits, have to be brought into the reckoning if we seek to assess the internal efficiency of a firm. Although there will normally be a high correlation between profitability and other productivities, for example, of labour, this is not automatic at least in the short run. And finally, to round out any picture of overall social efficiency, we have to bring in three further sets of economic criteria. These relate to opportunity costs (social, not purely internal), spillovers and market power. Moreover, it should be noted that, if anything, these problems are relatively straightforward in the case of a smallish company like Lesney. With a firm at the other end of the size spectrum – say a large multinational company with a wide variety of products – economic analysis of profits becomes far more complex. In particular, in multi-product and multi-national companies reported profits become a more than usually hazardous guide to efficiency. All of which means that in assessing business performance, profits must be interpreted with great care. And the greater the size, complexity, market power and political importance of a business, the more caution required in using profits as a test.

PROFITS AND BUSINESS OBJECTIVES

This brings us to a key issue referred to several times in earlier chapters, that of business objectives. How important, anyway, are profits and profitability in the plans, motives and policies of firms?

Immediately we come up against a mass of disagreements. For some people say that profitability is, as a matter of fact, the basic objective of firms, in the short run, the long run, or both. In denying this, others point to the widespread existence of other business goals. The protagonists of profitability then retort that these other goals all boil down to profit anyway, at least in the long run. Profit defenders may also say that even if businesses do not pursue profitability, then they *ought* to do so, either for their own sake or for the social good or, of course, for both (possibly adding some necessary conditions for the two to be reconciled, notably proper competition). But other people worry about this. They reject maximum profit-seeking (*a*) because of general feelings about humanity and ethics, (*b*) because they fear that the state will be unable or unwilling to enforce things like tough anti-monopoly measures and protection of the weak which are necessary if such business behaviour is not to be socially damaging, (*c*) because they feel profit maximisation would be economically inefficient in other ways (for example, where external economies are important) or (*d*) because they dislike the social system in which profits belong to private shareholders. The cacophony of opinions is almost deafening. Economists are involved in it as well as members of the public and businessmen. Nor is the situation helped by semantic confusions about such terms as 'goal', 'motive', 'objective' and 'norm' – or by the loose employment of concepts like 'optimum', 'maximising', 'satisficing' and 'constraints'.

In this chapter we are concerned with contemporary business policies and with the use of economic principles to clarify these policies. Wider social criteria are considered in the final chapter. But properly to understand business policies requires clarification of the *present* role of profits. Businessmen themselves, let alone outsiders, do not always express the matter very clearly. In practice, profits appear to relate to business objectives in four main ways. First, a business may aim for a minimum profit simply to survive. Survival itself is desired for a mixture of reasons. The profit rate aimed at is regarded as a precondition for survival. For a firm to think of profit only in such terms is a limiting case but some small businesses approximate to this. Second, the firm has a mixture of objectives which go well beyond survival to include stability (risk avoidance or reduction, stable profits) and, probably very important, increased sales and market shares. In a sense these things, too, may be instrumental to motives of managerial power, craftsmanship and financial reward. But the important point is that the profit rate to be aimed at is regarded as a precondition for achieving these objectives. Moreover, since the objectives are dynamic, the profit rate required to serve them will be dynamic, too.

A third use of profit may go hand in hand with the second. The main objectives of the business are still mixed, as above. But top management uses profitability as an essential yardstick in assessing the performance of sub-units or activities. Any good, marginalist-orientated management will use profitability as a test (probably not the only one, see Chapter 9) of what activities are doing 'well' or 'badly' inside the firm. An important point here is that profitability may be used to guide internal resource allocations without necessarily being an overriding aim for the entire firm. A final role for profit approaches the neo-classical model of the firm under perfect competition. A business may regard 'maximum profit', variously defined, as its dominant, overriding or even exclusive objective in the short run, the long run, or both. Although this again is a limiting case, it is approximated by a number of businesses, particularly in some instances where ownership and management are closely combined.

Several points should be noted. (1) Most large companies seem to fall into the intermediate position of treating profit both as an instrument for wider goals and as an internal yardstick. (2) Whatever the profit policy, the firm may have greater or less regard for humanity, obedience to law, payment of taxes and ethically acceptable behaviour. However, higher standards on such matters seem more likely, perhaps, when profit is viewed instrumentally rather than as a supreme goal. (3) Again whatever the policy, quantitative models of profitability can greatly help decision making. For example, such models can illustrate what profits a company would need in order, say, to provide a return to shareholders comparable with other companies, to maximise shareholder returns subject to various constraints or to underpin stipulated rates of growth. (4) In practice, a firm's position on the spectrum just outlined will be affected particularly by its size, the degree of competition, general economic conditions, ownership–control links and the style of management. Any profit standards it decides on will relate to its past experience, comparisons with others and expectations. (5) Even when profit is viewed as an overriding purpose, it is such profit standards or goals, rather than some hypothetical profit maximisation, that will tend to inform business planning. As Neil Chamberlain puts it: 'Achievement of the rate projected is considered satisfactory, even good. To do better is fine, but not expected.'[1]

From all of this an important inference follows, one which will hardly surprise the reader who has already encountered the problem of plural objectives in this book. Although profit is critically important right across the business spectrum, whether as totem pole, lifebelt, calibrator or precondition of everything else, as an overall business objective it cannot easily stand alone. Even the most profit anxious firm will often moderate its immediate profit-taking for the sake of long-term goodwill. Such a firm will tend to fear sanctions from important customers, nationalist governments overseas, anti-trust laws, powerful trade unions. Such 'constraints' cannot always be foreseen and embodied in the profit target. Nor can profit targets be considered apart from criteria of growth or market shares. These will probably accord with profitability in the long run, but not necessarily straight away. Moreover, a business that considers itself socially progressive will clarify internally its standards on such things as labour relations and personnel policy, quality, service and community responsibilities. It may indeed set up dynamic standards so that actual improvements in such matters can become a source of pride. On top of all this society itself may insist on new elements of social accounting by businesses in the future (see Chapter 12). Solely from the viewpoint of business objectives, then, profit at present enjoys a unique place, often, indeed, more important than the public relations rhetoric of some businesses would suggest, but not an absolute one.

MARKET KNOWLEDGE

Once its objectives have been clarified (although this is a continuing process), a business faces a key issue long emphasised by neo-classical economics, that of understanding the market. Such an understanding is clarified by a familiar bevy of economic concepts. Let us briefly recapitulate these (with due apology to readers who can recite them in their sleep). A *market* is a 'network of dealings in any factor or product between buyers and sellers' (Cairncross). *Competition* is the process of rivalry between firms using (*a*) product differentiation, (*b*) persuasion and advertising and (*c*) price. But competition also applies to the *factor markets* for resource inputs of labour, land and capital. *Demand* is the amount of something that buyers are able and willing to purchase, *supply* the amount of something that sellers are able and willing to offer for sale, both within a given time period. *Demand and supply curves* relate these amounts to various levels of prices.

All these concepts, though, are only a prelude to the most important idea of all in this field, that of *elasticity*. This is a measure of the degree of responsiveness of demand or supply to the various influences on them. For example, as every elementary economics student knows, the price elasticity of demand is the percentage change in quantity demanded divided by the percentage change in price. Other important elasticities of both supply and demand relate to changes in the prices of near substitutes, in advertising expenditures and in people's incomes. If the change in supply or demand is more than proportional to the change in such a variable, supply or demand are said to be relatively elastic; if less than proportional, relatively inelastic. In what follows we will concentrate on demand elasticities, although much of what is said applies to a firm's supplies as well. Obviously the key question at this point is, how many of all these vital facts about markets and demand do businesses normally know? How much can they get to know if they really try?

In the mid-1960s Professor D. C. Hague carried out a detailed study of how 13 United Kingdom firms made their pricing decisions.[2] Although the sample firms were few in number and small or medium-sized rather than large (and also probably relatively progressive), the Hague study provides a useful starting-point in appreciating the practical problems in understanding markets that most firms face. Professor Hague found that all the survey firms tried to calculate their market shares and believed they could reasonably estimate the market shares of their main competitors. Firms selling direct to consumer markets tended to use specialised market research techniques in order to assess the impact of advertising, performance, appearance, price and sales promotion methods. Industrial goods firms, though, relied heavily on the first-hand knowledge of their salesmen and of important customers. Several of the firms went to great trouble in analysing the design and material content of competitors' products, but none felt confident in their understanding of how these specifications related to competitors' prices. Among the very real problems in assessing competitor prices were optional extras, hidden rebates, discounts or special credit arrangements.

However, the Hague study concentrated on the question of price elasticities of demand. All the sample firms, it found, believed that they knew something about the relationship between the general level of prices for all products of a certain type and the total sales volume for that product. In other words, they felt they knew something about the market elasticity of demand. But the more important price elasticities for individual products or brands, their own or others', were another matter. All the firms agreed that this would be most valuable to know. Some tried to quantify the relationship for their own products. Only one or two appeared to do so with any precision. Only one firm hazarded a quantified guess as to the price elasticity of substitution between its own and a competitor's products. The firms always found it difficult to distinguish between the effects of a change in price on sales volume – and the impact of other variables like product design and advertising. On the other hand, most collected a lot of information about their competitors' marketing practices, product plans and financial situations. On the whole question of external information on markets (for pricing and other decisions) the Hague study concluded:

First, firms rarely have all the information about market competitors that they would like. Some information is not available; some is uncertain. Some requires the price setter to make guesses about, for example, what moves competitors are going to make. Some information will be obtainable, but will be too expensive. Even so, this is a field where improvements are possible, although price setters must always weigh the costs of getting more information against the benefits of having it.[3]

This is a far cry, of course, from the earlier micro-economic theory which saw the firm as confronted by a crystal-clear marginal revenue curve. In a world of imperfect competition and oligopoly, of risk and uncertainty, no such facile and precise knowledge of demand functions is possible. However, a businessman continually has to make assumptions about the price sensitivity of demand. At any point of time he 'guesstimates' whether a single change in product X's price, upwards or downwards, other things remaining equal, will induce a more or less than proportional change in sales. Supposing he guesstimates that if he raises the price by 10 per cent, sales will fall less than proportionately, say by 5 per cent (implying a price elasticity of demand of -0.5). This of course, would probably make such a price increase worthwhile to the firm. But supposing a price decrease of 10 per cent is only expected to increase sales by about 3 per cent (an implied price elasticity of +0·3). The combination of these two judgements is already an approximation to a limited range demand curve. The fact that the businessman does not depict his judgements on a graph, let alone use the phrase 'price elasticity of demand', is beside the point.

In a market where prices matter the businessman is highly unlikely *not* to be making assumptions of this kind. What the economist would suggest, as a minimum, is that there is virtue in making such demand/elasticity assumptions explicit, verbally or graphically, so that they can be further clarified, debated and, if necessary and feasible, tested. For example, supposing that over the past year variations in the price of X have been associated with varying sales as shown in Figure 7. Our businessman would be very dumb if he

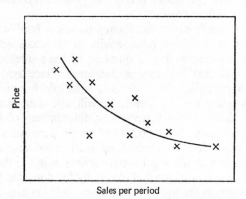

Figure 7 Hand-fitted demand curve

did not attempt to fit a rough-and-ready curve to these data as shown. This would approximate more closely to an 'objective' demand curve; but with one obvious and critical proviso: that other things than the price changes might actually have caused the sales variations. Once again, the businessman would make assumptions about the relative impacts of, say, changes in advertising, customers' spending habits, competitors' price changes. Once again, too, an economist would suggest virtue in at least making these assumptions explicit (even this may not be done). But by this stage, if the businessman really needed to know more, the economist would almost certainly advise recourse to more sophisticated techniques (see below).

Perhaps, though, the headache faced by the firm is not about price competition on near-identical products. Perhaps the problem rather involves more fundamental questions like: what business are we in anyway? How distinctive are our products? How substitutable with other products? In most markets there is likely to be some product differentiation. Even an absolutely identical piece of kitchen equipment or a liqueur or a pop record may be regarded as a somewhat different product if marketed in different places, at different times, by different suppliers, to different sorts of people or with different types of psychological promotion. That business competition frequently seeks to engineer such differences – with the object of producing an element of monopoly – is by now platitudinous. As Joan Robinson put it: 'The chief cause of monopoly (in a broad sense) is obviously competition'.[4] But before a firm can differentiate something, it must have an idea of the product's *existing* closeness or distance from other products. It is at this point that economics offers the key idea of *substitution*.

Once again, micro-economic theory makes a familiar assertion, this time that the complex relationships or contrasts between products can be crystallised into a question of their substitutability at the margin, and that this can be measured. Once again, too, the decision maker applies this economic principle intuitively or implicitly. Depending on the sector, he will ask such questions as: what is the relative competitiveness or differentness of holidays in Brittany, Majorca or Sorrento? How much personal service and local accessibility does a corner shop really need to make up for higher prices than at the local supermarket? What is the extent of competition between oil, gas and electricity for domestic fuel? What marginal changes in the use of tubes, buses and cars may result from relative changes in, say, transport subsidies, fares, motor taxes or congestion? How far are washing machines substitutes for refrigerators, record players for tape recorders, Cortinas for Marinas, even Marinas for Minis? Here again, economics makes a minimum suggestion: any assumptions on product proximity or distance should be made explicit. But economics also goes on to suggest that the precise relationships should be estimated. For example, a relevant issue is very likely to be the *cross elasticity of demand*, that is, the extent to which sales of one product, A, are affected by a change in the relative prices of A and of another product, B. Another problem is how far other variables – say in advertising, product quality or people's incomes – appear to have affected sales of A relative to sales of B.

To explain more sophisticated demand analyses – as carried out particularly in bigger concerns – would take us into the realms of statistics and econometrics. There are many excellent technical and descriptive books in this field that an interested reader can consult. No important economic concepts are involved beyond those we have been discussing: only a tremendous amount of sheer fact-finding, on the one hand, and of statistical finesse on the other. Suffice it to say that sophisticated economic models of demand have been developed for products like steel, motor cars, refrigerators, domestic gas and certain basic foods. Such products tend to have large sales, high sensitivity to macro-economic conditions, oligopolistic markets and giant-size suppliers. All of these characteristics make elaborate and expensive demand studies economically worthwhile and also more feasible. Such studies may concentrate on one variable, perhaps price. But they are more likely to cover a variety of possible influences on demand, notably changes in consumer incomes, advertising, indirect substitutes, demographic and sociological factors. The statistical techniques often include multiple correlation and regression analysis. Among the results are estimates of demand elasticities. For example, expenditures on food items may be systematically related to changes in real disposable income. The demand for steel is found to be apparently income elastic but relatively price inelastic. Refrigerator demand is found to be fairly elastic relative to changes in both income and price; cigarette demand inelastic relative to both. A particularly controversial case, that of demand for cars, involves reference to household income, price, the ages of buyers and their social class. In the United States estimates of the income elasticity of demand for cars appear to range from $+2.5$ to $+4.2$, of the price elasticity from -1.2 to -1.5, with income tending to emerge as a more important explanatory variable.[5]

Such findings can be useful to business planners. Provided the data going into the economic models are reliable and comprehensive and the results carefully interpreted – problems more difficult than those of a purely statistical kind – sophisticated demand studies help to build up a background understanding of markets. For example, they help a firm with its short, medium and long-term sales forecasts, its long-term decisions on strategy and investment, and its marketing policy, including considerations of pricing, advertising and sales organisation. On the other hand, sophisticated demand studies can often be like a Rolls Royce: too cumbrous, expensive or perhaps even outdated for the particular decision in hand, say on pricing. They need to be heavily banked with more political data on competitor companies, particularly in oligopolistic markets.

In the case of oligopoly, which is so frequent, assessments of the likely moves of competitors are vitally important. Where the stakes are high and competitors few, the interaction between rational analysis and the political judgement, flair and attitudes of top management can be specially subtle. To give something of the flavour of this interaction here is a highly simplified case study composited from the experience of a number of firms.

A STRATEGIC PRICING DECISION

In 1970 the Tilbury Company, one of the leading United Kingdom manufacturers of rogs, faced a difficult problem. The company held about 30 per cent of the total United Kingdom rog market, its main competitors being Astra, also with about 30 per cent, Ardua with 20 per cent and various smaller firms sharing the rest. Tilbury had a good reputation for product quality and had just developed an improved rog model which was cheaper to produce and potentially more attractive to customers. The company planned to switch completely to the new model. But the problem of what price to charge for it – involving considerations of cost, demand, competitor reactions and the company's basic strategy and objectives – led to serious argument.

Tilbury's production department made estimates of what it would cost to produce the new model, providing appropriately for the capital investment involved. These estimates were based on variable and marginal costs and they foresaw substantial economies of scale as output increased from 5 units to around 45 units – with diminishing returns setting in soon thereafter as bottlenecks developed within the envisaged capacity. The production department favoured a cost-minimising output level of about 45 units of the new model (implying a 45 per cent market share since the total market was estimated at about 100 units). They also reckoned that a price of about 1·8 would fairly reflect the new model's qualitative edge on the old one which was currently priced at 1·5.

But a key factor was obviously the likely effect of varying prices on sales. The sales department were asked to make estimates here relative to a possible price range from 1·5 to 2·0. Their estimates were very rough and much argued over. They were based on the initial assumption that Tilbury would be the only producer of the improved model within the relevant time scale and that competitor prices would remain the same. On this basis, for example, the sales department reckoned that, at a price of 2·0, 10 units would be sold (10 per cent market share), at a price of 1·7, 30 units, at a price of

1·5, as many as 90 units. In other words, demand seemed on this first look to be relatively price elastic – and increasingly so at lower price levels. Finally, putting together the production and sales estimates, Tilbury's accountants declared that the company could meet its minimum contribution rate (50 per cent of variable costs) at any price between 1·5 and 2·0, but that a contribution-maximising price, on all these assumptions, would be in the region of 1·6.

All of this, however, was simply a first cut at the problem on the admittedly unrealistic assumption of a nil reaction from competitors. So the managing director asked for a further appraisal to take account of the following factors: (*a*) major competitors able to introduce an equivalent new rog model fairly quickly at roughly the same costs; (*b*) possible retaliation from these competitors if they felt 'unduly threatened' by Tilbury's growing market share and profits. The further analysis then concentrated on what might be regarded as 'undue threats' to competitors, and on a careful appraisal of competitor strengths and weaknesses. It was agreed that with market shares lower than its existing 30 per cent Tilbury would hardly worry competitors, but that increasingly tough competition from them could be expected insofar as its market share edged upwards from 30 per cent to 40 and 50 per cent.

There seemed to be three main possibilities. Tilbury might pursue a moderate policy, simply aiming to retain its present market share of about 30 per cent. This would imply a price of around 1·7 and the likeliest result would be a similarly moderate response from competitors who would probably charge equivalent prices. The eventual result could well be stable shares and higher profits all round. Secondly, Tilbury might pursue an aggressive policy, aiming to push its market share up to about 50 per cent. This would imply a price of about 1·6 and would probably elicit retaliatory price cuts and heavy advertising from competitors. Tilbury's market share would be reduced if it held prices, or else it would be forced to match the price cuts. The result could be anybody's guess but, on the assumption that Tilbury were stronger than their competitors, they might end up with, say, 40 per cent of the market. If they were evenly matched, the original market shares might be eventually maintained but, of course, at lower prices and profits than otherwise. Finally, a highly aggressive policy, aimed at securing most of the market with a price of around 1·5, could be considered, its keynotes being 'surprise' and 'saturation'.

What should the directors decide? On product differentiation/ existing product line criteria, the price might be 1·8, on narrow cost-minimising grounds, something around 1·65, on the accountant's minimum contribution criterion, anywhere between 1·5 and 2·0, and on 'contribution-maximising' criteria, something around 1·6 – the last two on the basis of highly unrealistic assumptions about elasticities and nil competitor reactions. Taking competitor reactions into account, however, the price might be a 'moderate' 1·7, an 'aggressive' 1·6 or a 'super-aggressive' 1·5, depending on Tilbury's basic strategy and its willingness and ability to take risks vis-à-vis competitors . . .

The reader is advised to think carefully about the circumstances in this case. What would he himself decide, on varying assumptions about Tilbury's objectives? What was the point of rational analysis here? Obviously it was not to provide 'the right answer', whatever that might be, but rather to help clarify alternatives and sharpen top management choice. A few points also emerge about the specific usefulness of economic analysis in such far from untypical situations of oligopoly and risk. First, in making sense of the competitive and market environment of a company like Tilbury, traditional economic categories of competition, market power, product differentiation, substitution, etc., are essential for any kind of clear thinking at all. Second, the more precise the estimation of demand elasticities, the more fragile the political assumptions behind these estimates may well be, although this does not necessarily mean they should not be made. Third, even in the final summing-up process before the final decision the pervasive concept of elasticity reappears. This time it is the elasticity of Tilbury's market share in response to its possible price decision (as illustrated in Figure 8) that is at the core of top management's final weighing-up of the odds.

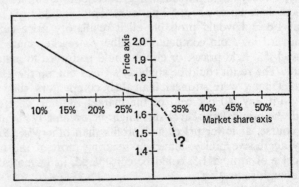

Figure 8   Elasticity of market share relative to possible price changes; the Tilbury Company

Note on Further Reading

For discussions of the role of profits in business planning, see relevant chapters of Joel Dean, *Managerial Economics*, Englewood Cliffs, N.J., Prentice-Hall, 1957, and C. I. Savage and J. R. Small, *Introduction to Managerial Economics*, London, Hutchinson, 1967.

For practical applications of demand analysis, see D. S. Watson (ed.), *Price Theory in Action: A Book of Readings*, Boston, Houghton Mifflin, 1969, and Ralph Turvey, *Demand and Supply*, London, George Allen & Unwin, 1971.

On business forecasting of markets and sales, see introductory description in Savage and Small, cited above. For case illustrations, see W. W. Haynes, *Managerial Economics: Analysis and Cases,* revised edition, Dallas, Business Publications, 1969, Parts 2 and 4. For a good general introduction to the techniques, see Colin Robinson, *Business Forecasting: An Economic Approach*, London, Nelson, 1971.

K

Chapter 9

Big Business Budgets and Plans

A firm's profit policies and market assessments, as discussed in Chapter 8, are vital elements of a bigger process to which we must now turn, that of its overall budgeting and planning. It is convenient to concentrate for this purpose on large firms. The reader will recall that in Chapter 2 we glanced briefly at the 'Galbraithian' and 'counter-Galbraithian' theories of big business power. To a large extent, of course, this controversy hinges on how far large businesses are in fact able to control their environments, i.e. to plan. In Chapter 2 we also glanced at the related question of the internal allocation system of the large business and of its internal resource flows and dispositions, a matter of increasing economic interest in a world straddled by giant conglomerates and multi-nationals. In Chapter 7 we raised the question whether the large, diversified business can be controlled efficiently at every-increasing levels of size. Can it maintain efficiency over time, avoiding ossification and even decay? In order to achieve its objectives, whilst co-ordinating scores of thousands of employees, many hundreds of products and, perhaps, too, operations from New York to Milan, from Birmingham to Hong Kong, the large corporation has to employ all types of allocative instrument. But what mixture of internal financial pressures, hierarchical command and carefully cultivated internal goodwill can it use? What conflicts exist between these allocative principles in a giant business and are these conflicts resolvable?

THE CHOICE OF BUDGETING SYSTEM

There is a clear way in which all these issues come to a head and one that is of particular concern to micro-economics; the corporation's choice of budgeting system.

Budgeting is a process for systematically relating financial flows to the attainment of plans. Starting out from fundamental business objectives, as discussed in Chapter 8, the budget concentrates on agreed targets and plans for a year ahead, often longer. The budget of a business or business sub-unit outlines the financial implications of these future plans in terms of projected balance sheets, profit and loss statements, sources and uses of funds – and sometimes, too, other quantities, for example market shares or flows of manpower and materials. Capital budgets concentrate on long-term investment projects.

For a large business the budget serves several purposes. It commits people to agreed tasks, serves as a benchmark for assessing variations from plan ('management by exception') and provides an *ex post* yardstick of how well activities or divisions have done and of whether they ought to get more resources. But the budgeting system also crystallises the problems of interdependent or conflicting allocation systems. How fully should sub-units of the business participate in evolving the targets and plans affecting them? How can local knowledge be reconciled with central optimising and co-ordination? How closely should subsequent performance be watched from the centre? How reasonable is it for top management to use conformity to budgets as a test of the performance of (*a*) divisions, (*b*) divisional managers and (*c*) future resource allocations? How can the central co-ordinating device of the budget reconcile central authority, financial pressure and local goodwill, assuming that all these are necessary?

One influence on the choice of budgeting system is the firm's stage of development. This must be looked at historically. For example, on the basis of intensive studies of Du Pont, General Motors, Standard Oil Company (New Jersey) and Sears, Roebuck, and also of short studies of a further 70 large United States companies, Alfred D. Chandler has identified four main phases or 'chapters in the history of the large American enterprise'. These were (1) the initial accumulation of resources, involving rapid growth into vertically integrated businesses covering national markets, (2) a period of rationalising and digesting the resources thus rapidly and often haphazardly acquired, involving the creation of formalised and functionally departmentalised administrations, (3) further growth in response to increased competition, by now taking the form of diversification in related or even entirely different fields, sometimes overseas, and (4) further rationalisation of these diverse and swollen empires into federations, more or less centrally controlled, of product divisions. According to Chandler, these phases varied in timing and detail, depending on both the character of the industry and the abilities of particular firms. But the overall patterns from the late nineteenth century to the post-1945 years were, he suggested, reasonably clear.[1] These trends have been more recently applied by Channon to the development of British industrial companies over the past two decades.[2] They help us to interpret the historical contexts within which big firms have to develop their budgeting and planning systems.

An important influence on the choice of allocation system is the degree of affection, loyalty and co-operation that a large business can expect to be able to build up. Joseph Schumpeter's remark that large capitalist enterprises are hard to love may contain a kernel of truth. The slogan, 'Ask not what GEC can do for you, ask what you can do for GEC', is perhaps less than compelling. For that matter, whether this slogan becomes more attractive as applied to, say, British Steel or an Area Gas Board is debatable. The sheer complexity, the pace of change, the mundane quality of the final products, the impersonality of markets, the frequent remoteness of final consumers and, not least, the factor of sheer size mentioned in Chapter 7, such problems make it genuinely hard for people to feel affection for large business enterprises. In social organisations, even quite large ones, such things may perhaps come easier. For example, a large local authority may be able to rely on a strong political ethos, local and regional loyalties, and motives of service and professional pride on the part of its officers (although these, too, have occasionally awkward allocative implications, see Chapter 11). A large hospital or charity relies heavily on motives of service, care and professionalism. Lacking these potential reserves, a big business has to work harder to build up corporate loyalty and identification. The way in which some have attempted to create an 'organisation man' has often been parodied. On balance, a big business probably has to rely more heavily on instrumental attitudes related to financial rewards and penalties – and to a certain extent, too, on sheer central power – as compared with other sorts of large enterprise. This strongly influences its choice of budgeting system.

A third major influence on the choice is the degree to which the activities of a big business genuinely interrelate. In modern complex economies, with fast-changing markets and technologies, such interrelatedness can take many forms. At one end of the spectrum is the business with a single or dominant activity. The impetus of this one activity, together with marked production economies of scale, suffices to create giant-size firms in such industries as oil, steel, motors and aircraft. At the other end of the spectrum is the 'pure conglomerate', a form of business organisation somewhat rarer in the United Kingdom and Europe than in the United States. The classic US example is ITT, with its interests in telephone equipment, car rentals, home construction, foods, insurance, mutual funds and hotels. Between these extremes lies a rich diversity of types of market, technological and vertical relatedness.

Many firms produce a variety of products for one general market and use much the same process in so doing, for example, food processing firms manufacture canned fruit, canned vegetables and also frozen foods. Some firms satisfy joint consumer demands by producing complementary products. Others engage in joint supply, processing by-products of their original lines. But many firms have used their existing technologies and market skills as launching-pads for bolder expansion. They have either (a) applied their existing technology and research to new markets (either genuinely new or just new to them), (b) adopted new products and technologies in order the better to serve their traditional markets or (c) integrated backwards and forwards as between supply, manufacturing and distribution. It is these last forms of much looser interrelatedness which characterise some of the biggest diversified firms. Sometimes all three growth strategies – of entry into related markets, use of related technologies in habitual markets and straight vertical integration – have been combined. It is into this category of loose interrelatedness on varying and often shifting criteria that such major UK companies as GEC, ICI, Courtaulds, Unilever, GKN and Cadbury–Schweppes wholly or partly fall. These complex and often fast-changing business systems incidentally make it difficult to draw defensible and consistent dividing-lines between diversifications as more or less 'logical', 'interdependent' or 'economically legitimate': a headache for the opponent of monopoly power. They also powerfully affect the nature of the firm's internal allocation system.[3]

In practice, all large companies appear to maintain at least two central controls, over senior appointments and large-scale investment projects. To do less would defy all sense in having a unified organisation at all. Most go well beyond this but in intricate ways. A study of 25 of the 100 largest UK manufacturing companies found indications that about half were highly centralised – with large and influential head office departments, centralised product/market strategies and a strong involvement of top management in the affairs of the divisions. Such centralised companies either had a dominant product, with inter-divisional flows representing a very high proportion of total output, or a dominant technology, with diversified products concentrated round a central core of sophisticated technical skills. In the former case, centralisation might be mainly dictated by an essential network of cross-ways internal transactions, in the latter by a central grouping of essential productive knowledge. By contrast, in the less centralised UK manufacturing firms, inter-divisional product flows were less marked, even if one product dominated. Typically, though, such firms had recently diversified – on the basis of related markets and/or vertical links, as in textiles, food manufacturing and distribution, paper, printing and publishing. On the other hand, these companies were expected to become more centralised as time went on.[4]

The same survey found that most of the top managements of these UK companies used a mixture of (mostly financial) tests in judging their divisions, particularly return on assets, sales margins, costs and market shares. Their budgeting processes mostly involved active participation by the divisions. Indeed, divisional bosses often sat on top committees, sometimes even on the main board. Significantly, the divisional managers were mainly rewarded by salaries, promotion prospects and perquisites. Most of the top management interviewed expressed distaste for the idea of rewarding their divisional managers in a fluctuating manner related to divisional performance ('payment by results'). The survey regretted that in these latter respects the UK companies appeared to 'lag behind' the practices of many American corporations.[5]

PROFIT-ORIENTED DECENTRALISATION:
THEORY AND PRACTICE

This brings us to the crux of the debate about internal allocation systems in giant businesses. So long as companies are tightly integrated around dominant products and technologies, production criteria necessitate major central services and high internal product flows. A high degree of interdependence between, and central oversight of, sub-units is essential (oil, motors, railways, fuel and power utilities, large parts of chemicals). The question of how to marry such central control with good morale and co-operation, although probably more and more difficult at increasing levels of size (see Chapter 7), is familiar enough. But, as the web of diversification spreads wider, the difficulties appear to be compounded. Where the only unifier is central managerial and marketing skills, linked with a zest for size and power, central authority may grow harder to enforce. Common loyalties and friendships of the kind that lubricate all allocation systems may be harder to build up. Yet if the headquarters are to keep on top – let alone secure any company-wide internal economies from the diversification – something more than a loose confederation is essential.

At this point a theoretical answer appears: to summon back from classical micro-economics the model of a decentralised allocation system relying on competition, market signals and profit motives. But this model is to be transplanted into the internal workings of the big business. Each division, according to the theory, is to have a profit target spelt out in the budget. Top management will later assess the division's performance by using this profit yardstick. Not only the subsequent allocation of resources between divisions, but also, perhaps, the financial rewards of their managers will depend on this. According to the theory, operations can then be decentralised, divisional managers kept on their toes and top management enabled to concentrate on long-term planning and strategy. Some versions of the theory go further. One protagonist implies a high degree of internal social engineering: 'Management can increase the pressure to almost any degree it likes, simply by increasing the percent bonuses paid to the "winners" and/or increasing the percentage of low performers who are demoted'. The result could be 'as strong or stronger pressures for performances as those affecting the lemonade stand or the dairy farmer – the pressure of personal survival even when the survival of the company as a whole is in no way threatened'.[6]

Can such a decentralised quasi-market system inside the giant business enterprise really work? How does it relate, in practice, to the operation of budgeting systems? There are many problems. For example, there is no getting away from the dilemma of central versus local power. For, on the one hand, purely centrally imposed targets would seem autocratic and would throw away the advantages of divisional managers feeling actively involved and emotionally responsible. They would also presuppose, perhaps questionably, that 'head office always knows best'. But, on the other hand, for divisions to decide their own targets would virtually deny the existence of any central objectives, whether on profits or anything else. So in evolving the profit targets some sort of compromise – involving an interaction between head office and divisions – seems unavoidable. But joint local-headquarters planning may blur the clear edges of responsibility and compromise the 'arm's length' market theory. Moreover, it may create a centralising force simply because in the last resort head office has more power.

Again, how does one arrive anyway at a divisional profit target that is 'reasonable' and 'fair'? There will be the familiar problems of varying market conditions requiring different targets, of allocating overheads between divisions and of valuing divisional assets of widely varying structures and vintages. As Neil Chamberlain points out, 'whatever decisions along this line are made . . . it can be expected that some divisions will benefit more than others'.[7] But the problems of operating a quasi-market internal system go still deeper. Can profitability, particularly in the short run, be taken as a fair measure of overall divisional performance anyway? Doubts on the level of the whole business (see Chapter 8) may well be reflected at this level. Perhaps most important, there are the possible demands of company-wide financial 'optimisation'. Whatever the precise role of profit in head office thinking (again, see Chapter 8), it will probably be of the first importance, frequently decisive. This implies that top management may want to manipulate inter-divisional resource flows in the interests of overall profits. But the resulting cross-subsidisation and centrally imposed financial flows, even including deliberate loss-making on some activities, takes us a long way from the quasi-market decentralised model.

A searching study of the organisation and finance of multinational companies by Brooke and Remmers illustrates some of the cross-currents. Brooke and Remmers found that 'the practice of firms is more centralising than the theory'.[8] In multinational enterprises, according to their findings, initial consultation on budget plans and targets between geographic/product divisions and the headquarters appeared to be close. There was 'firm, though subtle pressure' on sub-units to conform to the parent company's expectations of overall performance. Once defined, budgets were used as a quasi-contractual device to ensure commitment. Head office 'management by exception' necessitated much feedback data from sub-units to head office (needless to say, this tended to be resented). Changes in external conditions often required further dialogue on budget revisions. Moreover, central control over investment was 'almost always closely held at head office'.[9]

The multinationals, according to Brooke and Remmers, found it difficult to apply purely profit tests of divisional performance for two reasons. First, a pure profit test would over-emphasise short-term gains. A manager keen for head office approval, extra funds, perhaps even extra pay, might simply neglect less quantifiable priorities in labour relations, public relations or research, with potential long-term damage to the company. 'One of the inherent weaknesses of decentralisation is that if managers are judged by absolute profit returns there is always the danger that the subsidiaries will pursue goals which conflict with overall corporate interests.'[10] Second, headquarters often influenced the profits of overseas subsidiaries for the sake of reduced risks or increased profits for the whole company. But such central decisions for purposes of tax avoidance or currency manipulation – involving things like transfer prices and the timing of payments between divisions – could distort the profits of a subsidiary to such a degree that they would be 'virtually meaningless as an indication of efficiency'.[11] A possible way out of this difficulty was to have a dual system, with superimposed quasi-market shadow prices being used as a 'fair' test of performance – as opposed to the real, central profit-oriented financial flows. On the other hand, this expedient could be cumbrous. Overall, Brooke and Remmers concluded in this part of their study that there were strong long-term trends towards centralisation in multinational businesses.

THE ECONOMICS OF 'WHO IS RESPONSIBLE?'

Jim Brown was general manager of the Zed Cleaning Products Group, a subsidiary of the Multi-purpose International Corporation. He was worried about the performance of Division A in his group. Division A had done badly, so it seemed, in 1984, in relation to its budget plans, in terms of return on assets, absolute profits and market share. On all these criteria the Division's performance had fallen short of the targets agreed between its general manager, Mr Brown himself and the head office of MPIC. Moreover, the Division had performed badly compared with Division B, which manufactured and distributed exactly the same product in another region. Table 9 summarises the key ratio comparison between the two.

Table 9

	Actual 1983 %	Budget 1984 %	Actual 1984 %
Division A			
Return on assets	16	18	15
Profit increase	14	15	4
Market share	40	45	41
Division B			
Return on assets	18	20	19
Profit increase	20	22	24
Market share	25	29	30

In evaluating this situation, Jim Brown knew that he had to bear in mind some managerial factors. Bill Smith, manager of the apparently laggard Division A, a careful administrator, had recently been put in to improve its operations. Jack Robinson, manager of the apparently successful Division B, was well-known in MPIC as a thrusting, ambitious manager, keen to impress head office. There were also differences between the competitive conditions in the two Divisions, although head office claimed to have taken these into account in its thinking about the targets. The managing director of the Corporation was shortly making his annual tour of inspection and Jim Brown was frankly worried that he would pounce on the apparently indifferent performance of Division A. Jim Brown put in a telephone call to Bill Smith, Division A manager, to get a feel for what his line of defence might be and to express concern. The following is an extract from their telephone conversation.

BROWN: Honestly, Bill, I'm worried what the MD is going to say about your Division's showing this year, it doesn't look good.

SMITH: Well, you know, Jim, I never liked those budget targets laid down last year. You remember I always said they were too high . . . that head office were putting the screws on.

BROWN: The fact is, you agreed those targets, Bill.

SMITH: Hmm . . .

BROWN: The fact is, after all, the sort of improvements you were asked to make were very much in line with Division B's – and look how they've done . . . Now I know you face some difficult problems that they don't but all the same . . .

SMITH: You bet I face bigger problems, Jim! For heavens' sake, to start with I've already got a much bigger share of the market. Whereas Jack Robinson and his lads are starting from much lower and everybody knows that's so much easier.

BROWN: All right, Bill, you've got a point there, but the head office economists seemed very sure that competitive conditions in your region warranted those targets . . . I know you believe you've got a better idea of your local competition than they have [expletive from Smith] . . . But again, the real crux is your return on assets . . . Even if you couldn't push up market share all that much, couldn't you have cut costs and got more out of the pot that way?

SMITH: I can point to major savings on overheads and all the rest since I took over, Jim . . . But you know perfectly well that what dished me this year was that strike when all my fitters downed tools . . . None of us foresaw that little lot when head office pushed out all those damn budget targets last year!

BROWN: Yes, Bill, I don't think the MD will blame you for *that* . . . In fact, so far as your own image is concerned, please don't worry about that strike, after all everybody knows the state

your Division's labour relations were in when you took over . . .
What I'm really worried about, though, is that what with the poor
profit showing, the strike and all the rest, we're going to find it
hard to persuade head office to allocate more funds to you as
compared with Division B . . .

SMITH: Well, may I suggest that you consider making a case to
head office to agree to revise those targets and take a broader
view? After all, it'll take me time to rebuild this Division's
relationships, and I'm spending fairly heavily on that alone . . .
which has depressed my ROA showing to start with . . .

BROWN: Hm, I'm afraid Head Office want better group profits *this*
year, Bill, and you'll have a lot of convincing to do on that one,
although you have a point . . .

SMITH: I mean, I know Jack Robinson is a good fellow, he's a
great chum of mine and all that, but how do head office know his
Division isn't getting a glamorous profit by storing up some
trouble for the future, the same as I've inherited?

BROWN: I can't comment on that, Bill . . . Anyway, I suggest you
get your arguments ready quick and we'd better have another
chat before the old man lands on us and goes up the wall over
your results . . .

The reader is advised to consider the implications of this telephone conversation carefully. Obviously, the situation is stylised.
For example, the financial complications of Division A's relationship to other parts of MPIC have been ignored; comparisons
between Division A and Division B would be relatively easy because
they are producing the same product in the same country; and even
the environmental contrasts between their regions are simplified.
In reality Divisions A and B might have differing financial relationships within MPIC's overall system and, moreover, they might well
be producing a different product or product line under substantially
different market and environmental conditions, perhaps even in
different countries. Such complications would make the issues of
how far Bill Smith and his managers are responsible for Division
A's results – and of how far these results can be fairly compared
with Division B's – still more difficult.

The telephone conversation between Jim Brown and Bill Smith,
much more than the firm's public or internal formulas, provides
a real cutting edge along which the interplay of allocation systems
can be judged. As the two men talk, the tension between coercion,
competition and co-operation is palpable. To start with, Bill Smith
is far from being crudely or completely coerced, whether on the

budget targets or anything else. If he and others were, there would be no room for local initiative, MPIC would become excessively centralised, good managers would leave, only 'yes men' would stay. On the other hand, an element of coercion is implicit. In the last resort, after all, Jim Brown, and still more the managing director, have more power than Bill Smith, if only because they can largely determine his future prospects. Again, the element of internal competition is strong, indeed to some extent explicitly encouraged by top management. For example, Bill Smith and Jack Robinson certainly regard their Divisions as competing for top management approbation and resources and they may well regard themselves as rivals for promotion also. Yet this element cannot be pushed too far either by top management. Divisions might try to do each other down; MPIC might sub-optimise even in purely financial terms; both Bill Smith and Jack Robinson might be driven to 'fiddle' the system unduly in efforts to boost their real or apparent results; they both might get ulcers; feelings of equity and co-operativeness might suffer; and the accounting system might grow ever more complicated in efforts to prevent abuses and make up for unfairnesses. Incidentally, similar results may follow if internal competition is pushed further down to the labour force, for example through an over-emphasis on 'payment-by-results' schemes.

But of course the third element, that of goodwill, loyalty and moral consent, also has limits. In a concern like MPIC to rely too much on such feelings might invite excessive managerial slack. On the other hand, they are critically important. To be realistic, Bill Smith cannot be expected to love the managing director, or, for that matter, Jack Robinson. But if Bill Smith and others find it difficult to like or morally respect their superiors and colleagues – and still more, if they cannot really believe in and respect MPIC as fair, decent and friendly – the consequences could be corrosive. In the telephone colloquy all these forces are at stake.

A third issue is focused quite explicitly: how much control over their performance do Bill Smith and his Division really have? For Smith, the proverbial 'man in the middle' of the big organisation, this question has three aspects. How far am I responsible for the targets and their execution as compared with my seniors and head office? How far am I responsible for the overall performance of Division A? And how much control does my Division really have over its environment anyway? The first of these questions involves the informal, perhaps more than formal, interplay of central and local power, the second involves Bill Smith's own power in the Division and, very important, his time span as general manager, and the third question involves the 'Galbraithian issue'. With regard to the latter, Bill Smith's own judgement on the external power of his Division as part of MPIC will informally distil the dimensions calibrated by the head office economists in more systematic terms. These external power dimensions will include distances from near substitutes, market shares, number, relative size and characteristics of direct competitors, risks of new competition, future market growth and socio-economic characteristics of customers, as also the distribution of economic power between MPIC and its suppliers, perhaps particularly the trade unions. In these senses Bill Smith and Division A's problem is but a microcosm of the planning problem of MPIC as a whole.

CONCLUSION

It has been shown that the budget brings to a head the question of how a business perceives its environment, how much power it sees itself as having, how much it seeks to use that power, what standards it aims at and how it achieves internal co-ordination. Built into the budget are comparisons with historical data on performance (including that of competitors and large companies generally), expectations as to the future and attitudes, more or less aggressive, towards the deliberate moulding of that future. As Chamberlain puts it, the budget represents a continuing attempt to explore the meaningful limits within which a firm controls its environment. 'Both discretion and external limitations are present, and the mix of these two necessarily varies from business to business and from time to time. Business budgeting and planning attempt both to enlarge the area of business discretion and initiative and to capitalise on whatever measure of these assets is already enjoyed.'[12] Bearing all these issues in mind, it is hard to disagree with Chamberlain's conclusion that 'the budget may become as useful an analytical concept to economists in understanding the firm as it has proved a functional device to management in administering it'.[13]

Chapter 10

The Provisioning of Social Enterprises

We have now discussed how businesses try to understand their environments, to increase their market power and to plan. The analysis has concentrated on the firm in dynamic relationship with its environment, on the ways in which it obtains what it wants. The time has come to apply this analysis to social enterprises: that is, broadly, non-central government organisations mainly in the social services, housing, health, education, the environment and the arts.

Traditional micro-economics has tended to ignore co-operative, charitable, voluntary and semi-public organisations. Even where the economic problems of intermediate organisations are considered, the main emphasis is on their housekeeping role, their purely allocative efficiency within an established framework of public wants and central government control. But before considering how social organisations allocate resources (see Chapter 11) one should analyse how they obtain such resources in the first place. Once this issue is raised, it becomes clear that social organisations are also in the business of struggling for what they want. They, too, play a dynamic, activist and even quasi-entrepreneurial role, creating as well as responding to social demands. No more than the business firm is the social enterprise merely an agent of environmental forces. On the contrary, it is frequently a persuader, a mobiliser, an innovator. And in order to fulfil its objectives the social organisation is very much in the business of competing for scarce resources. Indeed, the provisioning problems of enterprises concerned with people's shelter, welfare, spiritual growth and mutual aid obviously long pre-date the post-Industrial Revolution business firm.

Municipal, co-operative and charitable organisations occupy important middle territory in any developed pluralist society. This territory has open frontiers on all sides: with families, neighbourhoods and primary social groups, with businesses and markets, and with the state. It is to all these sectors that social enterprises must look in their efforts to obtain resources of money, materials and manpower.

Local authorities, of course, are in a special position since they have a major part of their finance guaranteed, either from central government grants or established local taxes. The fact that local authorities raise taxes to some extent makes them a special case for the purposes of this chapter. But apart from this important difference, there are strong similarities between the provisioning problems of all kinds of social enterprises. The quest for public subsidy engages a local authority asking central government to increase grants, a charity trying to get money out of a local authority, an arts group begging for support from, say, the Arts Council, or, for that matter, a pressure group trying to get public resources channelled towards, for example, the mentally ill or overseas aid. Again, the problems of deciding whether to charge for some social good, and if so what, extend widely across the spectrum of social organisations. So does the continuing search for support from individual citizens in the shape of gifts of money, materials and labour. It is this triple dependence – on markets, public assistance and voluntary gifts – that presents some of the most difficult economic and managerial problems with which social enterprises are faced.

THE RESOURCE GAP

Economists have observed some general trends. Over the past century or so local authorities have greatly increased their share of resources in most countries. This mainly reflects rising social costs in urban, fast-growing societies and the rapid expansion of collectively provided welfare services. In many countries local taxation has proved a sticky and restricted source of funds, although modern experience on local taxation varies enormously from country to country. Generally, relative dependence on central government grants (or on central subventions from assigned national taxes) has increased. So, frequently, has the local authority propensity to borrow in the capital market. But there have been wide variations in getting and spending between local authorities within a given country. For example, a large-scale study of city expenditures in the United States found that varying population densities and social compositions appeared to play a major role in such variations. This still left large unexplained variances, though. These the study was forced to put down to inter-city cultural and political differences.[1] In the United Kingdom a study of local authority services complained about 'territorial injustice' in the sense that resources and spending on equivalent needs appeared to vary so widely from one part of the country to another. Again, this appeared to relate partly to differing politics, partly to contrasts between countryside, suburbs and inner city areas.[2] But overall, the expansionist drives of local government in its quest for resources have been strong.

The changing resource shares of charities are less chronicled. In the United States private philanthropic gifts of money appeared to maintain or even slightly increase their GNP ratios between 1929 and 1959.[3] Among the factors possibly affecting this ratio the relevant study singled out increases in real incomes and new tax concessions for financial philanthropy. It doubted whether the big increase in government welfare expenditure had been a dampening influence. 'The entrance of government into philanthropy on a grand scale, like the general rise in income, has not altered the fact that resources are always scarce, that the general well-being can always be improved, and that satisfaction of the disposition to improve it can always be rewarding.'[4] In the United Kingdom the overall financial share of charities relative to GNP may have slightly receded. Some charities have increasingly relied on local authority money in return for providing agency services in social welfare. As the welfare state has expanded, many charities appear to have ossified. But others have simply become more voluntary labour intensive, filling in gaps in social care and acting as pressure groups on the public sector. For example, it is voluntary organisations that have pleaded, more or less successfully, for more governmental as well as private resources to help the homeless, the mentally ill, deprived children, black minorities and the gigantic cause of overseas development.[5]

Economists have reacted in different ways to the resource problems of social and public services. Some economists tend to discuss what would be a 'rational' or 'optimal' division of labour between government action, philanthropy and the market. In particular, they argue for a greater use of pricing and markets, for example in housing, pensions, education and health. The classical liberal economist is a professional (and often extremely useful) winkler-out of wastes and perversities in the systems of local and charitable as well as central bureaucracies. He sees market/pricing solutions as offering more variety and choice, a more rational allocation and perhaps, too, a greater overall supply of resources. Another tendency among economists, typified in modern times by Myrdal and Galbraith, is to argue for (a) a more equal distribution of resources, nationally and globally, necessitating collective action, and (b) an increased priority for social goods. The 'Galbraithian' argument is that in the battle for resources between business-propelled private consumption and public/social causes there is a built-in tendency for the latter to lag behind. Mass advertising, individual status-seeking and commercial pressures, so it is argued, continuously inflate the consumption options and expectations of the already affluent. But the consequent loss of other choices, for example for pedestrian mobility, children's playspace or mutual care in small communities, is relatively unarticulated. Meantime, comparatively speaking, continuing poverty at home, let alone overseas, is unadvertised, hidden away or remote. In this view there is a systematic tendency for social opportunity costs to be under-stated.[6]

Whatever opinions are held on this bigger issue, one thing is clear: there are surging, and often clamorous pressures which cause many social enterprises to want to expand. These pressures are partly political: the 'empire building' of administrators and politicians, their frequent sensitivity to electoral pressures, their social convictions. Wider pressures include the rising proportions of social dependants, both children and the retired; the increasing standards of provision expected in public services; the discovery of new social wants; and the social costs of growth and urbanisation, for example congestion, pollution and perhaps even increased crime, which demand public remedies.

To all this must be added a difficult economic problem. Most social enterprise activities are highly labour intensive. It is not easy to increase the productivity of nurses, teachers, dustmen or social workers without damaging quality or even destroying the product. Potential economies of scale are often very restricted. Unit costs would be unlikely to fall dramatically if, say, hospitals, schools or residential homes were to increase significantly in size. Indeed, the quality of care often seems to depend on small and decentralised units, particularly in education and social welfare. But these features of labour intensity, stable productivity and few scale economies combine to give a further twist to the social enterprise 'resource gap'. For other sectors of the economy which do not face these problems are able to provide their employees with big pay increases as a result of continual productivity increases. For reasons of recruitment and equity there is then strong pressure on social enterprises to provide comparable increases to their own employees, but they have less ability to do so. This provides yet another reason for the social enterprises' constant search for more resources from central government, local citizens and clients.

L

SOCIAL PRICING CRITERIA

One way in which social enterprises can recover funds is by charging for their services. By definition purely philanthropic organisations will not do this, but many other social enterprises will and indeed must. The decision whether to charge, and if so what, is one of the most difficult with which they are faced. It is a decision which can be considerably clarified by economic analysis.

Whether the service is rented housing or a public recreation centre, day nurseries or theatrical performances, a useful first step is to estimate the likely demand functions. Background information is required on potential users and their likely responses to quality variations, advertising, the imposition of charges and, of course, varying levels of charge. An obvious question is, supposing there were charges, what would the demand curve look like? The demand curve, summarising people's willingness to pay for the service, is one indicator of its potential social value, although there are others. That is why, duly corrected and supplemented by other indicators, the demand curve is frequently used in cost–benefit analysis (see Chapter 11). But for the moment the main significance of the demand curve is that it is one guide, among others, to social pricing decisions. It is in the light of the demand curve that social decision makers will be able to juggle with the implications which either no charges or varying levels of charge, will have for (a) revenues, (b) levels of use and also, to some extent, (c) citizen welfare.

For example, supposing the estimated demand curve for a new bridge or public park is as shown in Figure 9. For people who are willing to pay, the potential total value, if the bridge or park is provided free, is roughly represented by the entire area under the demand curve ODE. At a charge OP, however, usage will be reduced to OQ. Total expenditure by users (gross revenue to the agency) will be represented by the area OPRQ. Total value to users will be roughly represented by the area ODRQ. Subtracting total user expenditure from total user value then gives us the important triangle, PRD. This triangle represents what is called *consumers' surplus*. Consumers' surplus means maximum willingness to pay minus total expenditure quantity if a single price is charged.[7]

Armed with such estimates, if only in rough form, decision makers will be able to discuss in a rational manner what their pricing objectives, if any, might be. Possible objectives might be (a) to maximise consumers' surplus without qualification, i.e. make no charge; (b) to maximise consumers' surplus subject to a minimum

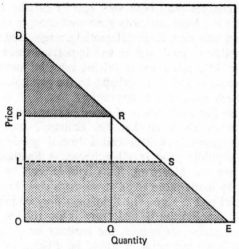

Figure 9 Consumers' surplus

revenue constraint (for example, this might suggest a lower charge than OP, OL, and a consumers' surplus of LDS); (c) to maximise consumers' surplus subject to a capacity constraint; (d) to maximise revenue subject to some minimal use of capacity, and so on. But in considering all this a further factor should not be forgotten: the possibility that having charges of any kind may deter some people altogether.

This brings us to the second set of criteria in social enterprise pricing, those of redistribution. Redistributive intentions may be one influence, perhaps a critical one, on the decision whether to charge for a service, what to charge and whether to charge differentially according to 'need'. Here one factor which is usually irrelevant in business pricing is vitally important: the actual numbers of people likely to be deterred at any price, however low, and then at successively higher levels of price. Also important will be the social characteristics of such non-users. Normally, the higher the charge, the fewer the users who are poor (or perhaps also disadvantaged in other ways). But sometimes the extent of any inverse relationship between price and 'need' may have to be more precisely gauged. In some cases the income levels of intended users may require to be systematically taken into account, for example in fixing standard charges representing a 'fair' ratio to income. Income levels and family responsibilities will be vital yardsticks in one extreme case: that of particularly costly and continuous services where charges may bear very heavily on the user. Classic examples here are local authority rents and charges to parents for children taken into care. Here differential charges tend to be made, related to 'ability to pay'. But in less important cases the 'equity' argument for differential social pricing may be swamped by its administrative costs and also, perhaps, by the psychologically deterrent effect of any associated means testing.

To complete this bald outline of social pricing criteria we need to remind ourselves about another key economic concept, that of *public goods* (sometimes also called 'social goods'). A classic example of a public good is a lighthouse. A lighthouse provides unqualified benefits. Moreover, if its light is seen by one ship, it can be seen by many more ships at no extra cost. In other words, marginal social cost is zero. The lighthouse may be jointly used by several ships simultaneously and there is no rivalry in such use between them unless, of course, the harbour becomes congested. Also, a very important point, it would be difficult to exclude any ship from using the lighthouse. In view of these attributes, it is neither desirable nor necessary nor even very feasible to charge ships for using the lighthouse. Charges are undesirable because they might deter users and so increase danger. Charges are unnecessary because costs do not vary with use, and they are probably impracticable, too, because to restrict use of the lighthouse and collect charges would be so expensive. These attributes of zero marginal costs, jointness and non-rivalness in consumption, and non-excludability are what chiefly distinguish public goods.[8] For all such attributes to co-exist in a pure form is rare. As they are departed from, so it becomes more reasonable to consider levying charges – subject, of course, to the demand and distributive criteria already outlined.

But there is an important proviso. Even where some of the purest attributes of publicness disappear, great caution about charges may still be justified. For example, marginal social costs may be positive and it may be perfectly possible to exclude some users, if so desired. But, nonetheless, external benefits or advantages to third parties may be important. Examples are adult education and immunisation against communicable diseases. In such cases nil or low charges may be justified simply in order to encourage fuller use of a service, partly for the sake of the favourable ripple effects on others in the wider community. Such favourable externalities form another aspect of publicness with which social pricing policy must be concerned.

SOCIAL PRICING IN PRACTICE: RECREATION, SOCIAL SERVICES, HOUSING, THE ARTS

How do the criteria of redistribution, publicness and externality work out in practice? Let us consider some examples of social pricing drawn from local government and related services. To start with a polar case, take refuse collection. Refuse collection involves no redistributive criteria: it is no more important to collect poor people's refuse than rich people's. In theory some people could be excluded but this would defeat the public health objectives which imply that everybody's refuse must be collected. The correct way of paying for such a non-redistributive, compulsory and highly public good is not through charges at all but taxation. Another polar case is a municipal restaurant. Here redistributive criteria are probably unimportant. Moreover, degrees of publicness are low. That is to say, (a) people can be excluded so charges are feasible, (b) there is an element of consumption rivalness so some sort of rationing seems necessary, and (c) there are virtually no externalities so cost recovery simply from users seems equitable. A municipal restaurant, there-fore, could be regarded as a quasi-commercial operation, justifying cost-plus, marginal cost or even market-based pricing. But these are limiting cases. The whole point is that many social goods exemplify cross-currents between the criteria of redistribution, publicness and externality, and it is here that the difficulties arise.

Take, for example, a municipal swimming pool. This is like the restaurant in that excludability is high so charges could be made. Again, too, there is an element of consumption rivalness. For although, perhaps, swimmers do not mind (and may even welcome) others simultaneously using the pool, congestion is possible. To deter this a charging system may be desirable, probably of a peak price or seasonal kind, for example, charging more at the week-ends. But beyond this point analogies with the restaurant break down. For the swimming pool may be regarded as providing external benefits. It provides public health advantages, perhaps particularly for children, with diffuse effects on the community. If the municipality is trying to build up a sporting reputation (say with the Olympics in mind), this too would constitute an externality. Externality considerations of this kind suggest that any charging should be at less than full cost. At the same time, though, re-distributive intentions are likely to be marginal. If it is hoped not to deter any particular group from using the pool, say schoolchild-ren or students, specially low charges might be made to them. The answer, therefore, may be rather less than full cost pricing, with special concessions to encourage full capacity use and for certain social groups (but the local authority should have some rational idea of the demand function, see the previous section, before it makes the final decision). From this brief outline it can be appreciated that the swimming pool is a useful example of an intermediate, mildly public good. Other recreational facilities tend to fall into the same category. The reader is invited to apply the same analysis to, say, access to stately homes or historical sights, the use of public lavatories and washing facilities, or municipally provided squash and tennis courts.

Now let us make a big jump further across the spectrum towards services where degrees of redistributive intent and/or publicness are considerably higher. Take, for example, marriage guidance. Since the counselling of married couples is a divisible, private activity, technically speaking, charges could be made. But many people who need and desire such help are likely to be relatively harassed, poor, embarrassed and inarticulate. They might be deterred by a charging system even if (or perhaps particularly if) this was means-tested. Moreover, the potential external benefits to children and society of protecting married happiness and family life must be rated highly. In this sector, too, there has traditionally been a heavy reliance on trained but voluntary workers to provide the counselling. As a result of all this, nothing is charged (although in some cases, perhaps, voluntary contributions may be accepted from clients). Compare this with, say, day nurseries for infant children from high-risk, emotionally stressed or single parent homes, where perhaps the mother has to go out to work. Here, as with marriage counselling, there are high degrees of both redistributive intent and externality (if only because neglected and deprived children may turn into unhappy and even delinquent adults). But there are important differences. Since day nurseries are usually heavy users of space, equipment and professional workers, unit costs are higher than for marriage counselling. Also, people are more likely to use day nurseries for their infant children on a continuous basis over long periods. These considerations suggest that some sort of charging system would be justified and economic, but with two provisos: (1) less than full cost recovery overall since an element of public subsidy is justified by the external benefits, and (2) differential charges related to ability to pay, in the interests of equity.

Readers will perceive that the criteria are complex in operation. They may find it instructive to apply them to some other locally provided social services, for example meals on wheels or home helps for the elderly and housebound, special equipment for the chronic disabled, or foster homes for children in care. They will find that the concepts of redistribution, publicness and externality, as understood by economics, provide a useful conceptual framework, but certainly no automatic formula, for the decision whether to charge and, if so, what.

Now consider a more complex case, that of a theatre company or symphony orchestra deciding on ticket prices. In modern times performing arts organisations in both the United States and the United Kingdom have experienced large and increasing 'income gaps', namely shortfalls between ticket earnings and costs.[9] The harassed arts administrator is unable to finance increased pay for actors, musicians and other employees by increasing their productivity and so reducing unit costs. A Chekhov play or Mozart symphony cannot be played faster or four times a day or with fewer artists or, for that matter, to 5,000 people. But fast-rising earnings elsewhere create a moral pressure not to let arts employees' earnings fall too far behind. As a result, live performing arts costs tend to rise relatively to costs elsewhere in the economy – a classic case of the 'service gap' already referred to. Should the arts administrator, then, simply increase ticket prices commensurately, thus pushing them up relative to other prices? He will probably be reluctant to do so. The evidence on demand functions for the live performing arts is conflicting. Indirect competition from the mass media 'canned' arts, relayed through records and TV, with their dramatic productivity breakthroughs, has grown. If the arts administrator increases relative prices, it would probably be more difficult to extend the social appeal of the live arts to many who might be stimulated by them. Audiences might become even more restricted to the already cultured and rich.

So what is the arts administrator to do? In practice, he may be well advised (1) to continue to rely to some extent on his artists' willingness to accept financial sacrifices for the sake of their art (and also of full houses); (2) to increase his marketing efforts with the object of shifting the demand curve to the right; (3) to apply price discrimination, for example by charging lower prices to weekday audiences or pensioners, and by 'squeezing' wealthy patrons; and (4) insofar as earnings still fall short of costs, to seek public subsidies on the grounds that the live performing arts create external benefits which cannot be fully recovered from ticket prices. Again, live arts performances are a good example of a semi-public good. Normally, there is non-rivalness in consumption. People at a concert are not put off by each other and may even enjoy the jointness (unless there is chronic coughing). Restrictability is high, indeed it needs to be, and exclusion costs low. But there may be favourable externalities – for example, benefits to a town's tourist trade, to the balance of payments from foreign visitors, perhaps even to future generations insofar as cultural traditions they may enjoy are kept alive.

The case of housing raises more fundamental issues in social pricing. The reasons why local authorities and voluntary bodies provide low cost rented housing are familiar. There is the insistence of social policy that people have basic rights to shelter and a home. There is the well-tried economic argument that because of the relatively fixed supply of land, there is a strong scarcity and monopoly element in pure market rents, leading to rents which tend to be particularly high in modern cities where the pressure on land is acute and the resulting demand–supply disparities particularly great. There is also the tendency of modern economics to extend social accounting to the social 'bads' associated with high rents and housing scarcity – particularly homelessness, overcrowding and family stress, sharpened poverty and child deprivation, perhaps even accentuated crime.

All this makes a strong case for public intervention. Yet elementary economics hardly supports the 'half-way house' of merely seeking to control market rents. If the supply–demand disparity is sufficiently chronic, controlling private rents tends to involve elaborate enforcement machinery, anomalies and evasions. But if the rent controls really bite, the lower returns to private landlords mean that properties are run down and the supply of rented housing is further reduced. This suggests that outright social provision would probably be more efficient. It is these arguments, too, that influence the critical problem of deciding what rents should then be charged.[10]

There are two main alternatives: (*a*) to apply 'corrected' market prices or (*b*) to develop entirely non-market prices based on 'need' or 'ability to pay'. The idea behind (*a*) is that shadow prices can be estimated: ideally, what rents would be if an unconstrained and competitive market in rented housing existed. The conditions for such a market, notably an elastic land supply, tend to be theoretical. So in practice alternative (*a*) means comparing market rents in areas of chronic scarcity with those in relatively less pressured areas, and adjusting the former to the latter. This at least drains off some of the profit created by extreme scarcity and has been broadly the approach attempted in controlling private sector rents in the United Kingdom. It does not, however, deal completely with the monopoly rent problem, let alone the social costs associated with any kind of scarcity in something so basic as housing.

So alternative (*b*) is normally preferred. In the local authority sector the normal United Kingdom practice has been to relate general levels of rents in some way or other to costs, to provide some general subsidy and then to provide rebates or housing allowances which will take account of individual households' ability to pay. This involves delicate issues: for example, on differing standards between old and new properties, on cross-subsidisation and on the question of what is a 'fair' proportion of net income, taking account of family responsibilities, to be spent on rents (as distinct from, say, mortgage repayments). But the essential point is that all such issues have to be resolved in terms of criteria of 'equity'. In practice, of course, it is the preferences of elected politicians, influenced by electoral considerations and consensus bargaining, that determine these criteria. Moreover, because housing policy has to be a national affair the pricing discretion available to local authorities tends to be small.

As far as housing associations are concerned, the problems are often simpler but more stark. Consider, for example, a housing association which is trying to help low income people in acute housing need in an inner city area. Given high property prices and housing costs, non-profit, 'pure cost' rents would still be far too high for, say, a typical pensioner or low-paid worker (although not necessarily for professional people who need housing). In the United Kingdom general public subsidies or tax concessions to housing associations serve to reduce rents only moderately below 'full-cost' and may still leave major gaps. So the association may seek charitable donations but, more important, special subsidies from its neighbouring local authority. These will enable the housing association's rents to edge closer to the local authority's. Correspondingly, the association will probably have to fit in with the local authority's ideas on whom it should rehouse. There may be certain social groups, say single people, priority public service workers or social deviants, whom the association is specially equipped to help. The essence of the pricing problem, however, is clear. Whether it fixes the rents only moderately below market prices, or closer to public sector rents, the housing association's pricing discretion will normally be small. Correspondingly, its financial situation will be tightly constrained. Caught between inflated property prices, restricted public subsidies and limited charitable donations – not to mention long queues of needy applicants – the inner city, direst-need oriented housing association will still have to recover most of its expenditure from rents. And these will often be higher than it would like.[11]

GRANT RAISING

By definition, many social enterprises, particularly charities, are neither willing nor able to charge for their services. Instead, they tend to rely on public grants and on voluntary grants from individual citizens, mainly of money and time. Charitable organisations can be said to compete for such grants in three main ways. First, they compete among themselves for citizen support, perhaps directly, as with charities for the blind, but probably indirectly insofar as charities and their objects are highly differentiated. Second, insofar as they seek to persuade government, local authorities and other public bodies to give money either to themselves or to the causes they promote, charities compete with other uses of public money. Third, insofar as they seek to obtain resources from individual citizens, often for new causes or in new ways, voluntary bodies compete with the other demands which are made on people's money or time, including those from commercial sources. These elements of competition are often acute. But similar problems in obtaining voluntary contributions are experienced by organisations other than charities : for example, by arts enterprises (as already mentioned), churches, community action groups of various kinds and also a number of statutory organisations, such as hospitals and schools, which rely on voluntary workers for special purposes.

Let us first take money gifts. The methods by which grant-using organisations raise money subtly illustrate the permutations of the Boulding triad of coercion, exchange and solidarity (see Chapter 2). The coercive element is present insofar as 'arm-twisting', high pressure salesmanship techniques are used, as in some American 'constituency campaigns'. The exchange element is employed insofar as donors are implicitly or explicitly offered public recognition of their philanthropy or increased social prestige as a result of giving. Another variation of the 'giving to get' theme occurs when charities marginally engage in market operations. In the luxuriantly diverse world of charity shops, charity Christmas cards, charity balls, bazaars and jumble sales, money is handed over as part gift, part exchange. As for the vein of solidarity, this is consistently drawn upon by appeals to conscience, guilt, moral duty and human sympathy, whether for starving people in Africa, cancer research or mentally handicapped children, and in quieter and more consistent collections and covenants for churches and other bodies. In varying mixtures and degrees, too, the principles of solidarity and sympathy are employed in ad hoc fund raising campaigns for, say, an ancient cathedral, World Refugee Year or established charities for 'down and outs' or overseas aid ('For God's sake, give us a pound', 'Oxfam hates starving children', 'Ignore the hungry and they'll go away', etc.).[12]

Although some voluntary organisations have carried out systematic research for themselves, little is known about the supply of money gifts in general terms. For example, is the overall supply income elastic or not? There are a few faint indications. One study has suggested that tax-deductible philanthropic contributions in the United States may have been relatively inelastic to income changes. This study also suggested that money gifts had responded with less-than-unit elasticity to increased tax concessions for private philanthropy in that country.[13] Since money gifts tend to be a tiny proportion of people's incomes – and also appear to be strongly influenced by social custom, ritual and random factors – they seem unlikely to be revised very sensitively in accordance with changes in real incomes (or even, as in the American case, with changes in the tax-adjusted 'price of giving').

Obviously, much charitable fund raising aims to raise large amounts from a relatively few rich donors. Indeed, the extent to which this can be done has been quantified. But the question whether better-off people give away higher proportions of their incomes is still an open one. Comparisons are difficult. The manner of giving may vary by social class as well as ethnic, educational or religious factors. For example, the rich probably tend to channel their gifts systematically and continuously by cheque and covenant (particularly if they can claim tax deductions thereby as in the United States), whereas money gifts by the less well-off may be relatively spasmodic, informal – or continuous but cash-based. But again, money-giving propensities by and within religious groups – in support of their schools, welfare activities and general work – often seem to be above-average, regardless of income.[14]

An important part of the micro-economy of grants consists of voluntary gifts of time. The organisation-building qualities of labour gifts in all sectors were referred to in Chapter 2. But clearly it is labour gifts to social enterprises – notably local charities, youth clubs, hospitals, and community and neighbourhood groups – that most clearly illustrate the theme. There is a wide spectrum ranging from a highly qualified person accepting a less than market salary to work for some social cause, right across to mutual help patterns in local communities that merge almost imperceptibly into neighbourliness and friendship. In the United Kingdom, surveys in some areas suggested that about 10 per cent of adults did regular unpaid work for formal voluntary organisations, although the proportion making regular time gifts of all kinds was much higher, at over one-third.[15] Once again, there seems to be a strong tendency towards formal, organised voluntary work by the better-off and more informal neighbourhood patterns among the poor.

The evidence suggests that informal community care – for example, neighbourhood support for the old, lonely, sick and handicapped – may well be higher in communities that are small, well-knit, stable and socially varied, with mixtures of young and old, rich and poor. But it is precisely these sorts of communities that so many trends in high growth, mobile and urbanised societies appear to militate against. Big city pressures can be viewed as isolating people as well as creating middle-class, working-class and racial ghettos. Professional and executive people, increasingly mobile nationally and even internationally, transient residents in single class and even single age-group suburbs may be further divorced from social responsibilities. And so on. Therefore, some activities which could be spontaneous and voluntary have to be expensively professionalised through statutory welfare services – a real social cost of unbalanced economic and urban growth.

This has several implications for social enterprises which seek to increase labour grants in order to deal with such problems as loneliness, racial segregation, family stress and child deprivation. On the one hand, fire-fighting strategies concentrate on getting more volunteers, mobilising the young through organisations like Task Force in the United Kingdom and developing webs of interdependent help between the voluntary and statutory services, for example in hospitals, education welfare and community development. On the other hand, to increase the overall supply of voluntary gifts much further does not seem to be easy in modern, affluent urbanised societies. One sign of this is the way in which community development schemes, designed to build up self-help and voluntary activity in depressed areas, often seem to founder once the enthusiastic 'outsiders' who have started them off depart. The overall propensities to make free labour grants probably depend on factors which are slow to change such as patterns of family life, the amount of leisure time, the social ethos and the extent to which social interdependence is made palpable for people primarily, perhaps, through small communities. Correspondingly, it may make sense for many social enterprises to urge radical changes, particularly in education, community planning and overall social priorities (see Chapter 12), with a view to increasing the overall supply of voluntary social gifts of time in the longer term.

CONCLUSION

This brief chapter on the provisioning problems of social enterprises has left many important aspects untouched. For example, we have not referred to the question of trade-offs and conflicts between market, public and voluntary sources of support and the related issue of 'optimal provisioning mixes'. Nor have we mentioned such interesting topics as lobbying for government grants, the problems of duplication or concentration among public and semi-public grant making bodies or the resource-getting methods employed by new, unorthodox or even unpopular sorts of social enterprises.

Nonetheless a common framework of analysis has been outlined. It has been shown that economics considerably clarifies (a) the nature of the resource gap faced by social enterprises, (b) the varying proportions of resources required from market, public and voluntary sources and (c) some of the ways in which resources are to be obtained from each main source. As we have seen, such economic analysis attends carefully to any redistributive objectives that social enterprises may have. It employs concepts related to supply and demand, consumers' surplus, externalities and public goods. And it also takes account of wider developing work on the grants economy. There can be little doubt that some highly sensitive and testing problems arise in this field.

Chapter 11

Social Enterprises: Allocation Problems

Once social enterprises have obtained resources, how should they allocate them? To a large extent the basic economic concepts discussed earlier, of marginalism, opportunity cost, time preference and risk, provide a rational framework for resource allocation in social enterprises as elsewhere, as we have seen. But for social enterprises some special economic approaches are required. It is convenient to discuss these approaches under the headings of cost–benefit analysis, distributional impacts and output budgeting.

COST–BENEFIT ANALYSIS, THEORY AND PRACTICE

Let us start with the pure notion of cost–benefit analysis and then work through to the applications and modifications. The basic principles here were glimpsed in Chapter 3. Since they are particularly complex the interested reader is referred to some of the excellent introductions that exist (see the Note on Further Reading at the end of the chapter). But the basic objective of cost–benefit analysis can be summed up fairly easily. It is to assist decision making by carefully analysing all relevant costs and benefits so as to express them in terms of money. This involves various approaches. For some social costs and benefits existing money values may be acceptable. For others existing money values are inadequate. Either the markets in question are highly imperfect and monopolistic or else important externalities, good or bad, are not reflected in prices. In such cases the analyst has to revalue or 'correct' existing market prices. The biggest problem, though, arises over those social costs and benefits, often the most important, for which market prices are non-existent. Here, according to the pure version of cost–benefit analysis, socially acceptable money valuations are to be derived in a variety of ways. Essentially, though, the method will involve observing people's past behaviour or present preferences, assessing the implicit valuations they put on costs and benefits and then expressing all these valuations in terms of the common language of money. Finally, the costs and benefits to everybody are to be wrapped up in an overall cost–benefit ratio. Ideally, it is this monetised summation – or, in the case of alternatives, series of summations – that would determine the social decision makers' choice.

A number of possible misconceptions should be cleared up straightway. First, the pure version of cost–benefit analysis does not pretend to do anything more than play back, in suitably clarified, refined and usable forms, the valuations people already make. There is no implication that these existing valuations are necessarily morally correct in any deeper sense. Second, the use of money as *numeraire* is merely a convenience. As economists sometimes point out, beads, cowrie shells, or whatever, might do just as well. Third, the assignation of money valuations to costs and benefits does not imply (except, perhaps, in a few cases) that the goods and bads in question are intended to be bought, sold or compensated for in actual markets. The idea is simply to sum up the individual valuations of a lot of citizens in a manner which will be helpful to public decision making.

There are several serious problems inherent in the pure version of cost–benefit analysis. Although not fatal, these tend to diminish its usefulness. For one thing the theory ignores distributional criteria. That is to say, it takes an existing distribution of power and resources as a datum, assuming that £1 is worth the same to a rich man as a poor man and assigning no value to a changed or less unequal distribution. Yet as we have seen, explicit redistributive objectives are a frequent criterion of social decision making. Another problem is that the pure version of cost–benefit analysis applies a purely individualistic calculus. The costs and benefits to individuals are added up with insufficient regard for interdependent preferences. The tendency for our valuations to depend on those of others because of gregariousness, snobbery, generosity or other factors, tends to be under-emphasised. Again, in treating people's valuations as 'given', the pure version of cost–benefit analysis tends to ignore the extent to which attitudes alter. People may change their minds precisely as a result of publicity and debate in the decision making process, for example when a controversial town plan is being discussed in a particular area. Or again, people's valuations may shift after they actually experience new goods and bads. Such dynamic factors are hard to incorporate in the analysis. Not least, there is a severe practical problem. To be useful, cost–benefit analysis should be able to provide comprehensive and timely data for decision making. But some valuations can only be developed with great difficulty and expense and after prolonged research.

To illustrate some of the possibilities and problems, let us take a frequently important issue in local affairs, that of road traffic. Supposing Middlechester is subjected to heavy through-traffic. This has led to discussion on two alternative improvements, a one-way traffic system or a new bypass. A cost–benefit analysis of these alternatives is undertaken. On the basis of present knowledge and techniques, how would this proceed? Let us start with the relatively straightforward items in the analysis, not necessarily in order of importance. One possible benefit from the proposed schemes would be time savings for road users travelling through or inside Middlechester. In the cost–benefit analysis the time savings for business users would be related to market values, for example, the financial advantages of quicker deliveries and better use of commercial transport fleets or, in the case of a businessman, more time at work (valued at normal hourly income). The valuation of time savings for private motorists would be more difficult. One approach might be to infer the values transport users generally put on time savings from their past choices as between faster (more costly) and slower (cheaper) transport modes. National studies of this kind have suggested norms, for example a rough guide of half national average earnings, that can be applied to cases like Middlechester. Next, an assessment would be made of the financial impacts of the two alternative schemes on Middlechester shopkeepers, business interests and local employment. From this viewpoint, incidentally, the scheme offering more road access to the town might have greater advantages. Another important and obvious item would be the relative financial costs and benefits to the public authorities: on the one hand, the costs of the schemes themselves, both to the local authority and central government, on the other the trickle-through advantages to Middlechester's income from rates.

Turning to the more difficult valuations, there is the impact of traffic noise on local residents. Presumably the present seriousness of this is a major reason for considering the new schemes. The cost–benefit analysis would take account of the developing technology of noise measurement. Several approaches might be used to estimate the cost of noise (benefit of noise alleviation). An opinion survey might try to gauge the intensity of residents' discomfort relative to different types of noise at different times of day or night, perhaps in different parts of the town. Such a survey might also test out residents' attitudes to various methods of noise alleviation (sound barriers, double glazing, etc.). The most preferred and effective method might then be costed. Its cost would then be added to the costs of the one-way scheme, i.e. regarded as a benefit from the bypass. Next, the cost of accidents to life and limb (benefits of greater safety): we have already referred to confused public valuations in this field (see Chapter 4). Here the analysts might be torn between valuations related to past public expenditures on accident prevention, insurance values, or compensation to injured persons. Being aware of the problems (and, let us hope, humane), the analysts might be inclined to use the highest existing valuations. Perhaps, too, they might suggest even these as a minimum figure ('rightly or wrongly, the existing social valuation of people's lives and limbs cannot be *less* than X').

Finally, some other important but also difficult cost and benefit items could hardly be ignored. These would include the likely effects on (*a*) pedestrians (mobility, comfort), (*b*) social life (neighbourhood integration/severance), and (*c*) the aesthetic appearance of the town. Again, such matters might be tested through opinion surveys of local citizens or by reference to the town's political decision makers. In relation to (*a*), the cost of providing necessary and acceptable pedestrian protection (subways, crossings, bridges, traffic controls) would be debited against the one-way traffic scheme. Any money valuations assigned to (*b*) and (*c*) would be notional and, of course, particularly subject to debate. Having monetised all significant costs and benefits in some way or other, the analysts would estimate their incidence over time. A discount rate would be applied to arrive at net present values and the latter might well be ranged to allow for risk (on discounting and risk, see Chapter 6). The final outcome of this pure version of cost–benefit analysis would be a set of monetary valuations for the one-way traffic scheme and the bypass – in each case an overall, discounted, (probably risk-adjusted) cost–benefit ratio.

STRENGTHS AND WEAKNESSES OF SOCIAL MONETISING

It must be stressed that this is an extremely summary outline of the processes involved. It should, however, help the reader to glimpse the main strengths and weaknesses of the pure version of cost–benefit analysis. The principal strength is that a disciplined framework is provided for analysing relevant factors and verifying the interests and practical preferences of everybody concerned. In this sense cost–benefit analysis attempts to be both rational and democratic. It is sometimes argued that cost–benefit analysis does a disservice to decision making insofar as it throws up a mixture of items, some readily quantifiable, others much less so. For attention

M

will then be concentrated, so it is said, on the former to the detriment of the latter. True, it may. For example, in the case just quoted the reader will note that the benefits of a one-way traffic system (perhaps to through-traffic and local commercial interests) are easier to quantify than its costs (noise, neighbourhood, pedestrian and aesthetic effects). This asymmetry may tempt the analysts, local decision makers and others to over-emphasise benefits and underestimate costs, with highly inequitable and inefficient results. Moreover, it is easy to envisage situations where a reverse asymmetry might apply (slum clearance, environmental protection, social facilities for teenagers). But this danger is inherent in countless choice situations. The criticism implies that even relatively straightforward quantification should be refused lest this be foolishly misused. This seems hard to justify. The risk that analyses may be badly presented by experts or misapplied by decision makers should not deter efforts to analyse and quantify as far as possible (we shall return in a moment to the question of what is 'possible').

Nor is there much to be said for the argument that if the Middlechester local authority finally decide to go for a bypass – because they value the less readily quantifiable community and environmental benefits more highly than the 'harder' financial ones – this casts doubt on the usefulness of quantifying the 'harder' items in the first place. The fact that decision makers finally set a higher value on A than B hardly implies that B should not be calculated. On the contrary, the calculation of B may be an essential first step towards concentrating attention on A and deciding really how much we value it. An advantage of cost–benefit analysis is its recognition that when public policy makers make decisions they cannot avoid implicit quantification. Such unavoidable and implicit quantifications, resulting from, say, relative expenditures on life savings, children or old people, housing or national parks, have often been referred to in previous chapters. Cost–benefit analysis provides a framework within which these quantifications can at least be made explicit, debated, tested, made more consistent and not least, checked against some indications of what citizens themselves appear to prefer.

On the other hand, the Middlechester case pungently illustrates the fundamental limitations already referred to: the neglect of distributional criteria and social interdependence, the assumption of 'given' preferences, the acute difficulties of comprehensive analysis within a viable time scale. These limitations come to a head in that pivotal feature of the orthodox approach, its effort to reduce widely contrasted items to a common numerical scale. Some of the items just quoted are amenable to unambiguous monetary expression, for example the financial effects on commercial interests, local rates or employment. Some can be expressed in money terms with some plausibility, using well tried methods, for example the monetisation of certain types of time saving. But these valuations may still be questioned on equity grounds. For example, they may understate the interests of private motorists bent on leisure pursuits or of poorer property owners or council tenants. Yet again, some further items can be convincingly quantified or ranked in some way as a result of opinion surveys, political preferences or careful observation of past behaviour, for example, the pedestrian, neighbourhood and aesthetic effects. But once these quantified valuations or rankings have been translated into money terms so as to be commensurate with the other items, thorny questions arise. Looking at the whole picture, it is perfectly possible, in some way or other, both to value each item and then to collapse all the valuations into a single ratio or ratios. But there will be legitimate doubts on some of the individual valuations, and still more on the validity of the weighting criteria used to reduce such widely varying items and valuation methods onto a single numerical scale.

Can the advantages of cost–benefit analysis be developed whilst shedding such weaknesses? At this point an important choice in decision making techniques arises. The choice will not surprise the reader who has already confronted the frequent dilemma of rigour versus relevance, purity versus comprehensiveness, several times in this book. To be useful, cost–benefit analysis can retain its purity but limit its application. Alternatively, it can aim for the 'big time' but at the cost of abandoning its more ambitious monetising. This split between a low, well-lit road and a high, misty one is fundamental to the whole problem of economic decision making, as we have repeatedly seen.

Examples of a pure but restricted use of cost–benefit analysis by intermediate organisations are not hard to find.[1] For example, a large local authority is trying to evolve its attitude towards some new industry. Rigorous cost–benefit studies of the conventional sort, using input–output analysis, have produced relevant estimates of the ripple effects on local employment and income. Again, a local authority or amenity organisation seeks to estimate the demand for some recreational amenity, say a landscaped park. Despite the absence of a market, orthodox cost–benefit analysis can be used to establish a surrogate demand curve. This suggests how much people would be prepared to pay to travel to the park. People's willingness to pay for certain public goods can be ascertained by studies of their past choices and by opinion surveys. With reservations such studies can help to build up estimates of the value to the public of some facility, as a basis for investment decisions. If user charges are considered feasible and desirable, the study results can also be used to estimate likely consumers' surplus, revenues and utilisation levels as a basis for deciding what to charge (see the section on social pricing in Chapter 10). Again, the valuation of environmental costs affects many social enterprises – a city government trying to contain the motor car, a local amenity group fighting to preserve a quiet neighbourhood, a community action group trying to get action on pollution in a depressed urban area. Conventional cost–benefit analysis is beginning to put rough prices on what it would cost to counteract these nuisances, for example by soundproofing in the case of noise, cleaning and repainting in the case of dirt or, indeed, stopping both these nuisances at source. Such estimates of compensatory or preventative costs can be used to build up a case either against an environmental 'bad' in the first place or in favour of effective and publicly acceptable alleviation if it actually comes about.

All these are pure cost–benefit analyses, wrapping up neat parcels of social costs and benefits in terms of money. But useful though they are, they all have limitations from the viewpoint of wider strategy. For example, the local industry study cannot churn out money values for possible damage to coastline, animal life or local community relationships. Environmental studies can hazard guesstimates of the money costs of cleaning beaches, redecorating public buildings or stopping harmful effluents, although the technical problems in so doing are immense. But they cannot express in *money* terms, for example, the fears of old ladies walking through pedestrian subways at night or parents' worries over their young children travelling to school through traffic-torn roads. Nor can they tie up in money terms the extent to which, say, a new motorway prevents people from shopping and visiting neighbours. Nor can they convincingly monetise the degree to which carefully planned small neighbourhoods may facilitate infant recreation, social contacts, friendliness and mutual help. An overall cost–benefit ratio assigns no value to a redistribution of resources where such a redistribution is regarded as desirable by social decision makers. It does not even indicate the numbers of people affected by various items, let alone the movement of resources between persons, areas or social groups – a frequently vital matter for public decision makers. Nor can *money* values wholly (or perhaps even mainly) capture the benefits of, say, university education, slum clearance, counselling distressed families or helping the mentally ill.

For these reasons the pure version of cost–benefit analysis, however useful for a wide range of decisions and however important its further development, cannot handle some of the more strategic and sensitive areas of social choice. For these purposes it may be better to abandon the over-ambitious idea of an overall cost–benefit ratio, and hence of universal monetising, or at least to treat it with extreme reserve. Instead, modified forms of cost–benefit analysis and related techniques, often called by different names, have to be applied. It is to these that we now turn.

DISTRIBUTIONAL PROBLEMS

As we have seen, although the pure version of cost–benefit analysis disregards 'who gets what?' questions, these are often fundamental in social enterprise planning. In practice, there are several ways in which distributional issues can be handled, assuming they are considered to be important. First, the analyst can examine the implicit preferences as to distribution which social decision makers have shown in the past. It may be feasible to observe a run of past decisions made by senior politicians and bureaucrats as between, say, different social and geographical groups. Applying indifference curve analysis, the decision makers' apparent distributional preferences can be explicitly brought out and used in the evaluation of costs and benefits. Town hall top people or welfare administrators can then be helped to make their decisions more consistent, to articulate their redistributive aims more precisely or perhaps to revise them. Another approach, now used by some larger and sophisticated local authorities, is to construct geographical indicators of social need. These social need indices rely on various yardsticks, say low income and unemployment data, overcrowding and poor housing conditions, juvenile delinquency. Among the technical problems involved are those of obtaining sufficiently fine geographical areas and weighting the various criteria of need. Using factor analysis and cluster analysis, the areas are ranked against each other to see which have the heaviest concentrations of social need as defined. These contours are then employed to help social decisions on, say, the deployment of social workers or the location of new services. A further approach, already used in some social service and town planning studies, is to draw up a distributional impact statement. This tries to show the number of people in various categories – for example, pedestrians, car owners, residents of different areas, members of different social or ethnic groups – who are likely to be favourably or unfavourably affected by new schemes (or who are, perhaps, already so affected by existing ones).

Some approaches to cost–benefit analysis abandon all attempts at overall monetary ratios and are unashamedly pluralist. An example is the planning balance sheet approach developed by Professor Nathaniel Lichfield. This has been used to analyse town planning decisions in places like Cambridge, Peterborough and Swanley.[2] This approach first separates out all the categories affected by, say, a new town plan: for example, the local authority itself, landowners, owner-occupiers, motorists, shoppers, pedestrians, residents in different areas. The number of people in each category is shown. All the expected flows of costs and benefits are then considered. The expected flows (or 'transactions') analysed would include not only the real resource costs, interpersonal transfers and changes in market values affecting, say, the council, local businesses, shoppers and houseowners. They would also include intangible flows, for example the improved atmosphere in an office building as a result of a new park nearby or the noise suffered by a particular neighbourhood as a result of a new road. These flows are expressed in widely differing ways – in terms of (a) money items (b) time losses or savings, (c) physical units, (d) ordinal rankings as established by opinion surveys, or even (e) simple plus, minus or neutral signs, for example for the 'softer' items like aesthetic beauty.

Significantly, however, in this planning balance sheet approach, no effort is made to monetise the more difficult non-monetary items. Instead, these are left to speak for themselves. Significantly, too, great care is taken over the number of people in various categories who will be affected by the different cost and benefit flows (including, very importantly, the interpersonal transfers often ignored in overall cost–benefit ratio summaries). A series of balance sheets then incorporate these data. On the vertical side of the matrix are shown the categories of people, on the horizontal the types of flow. The entries in the various boxes include money figures (with minus signs prefixed where appropriate), other quantities, or symbols for 'neutral', 'better' or 'worse'. A final balance sheet summarises the relative scores of alternative plans so far as the different criteria – and categories of people – are concerned. The advantages of this sort of approach are that it concentrates on the social interactions and incidence of costs and benefits, avoids controversial monetising and expressly leaves to decision makers the final key weightings, particularly on distributional issues.

OUTPUT BUDGETING

Special cost–benefit analyses and distribution surveys can form a useful part of the background of social decision making. However, it is in the regular budgeting processes of social enterprises that the economic approach to resource allocation faces its biggest challenge. The budget concept has already been outlined in relation to businesses (see Chapter 9). As with firms, so with social enterprises, it is in budgets (short-term or long-term, current or capital) that political pressures, planning objectives and major spending decisions come to the boil. There can be little doubt that the economic ideal of resource allocation meets its severest test in the field of social budgeting. For it is not the rational evaluation of costs and benefits, but rather incrementalism – the view that conservatism and political bargaining dominate decision making (see Chapter 3) – that seems to be in firmest possession of this field.

Studies of public budgetary processes confirm that allocations to particular programmes are heavily overshadowed by the past. The main criteria appear to be, how much did X get last year? What proportion of the total 'cake' did they get? Percentage increases higher than last year's, or proportions greater than before, require enormous justification. Annual changes then appear to be very small or 'incremental'. Moreover, the public budgetary process is strongly influenced by financial control systems which concentrate on inputs rather than outputs, and on control rather than effectiveness. The process also appears to be affected by bargains between officials ('you scratch my back, I'll scratch yours'), 'fair share' philosophies between departments and the relative muscle of top politicians. Nor is this surprising. After all, many local authority departments are 'locked' into expenditure programmes as a result of statutory obligations; withdrawal from others may be viewed as politically unacceptable; and political pressures are an essential part of any democratic system.

Such an array of real or apparent obstacles to the economic approach in regular budgeting appears formidable. At first sight, indeed, the battle might seem lost even before it begins. Nonetheless, such an inference is mistaken. Once again an over-abstract concept of economics may obscure the chance of sensible improvements. It is a caricature to suppose that 'economic budgeting' requires detached and refined philosopher-kings brooding over reams of pseudo-quantified data. In a world of bureaucrats, politicians and incommensurables, the super-quantifying dream is more than usually inept. But this does not mean that rougher hewn economic approaches are impossible. Indeed, the very crudity and apparent 'messiness' of the social budgeting process may be all the more capable of improvement by moderate economic reforms.

This view has been stimulatingly expressed by the American economist, Mancur Olson. Olson has argued that inefficiencies in the supply of public goods are 'extraordinarily important'.[3] In his view, this is not because public authorities are inherently inefficient. Instead he ascribes part of the blame to the fact that most public goods are natural monopolies. In common with many other economists (see Chapter 2) Olson also considers that the professionals supplying public goods tend to have too much leverage – and the clients or citizens for whom the public goods are intended, too little. But in Olson's view the main difficulty is a miserably inadequate measurement of performance. Even modest indicators of volume and quantity, specific to a service and non-commensurable, for example in health, social services, recreation and the environment, are too frequently lacking. This 'lack of objective bases for judging performance', Olson maintains, induces a feeling of unease which in turn leads to a 'labyrinth' of restrictions on public officials – restrictions which are tangential or perhaps even harmful to the real objective. 'The civil service rules, competitive purchase provisions, and red tape requirements no doubt prevent some of the chicanery that the lack of measured output could allow, but they also impose enormous costs, both in time and money.'[4] A further result, Olson claims, is too much emphasis on loyalty, conservatism and 'not rocking the boat' when it comes to assessing and promoting bureaucrats, and far too little emphasis on their productivity. But, far from despairing, Olson sees this situation as fertile with promise, at least for broad-based economic improvements. Precisely because the social allocation process is so confused, in his view, even moderate improvements in output measurement and social indicators would offer 'substantial increases in social efficiency'.

An approach is now slowly developing for this purpose, that of *output budgeting*. Output budgeting is in the same spirit as the more realistic and pluralist approaches to cost–benefit analysis mentioned above. Unlike the more elaborate 'one-off' exercises of cost–benefit analysis, however, output budgeting aims to be part of the regular budgeting process. It represents a major challenge before which traditional social budgeting seems likely to retreat. For traditional budgeting in this field has been mainly concerned with internal financial flows, with the money costs of inputs and with the necessary but narrow objects of financial control – making sure that money is spent strictly as intended. By contrast, output budgeting seeks to relate costs of all kinds (in some cases including social opportunity costs) to activities and objectives. In this sense output budgeting is both more comprehensive and more outward-looking. Advocates claim that output budgeting compels decision makers to think more clearly about policy objectives, that it improves information on the actual effects of social enterprise activities and so facilitates more rational and community-orientated resource allocation. A further advantage, perhaps, is that output budgeting is a logical extension and intensification of what some local authorities, public agencies and charities have been attempting for some time.

The problems are considerable. Frequently it is quite impossible to measure the final outputs of social and public services. Instead, intermediate output measures have to be used, although these can be very helpful. Examples of such intermediate or secondary indicators would be the number of students successfully completing examinations in schools or universities, the numbers of cases treated, ratios of inputs to patients and balance of care, i.e. the range and mix of services being delivered to particular groups, for example in hospitals. Another problem is to provide for quality standards. Yet another is to develop measures for the 'purer' public goods which are characterised by indivisibility and/or particularly high degrees of externality (see Chapter 10). For example, it may be virtually impossible to ascertain the number of beneficiaries from crime prevention or inoculation against certain diseases. In such cases wider social indicators have to be developed. Examples of social indicators include data on life expectancy, morbidity, suicide, illegitimacy and abortion. Other problems arise where objectives and outputs are interdependent as between different social programmes. Frequently, output indicators for a particular programme are both multiple and multi-dimensional. For example, in the case of public recreation, important indicators would include numbers of users, numbers of users in particular social categories, intensity of use and capacity utilisation, tests of user satisfaction or dissatisfaction, and related social indicators (better health, less juvenile delinquency?).

Advances in output budgeting so far appear patchy in education, health, police and environmental protection; fairly rapid in the more quantifiable area of public transport; very promising in the personal social services. The highly ambitious measurement projects in some public agencies – starting in the United States in the early 1960s under the heading of 'planning, programming and budgeting systems' and spreading to British central and local government by the

end of that decade – have run into massive problems. To give some
idea of the magnitude of the task, it has been reported that in the
early days of output budgeting linked with corporate planning,
the Greater London Council developed over 1,000 potential
measures, of which 450 related to workloads and throughputs, 350
to indications of social need, 250 to indications of effectiveness. But
of these only 86 had become operational by early 1974.[5] On the
other hand, more moderate steps, for example in identifying client
groups in the personal social services, have been urged on United
Kingdom local authorities by the Chartered Institute of Public
Finance and Accountancy. This body claims that even modest
improvements here would help performance comparison and
emulation between local authorities, clarify thinking about priorities
and targets and help towards a more equitable distribution of
resources.[6]

ECONOMICS, COMMITTEES AND LOCAL POLITICS

In 1984 the Multiple Services Committee of Middletown had an
exhausting year. To begin with, its key members had some strong
disagreements. The chairman, Councillor Upcoming, a colourful and
dominating woman, generally had her way with the committee. But
there were repeated arguments between Councillor Savewell and
Councillor Softheart. Councillor Savewell's utility function could be
written: minimise internal financial costs subject to an electoral
constraint; namely the fear of being voted out at the next election
for inadequate services. By contrast, Councillor Softheart's utility
function could be written: maximise services to the public, also
subject to an electoral constraint; this time the fear of being voted
out because of unpopular rate increases. Predictably, arguments
between Savewell and Softheart tended to be intense. Predictably,
too, the committee tended to decide on some compromise between
the extremes of social narrowness and extravagance personified by
the two men. But the really memorable events in 1984 were as
follows.

(1) *How Councillor Upcoming got money for the new sports centre*
The ruling party's manifesto had done no more than refer to
'improving the town's sporting and recreational facilities'. But
Councillor Upcoming became convinced that a fully-fledged sports
centre was highly desirable. Since virtually none of the other
councillors, except Softheart and a few loyal henchmen, were impressed with the idea, Upcoming knew she would have to fight hard.

She reckoned two or three key people would first have to be persuaded. Upcoming squared another powerful committee chairman by agreeing to back one of his key projects later. This colleague tipped off the senior officer of his department to work behind the scenes at officer level. He also obligingly lined up a number of other councillors to support Upcoming on the grounds of past helpfulness to them or future support. But the most difficult person to convince was Savewell. He maintained that the sports centre would be 'a colossal waste of money' and 'was not in the manifesto anyway'. Savewell was partially sweetened by a subcommittee chairmanship, and also by an agreement to cut down on some minor services. Another important factor in convincing both Savewell and a number of fence-sitters was a persuasive paper by one of the council's analysts suggesting that the sports centre would be good for local business and that the relevant site could hardly be used for anything else anyway. By now the way was cleared for a debate at the party caucus meeting where Councillor Upcoming's charm and eloquence, combined with the support or silence of her key colleagues and the work they had already done, produced a sweeping majority for the idea.

(2) *How the committee were knocked for six by government cuts*[7]
The worst thing that happened in 1984 was a sudden announcement of government cuts in future public expenditure. The committee had been working on a series of ambitious projects for the late 1980s but in a spasmodic and unconsidered way. A few councillors and officers had warned that the country's current economic crisis might stymie some of these plans. At the beginning of 1984, in fact, the council's corporate planners had suggested that the committee should do some fundamental thinking about priorities. Their paper had proposed various ways of doing this. One suggestion was that the committee might group expansion projects into 'need' categories as follows: (1) urgent improvements to existing services, (2) urgent new services, (3) less urgent improvements to existing services, (4) less urgent new services. Another suggested method of concentrating on priority thinking would be a simulation exercise, taking a notional uncommitted £100, asking committee members to allocate this among certain representative projects and then to debate their individual allocations until a consensus emerged. Yet another proposal (the one most favoured by the analysts) was that 10-year objectives for each main service should be proposed to the Committee, indicating the gaps between present reality and the objectives. If the Committee agreed to the objectives, members would

then be asked to take one of the gaps and rank certain other gaps as more, less or equally 'serious'. Repeating the process and using iteration, this would establish groups of gaps – across the whole spectrum of services – which the Committee regarded as equally serious. The process could be used to establish a reasoned hierarchy of priorities which would help planning, particularly if there were any unexpected limitations of resources.

Unfortunately, none of these proposals was adopted. The Committee were in a highly optimistic mood at the start of 1984; warnings of possible cuts were discounted; members were attached to their own pet schemes and had no appetite to crab each other and engage in disputes, which the proposed priority thinking appeared to threaten. Also, the corporate planners' detailed suggestions were suspected for being 'too theoretical'. Anyway, when the announcement of government cuts came through, the Committee were largely unprepared. Massive reductions in proposed expansions were suddenly dictated. The Committee duly protested. But at two emergency meetings they were compelled to make drastic cuts in future plans. This experience was described as 'sad, almost heartbreaking'.

The question raised in retrospect was, would pre-thinking on priorities have produced significantly different results? It was hard to say. Perhaps it would have done. The final decisions might have been less conservative: in the panic situation it was the long-established activities that were unquestioned, the new ones most vulnerable to cuts. To some extent the lack of previous thinking on priorities meant that chances of rationalising existing services – and of creating entirely new ones – were completely ignored: a situation solidified by the cuts. Certainly, committee members felt disquiet. 'It would have been a miserable business anyway but scalpels would have been better than hatchets . . .'

(3) *How the committee were able to increase welfare from the same resources*

The year ended on a happier note. A few councillors were worried that a number of important welfare facilities were not getting to people in the greatest need. From their grassroots contacts these councillors had heard that official publicity on the facilities was couched in 'bureaucratese' and off-putting to possible claimants and that isolated pockets of extreme poverty existed of which social workers were unaware. Following pressure from these councillors and detailed proposals from officers, the Committee agreed to a pilot study in a representative area. This was designed to check the sort of people who were receiving benefits, those who were not, and the ways in which the latter could be reached and the available resources more fairly shared. The results of this survey were surprising. It was found that access to the facilities was strongly concentrated in a small minority of people who were articulate, knowledgeable and good claimers, although not necessarily the most needy. The council's statistics had not previously shown the extent of client overlap or the actual distribution among persons of the facilities. Conversely, it was found that a considerable number of poorer and more needy people were unaware of the benefits or reluctant to apply for them for mixed reasons of pride, inconvenience, suspicions of officialdom or misunderstanding about their entitlements.

Having discussed this report, the Committee moved quickly. Further expansion of the facilities which would largely benefit the already fortunate group of people was stopped (actually to withdraw the services from existing recipients was felt to be politically impracticable). A sharper and saltier publicity campaign was undertaken; the Committee's objectives for the services were revised to take account of the likely unmet need; and new and improved statistics were introduced. The Committee were gratified. As the chairman put it, 'At least we are not in the dark any more, the jam is going to be spread a bit more fairly and we know who are the people to help as soon as we get more money . . .'

The reader is invited to reflect on this brief chronicle. Among his jottings might feature (1) the utility functions of local politicians, (2) the allocative effects of the electoral cycle, committee 'learning' during its period of office and councillor–officer relationships, (3) the problems of 'selling' rational/economic approaches in this area, (4) the allocative influence of both exchange and solidarity in political choice, (5) the 'conservative bias' and incrementalism versus opportunity cost and equity, particularly in relation to crisis-enforced allocations, and so on. But perhaps the most important lesson is that often, in this area, the most socially useful approaches are not, after all, the most elegant. On the contrary, the complexities, crosscurrents, unquantifiables and incommensurables are so great that the simplest improvements are often the most important. Just a little rationality – and the implications for equity and efficiency can be profound.

Note on Further Reading

For fuller introductory treatments of cost–benefit analysis see:

E. J. Mishan, *Cost–Benefit Analysis: An Informal Introduction*, 2nd edition, London, Allen & Unwin, 1975.

A. R. Prest and R. Turvey, 'Cost benefit analysis: a survey', *Economic Journal*, 1967.

Robert Dorfman (ed.), *Measuring Benefits of Government Investments*, Washington, The Brookings Institution, 1965.

Richard Layard (ed.), *Cost–Benefit Analysis: Selected Readings*, Harmondsworth, Penguin, 1972.

J. N. Wolfe (ed.), *Cost Benefit and Cost Effectiveness: Studies and Analysis*, London, Allen & Unwin, 1973.

For output budgeting and planning, programming systems see:

A. J. Culyer, *The Economics of Social Policy*, New York, Dunellen, 1973, Ch. 9.

F. J. Lyden and E. G. Miller, *Planning, Programming, Budgeting: a Systems Approach to Management*, Chicago, Markham, 1968.

Alan Williams, 'Output budgeting and the contribution of micro-economics to efficiency in government', *CAS Occasional Paper No. 4*, London, HMSO, 1967.

For social indicators see:

A. Shonfield and A. Shaw, *Social Indicators and Social Policy*, London, Heinemann, 1972.

Chapter 12

Organisational Reform

This book has used economics to explain and interpret what organisations do. Taking present institutions as given, we have concentrated on the varying objectives of organisations and on how they can pursue those objectives more efficiently. Wider social issues have hardly been considered. But we live in a society of complex and often increasing interdependence, a society where organisations can greatly damage each other and the community, sometimes glaringly but often subtly, cumulatively and even unawares. What should organisations do about these external effects? What changes in existing organisations are needed in response to the fundamental social problems faced by Western societies? What sort of *new* organisations may be needed?

To deal with these issues would require another very different kind of book. But to ignore them completely would be wrong. Not only present realities but also possible reforms can be greatly clarified by micro-economics. In this final chapter, therefore, we sketch out how the framework of analysis applied in the book relates to the wider issues. Some contemporary economists' criticisms of the present organisational system are briefly outlined, then some micro-economic lessons as to possible remedies. At this point the selection of both critiques and proposals inevitably reflects the author's personal preferences. In discussing what is wrong and what can be done to put it right some personal value judgements are unavoidable. These, of course, readers may accept or reject as they please. What is essential is to realise that the economics of organisations cannot be divorced from wider social values and purposes. Indeed, micro-economics provides an essential framework for clarifying and stimulating the inevitable debate on such issues.

ORGANISATIONAL POWER, EXTERNAL DISECONOMIES, SOCIAL CONFLICTS

A brief catalogue of contemporary social problems – related in some way or other to organisations in developed Western societies

– is not hard to construct. Many economists would probably start off such a list with the problem of *excessive sectional power*. They would worry about the damage from business monopoly – allocative inefficiency, 'X-inefficiency' and the ability to hold other members of society to ransom if so desired. As suggested in Chapter 7, though, in complex and fast-changing markets the evils, let alone the precise degrees, of business monopoly are slippery and hard to pin down. It is arguable that the real and more specifiable problem, sometimes linked with monopoly but not always, is size itself, related to conglomerateness and overall concentration of business power in the economy as a whole. We found indications that such concentrations do not necessarily increase economic efficiency, particularly when they swell out beyond the limits justified by production and technological economies of scale; that there are no 'built-in' limits to their further expansion; that even where they offer efficiency and national interest gains in the short run, the longer-term risks of sluggishness and ossification may be increased; and that meantime perhaps the giant businesses often wield too much market and social power. But neither monopoly nor the size problem is restricted to the business sector. Both are evident also in the trade unions, the professions and other fields. For example, in a society where striking doctors, engineers and power workers can bring chaos to hospitals, whole industries and giant modern cities, the risks of concentrated and aggressively used sectional power in a situation of increasing social interdependence hardly need emphasising.

Nor is the problem of excessive sectional power restricted to nation states. Recent estimates suggest that since investment by *multi-national companies*, is increasing faster than the economic growth of most advanced countries, the relative weight of business enterprises to nation states will continue to increase.[1] In the United Kingdom between 20 per cent and 25 per cent of manufacturing output seems likely to be supplied by foreign-owned concerns by 1981.[2] Although many economists argue that on balance multi-national companies may be a 'good thing', few dispute the serious politico-economic problems.[3] A recent study suggested that if multi-nationals really sought to 'optimise' their financial positions systematically – by juggling to their advantage varying national economic and fiscal systems – serious implications would follow for the balance of payments of many individual countries.[4] In less-developed countries the multinational threat to national sovereignty is taken very seriously. As Professor Edith Penrose has said: 'So long as the inequalities among the nations of the world are so great that a large proportion of the people of some are in real poverty, the governments of these peoples will be unwilling to give the rich and favoured foreign economic interests a dominating position in their economies'.[5] In the long run such problems could theoretically be transcended by decisive moves towards a world state. But assuming that national loyalties and identities remain strong – and that the chasms between rich and poor nations continue to be appallingly large – certain conflicts posed by multinational business operations seem likely to persist.

Social deviance by organisations is hardly a new problem. But consider the following examples of departures from laws and basic social norms in modern times. In the middle of the Second World War the large British company AEI covertly engaged in a financial manipulation in order to avoid taxes required for the war effort.[6] In 1961 a series of anti-trust hearings in the US Senate discovered not only that the General Electric Company had engaged in systematic illegal price fixing and bid-rigging, but that this had happened in such a manner that the responsibility of top executives was largely blurred. It emerged that in some cases the General Electric top men's instructions to their subordinates to obey the law had actually been accompanied by winks.[7] In 1971 the UK Committee on Consumer Credit reported on the widespread tendency for credit providers systematically to understate the true rate of interest and the true cost of credit to the consumer.[8] A further catalogue of illegality or moral deviance might include such phenomena as corruption and boundary-rigging in local government, harassment of poor tenants by speculative property companies, exploitation of migrant black workers in apartheid South Africa by established international concerns, the apparent increase in industrial espionage, etc., etc. The relative gravity of such deviations can be debated, as also the degree to which they may result from ignorance, competitive pressure, herd instinct or fear. But the economic implications of illegal or unethical diversions of resources of this kind can hardly be ignored.

Over recent years there has been increasing concern about *environmental diseconomies* imposed by organisations (as also by individuals), including the pollution of air, water and soil, the infliction of noise and ugliness, the creation of wastes and the uncompensated using-up of scarce natural resources. Although Pigou firmly placed such problems on the economic policy agenda some fifty years ago, it is only recently that economists have sought to measure such costs on any substantial scale. To take one example: in 1972 the US Environmental Protection Agency estimated, probably very conservatively, that by 1977 the total national cost of air

N

pollution in that country – taking account of abatement costs – would be of the order of $14,000 million.[9] Some forms of pollution are hard to measure or even identify. As Professor Thomas Schelling of Harvard graphically puts it: 'Ships at sea may go on flushing their bowels in the ocean like undisciplined children at a municipal pond'.[10] According to the predictions of the 'eco-doomsters', the consequences of all these problems within the next century could be disastrous. Some economists argue that the 'doomsters' underrate society's ability and willingness to adjust by developing new energy sources, controlling pollution, stabilising population growth and carrying out necessary social reforms. But even a moderate on this issue, Professor Beckerman, having slated the extremists, declares 'there is no doubt that there is a genuine pollution problem, that it must be taken seriously and that appropriate policies must be adopted to deal with it'.[11]

To conclude this brief catalogue of modern ills, there is the overall problem of *social unbalance*. Developed societies are characterised by large and increasing expectations for personal consumption, continued conflicts over the distribution of rewards, a growing demand and need for public services, a growing concern for the quality of life, and a moral challenge from Third World poverty. Moreover, progress on all these fronts is expected under conditions of full employment, consumer 'freedom', political democracy and minimal state control. It requires little economic wit to perceive that these demands are irreconcilable and that their cumulative impact is such as to exacerbate both inflation and social conflict. Such inflationary and socially divisive pressures on resources are particularly grave for externally vulnerable countries like Britain. None of which is intended to suggest, *pace* some recent discussion, that national output should necessarily become stationary; but rather that people are expecting far too much from that output and that the social priorities in its make-up and distribution appear to be seriously wrong.

Some economists now have a clear proposal as to what should be sacrificed. Apart from deploring the continuance of colossal arms expenditure in a world where millions starve, they believe that what is particularly required is to lower the expectations for increased personal consumption which are held by already well-off people in the rich countries. They suggest this partly on the grounds that ever-increasing personal consumption does not necessarily make people happier. This idea was eloquently expressed by John Stuart Mill over a century ago.[12] As Schumpeter put it, 'Satiety is a flying goal'.[13] Or in the words of a modern economist: 'An all-round increase in wealth is liable to be achieved by the agency of a general stimulation of dissatisfaction, so that at the end of the process no-one is any happier and the gap between rich and poor yawns as widely as ever'.[14]

Greater restraint in private consumption by the affluent is also advocated because of the problems summed up by Galbraith under the heading of 'public squalor'. Over recent history there has been 'an extraordinary growth of problems of a kind that are not spontaneously solved by market mechanisms'.[15] 'The higher the density of population, the more decisions and expenditures have to be made collectively . . . The more people, the more they are concentrated in urban areas, the higher the public budget becomes. And this pressure is quite independent of the need for kinds of environmental expenditure not undertaken in the past'.[16] 'Looking ahead, it may be reasonable to expect that the increasing interdependence and complexity of modern society will lead to a rising incidence of externalities, calling for increased concern of public policy with both the provision for social goods and the prevention of "social bads".'[17] On top of all this there is the familiar argument that poverty at home, let alone overseas, necessitates redistribution, mainly through taxation, from the affluent to the poor. But it is unrealistic to imagine that even draconian taxes on the very rich, however socially just, would have more than a marginal impact on poverty. Some sacrifice, at least of potential private advantage, would be required from large numbers of middle-class and better-off working-class people as well. For all these reasons, so it is implied, the thrusting, overheated engine of affluent consumer desires now urgently needs to be cooled and decelerated.

If this judgement as to social balance is correct, as the author believes, then virtually all types of organisation are implicated. For example, political organisations compete in 'Dutch auctions' by offering too much to their electorates. Manufacturers of consumer products may whip up new and arguably trivial consumer desires. Mass advertising, involving thousands of businesses, cumulatively pushes forward the more refined forms of consumer affluence whilst drowning out other forms of appeal. Trade unions leapfrog over each other in a frequently vain and socially harmful pursuit of pay differentials. Leaders of organisations often set a poor example by grasping ostentatious privileges. So far, micro-economics has largely concentrated on isolated parts of these processes, for example 'built-in obsolescence', tax avoidance, wasteful advertising or competing wage demands. Comprehensive analysis of the roles of organisations as initiators, carriers or exacerbators of social unbalance has yet to get under way. There is widespread concern in the organisational world itself about these problems, of course, but also a feeling of helplessness and a disposition to shift the blame onto others. The remaining years of this century will show whether the necessary reforms are achieved voluntarily or enforced through crisis – or alternatively whether the unresolved conflicts inherent in excessive and competing claims on the economic system will actually get out of control.

SOCIAL CHOICES OF ALLOCATION SYSTEMS

On possible remedies, what lessons can be learnt from a study of micro-economics as pursued in this book? The micro-economic approach of digging-down, and penetrating recesses first offers one obvious message. It is that sweeping macro-solutions are all-too-likely to be inadequate, perhaps even harmful, unless accompanied by changes at organisational levels. In other words, reform should be radical in the strict sense of penetrating to the roots. For example, in terms of that subtle, complex, historical phenomenon, the 'English disease', the various macro-therapies which have been proposed – control of money supply, nationalisation, competition, consensus indicative planning, floating exchange rates and the rest – would all be regarded as far too weak and/or clumsy on their own. Instead, the emphasis would be on changes from below as well as above, on intimate and decentralised remedies as well as central ones, on the need for each sector to undergo depth treatment. The organisation of industry, the company sector, the trade unions, local government, the education system, the welfare services, the professions – all would be seen as requiring fundamental reform.

A major theme of this book has been the study of micro-allocation systems as interactions of exchange, coercion and integration. This theme greatly clarifies the debate about institutional change. For there are, broadly, three ways in which the organisational world can be reformed and made socially responsive. First, markets, taxes and subsidies can be deployed so that it becomes financially worthwhile for organisations to operate in socially approved ways – and financially punitive if they do not. This method requires state action to create a web of financial incentives and disincentives through both competition and taxation. It also vitally depends on strong motives of financial gain on the part of organisations and decision makers. Second, there is state direction through laws, statutory controls and nationalisation. As a minimum this demands not only firm elected governments and effective laws but also efficient bureaucrats. The third method is that of internalisation: to seek social and institutional changes of such a kind that organisations will conform to social norms because they *want* to. For example, the education framework can be changed, the social results of organisation's actions can be made more obvious both to themselves and others, and an informed public opinion can be brought to bear on them. The reader will recognise at once the three basic social organisers of self-interest, coercion and integration. In practice, the methods of ensuring social responsiveness roughly equate to (1) markets, suitably socially doctored, (2) public bureaucracies, ultimately responsible to electors, and (3) induced solidarity and voluntary gifts. In other words we return to the problem of choosing allocation systems but now for social rather than merely organisational ends.

To a large degree, as we have repeatedly seen, these allocation systems are commingled and interdependent. So perhaps the next main lesson of micro-economics is that some sort of *mixture* seems necessary if our institutions are to be changed. Perhaps a viable strategy for reform cannot avoid being allocatively diverse, however clear its moral aims. Just to take a few examples: markets will not harness business self-interest in the right social directions if there is a lot of monopoly. But to cut down monopoly would require strong and continuous state action (often on a bigger scale than proponents of this approach assume). Again, there is much evidence that state direction will not work in a pluralist society without a good deal of voluntary co-operation. Such policies as incomes restraint, racial equality and high taxation for public services all seem to require micro-goodwill as well as macro-coercion. Nor can moral persuasion alone ensure general obedience to social norms. If organisations are to make their neighbour's and the community's interests their own to a greater degree than today, complex motivations are needed. It seems that the legal, institutional and social framework must favour social responsibility. Unless it does so, decision makers may simply feel that good behaviour on their part will make no difference, will even disadvantage them and will not be recognised by society anyway. Socially responsible actions are more likely if they are able to be seen – at the grassroots – as possible, effective, creative, productive of social esteem and even reward.

But there is also a sense in which each of the three allocative approaches, if pushed too far, can involve heavy and undesired social costs. For example, take the classical liberal's view of market forces and price–exchange systems as the principal weapon for social improvement. His view is that under certain conditions (which the state must ensure) if organisations behave self-interestedly enough, then a socially good result will follow. If the micro-units are not self-interested enough, they should be stimulated to become more so. Thus the classical liberal may well agree with Milton Friedman that 'few trends could so thoroughly undermine the very foundations of our free society as the acceptance by corporate officials of a social responsibility other than to make as much money for their stockholders as possible'.[18] He may well agree with Professor Harry Johnson that in Britain ordinary people do not care *enough* for their own material comfort and prosperity.[19] He will probably favour the extension of pricing systems into the social sector, the sharpening of financial incentives and disincentives and a widespread, indeed intensified, employment of motives of private gain.

However, a study of micro-allocation systems, business, public and voluntary, suggests serious doubts. As we have seen, many activities are incapable of articulation even through non-monetary exchange, let alone organised markets. Exchange and markets cannot bind together a community, care for the weak, redistribute towards the poorest, provide for our great-grandchildren or produce most categories of public goods. Perhaps the gravest weakness of classical liberalism is that it pursues an abstract division between 'economic' and 'social' factors. It seeks a business-productive system which both excites and is excited by acquisitive motives – but also, at least in some versions, a social system which is then to pick up the pieces. Close study of micro-allocation systems shows how unreal such a schism is. Once fully conceded, indeed further incited, the genie of acquisitiveness can hardly be restricted to businessmen and entrepreneurs. Profit obsessions in market places and stock exchanges cannot be insulated from society at large. Managers and workers who are encouraged to be more self-interested will probably fight more intensely both with each other and with rival businesses and trade unions. It seems all too possible that they will be also more inclined to avoid community ties, seek 'privatisation', chisel on taxes, begrudge collective action for pensioners, the handicapped and the poor. In a productive system even more dominated by self-interest, the individual would be still less likely to put down local roots, to live close to his extended family, to increase his leisure time, to make social gifts. He would be more likely to be materially dissatisfied, constantly straining for a contentment that always eludes him.

Proponents of exchange-competitive-market solutions, therefore, often appear to be unaware of delicate micro-interactions. But theirs is not the only would-be panacea to commit this fault. Comparable misunderstandings apply to the perpetual debate about government intervention. Depending on a person's ideology, state control of organisations is either dreaded or ritualistically invoked. Increased government intervention is viewed either as a threat to liberty or as a solution for virtually all ills. The less dramatic possibility that down among the grassroots state direction may turn out to be neither of these things is hardly considered. Yet the evidence of micro-economics on centrally directed allocation systems tends to suggest that in pluralist societies such as ours, rightly or wrongly, direct government control of resources has not so far proved to be super-efficient. There is 'control loss' as instructions work downwards; democratic accountability is hard to ensure; the bureaucrats and experts may get too much power; exchange systems tend to reassert themselves at various points; the possibilities of avoidance and evasion are considerable.

One may believe, as does the author, that increased state intervention is necessary as part of a constant effort to check excessive sectionalism, remedy injustices and redistribute national and international resources. But once again micro-observation suggests some important lessons. One is that public intervention should be subjected to greater disciplines of rational analysis and output measurement. This is largely to make it less production- and more community-orientated, as implied in Chapter 11. Another lesson is that one should not hope for too much from government. The state has only to assert itself for resistances and avoidances to arise at micro levels. The process seems to be a never-ending one. In a pluralist society the micro-forces of self-interest constantly re-emerge. Insofar as the state struggles for some idea of 'equity' it may win individual battles but never the whole war. Nor can the state win even particular battles on its own. The idea that millions of people can behave individualistically whilst comfortably leaving to the state the job of asserting community values and creating greater equality is no less schizophrenic than classical liberalism. The need to inculcate voluntary social responsibility, will still be profound. If an unashamed moral judgement can be cited: 'Legislation is necessary, but it is not sufficient for setting up true relationships of justice and equality . . . Without a renewed education in solidarity, an over-emphasis on equality can give rise to an individualism in which each one claims his own rights without wishing to be answerable for the common good'.[20]

The reader will perceive where this argument is leading: towards a mixture of allocation systems including a selective use of markets, increased and improved government intervention but, perhaps most important, a greater emphasis on induced social responsibility. It is to this third allocative approach, relatively neglected by economists, that we now finally turn.

INDUCED SOCIAL RESPONSIBILITY

The essence of the voluntary method is to design a framework of information, contact and concern so that decision makers (a) feel it is important to do the socially right thing as a matter of conscience, (b) clearly see how their resource decisions do in fact affect others, and (c) expect unpleasant social criticism if they err, social approbation if they conform. Let us briefly look at each of these elements.

(a) is required if only because, as Kenneth Arrow points out, conscious agreements to act in a social manner are often much too costly in terms of information and bargaining. Therefore, as he puts it, 'internalised feelings of guilt and right are essential'.[21] (b) takes us back to a basic precept of the economic theory of decision making: that all relevant costs and benefits should be considered. Few people would deny that at the very least it is 'relevant' for organisations to be made properly aware of any external damage or benefit they cause. Whether they then react in the right way may still be left to them but at least it should be made impossible to plead ignorance. The problem here is not only one of ensuring that information about social costs and benefits is provided to decision makers effectively, pungently and economically – a difficult task in itself. Changes in the timing of organisational decisions may also be needed, for example in trade union wage claims, so that social interactions are made clearer. Decision makers should be brought personally in touch with organisations and people who are less advantaged. This means local and immediate contacts. But it might also justify wider contacts, for example through some sort of compulsory national social service for young people enjoying higher education. As for (c), the eliciting of 'feedback' signals from the environment, this requires, among other things, that public opinion should be alerted and that new organs of social accountability, even new counter-organisations, should be developed. Taken together, then, (a), (b) and (c) suggest changes in education, social accounting, legal disclosure, mass communications, community planning and the organisational 'mix' itself – all designed to encourage voluntary restraint and social gift making on the part of organisations.

For example, in an economy in which social interdependences are brought home as if they really mattered, all large and public companies would submit annual social accounts. These would include productivity data, social end uses of outputs, balance of payments effects, notable external economies and diseconomies, and grants made and received. The infrastructure for such a reporting system would be provided by the state. For companies generally the profit mechanism in some minimal sense would continue to be essential, whatever the pattern of ownership and control. For small firms particularly a 'social market' solution might be expected to perform well enough. But for large and public companies the emphasis would be decisively shifted, legally, ceremonially and psychologically. Instead of crude growth and profits subject to social constraints, it would be rising productivity and social standards subject to profit constraints that would be highlighted. A further and perhaps more radical suggestion has come from Joseph Bower, Professor of Business Administration at Harvard University. He has suggested 'the elimination of corporate anonymity . . . We must remove the screens that detach social consequences from their origins in individual acts . . . Individuals must bear the consequences of their actions, and this may mean the necessity of ending the social, political and, in some areas, even the economic aspects of limited liability'.[22]

Nor should the trade unions be exempt from appropriate forms of social accounting. In Britain trade unions' organisation anyway requires fundamental reform in their own and society's interests. Following such structural reform they, too, might be required to make annual reports. But here the external distributional effects are often hard to pin down. Trade unionists have some legitimate excuses about a chaotic bargaining system. It is genuinely difficult to answer the question, 'How do we know that restraint by us will help the less well-off?' Professor Phelps Brown's suggestion for annual pay bargaining on a concurrent basis – related to estimates of the total 'cake' to be shared – is highly relevant here. This would mean that the realities of 'the A's getting less because the B's get more' would at least be made clearer. It is in the same spirit of ensuring that the social costs and benefits of their decisions are brought home to sectional interests at the moment of choice, and not cushioned by their isolation at particular points of time or obfuscated by real or pretended ignorance.

When we turn towards proposals for new organisations, as distinct from the reform of existing ones, the same theme of new pressures towards voluntary social responsibility is evident. For example,

Kenneth Arrow has suggested two new types of public institution to deal with external diseconomies. One institution would have the 'adversary or prosecuting attorney role' of establishing the social costs of an activity, entering a brief and suggesting general remedies, whether through tax, price solutions or regulation. The other body would be a quasi-judicial agency to receive evidence and make final decisions, serving to build up an interrelated code based on cost–benefit analysis.[23] Again, there is the frequent proposal for public information services to inform and champion the consumer. Some, like Emmanuel Mesthene of Harvard University, have gone further and argued for 'a large-scale and extensive system of public information – analogous in scope to the institution of commercial advertising . . . free of both private pressures and shifting political orientations . . . as aggressive in getting messages across as present-day advertising'.[24] In the same genre come pleas for the full-scale advertising of social goods. Equally stimulatingly, Robin Marris has argued for 'social benefit corporations'. 'It seems that unless we can develop a type of business organisation whose stated and legitimate purpose is to create social benefit for society, while in the process creating a just income for its members . . . we shall suffer a conflict between national aims and business ethics.'[25] Significantly, though, Marris puts his suggestion in pluralist terms: 'Some social benefit corporations might be rather like communes. Some might be rather like Yugoslav self-managed enterprises, but with more emphasis on responsibility to society at large. Some might be like the better class of government agency. Some would be old-style, small profit-seeking enterprises'.[26]

Finally, it should not be forgotten that most people belong to a variety of organisations at any point of time and certainly over their lifespans. The relative priority of these organisations in their lives is important. It is not necessarily right that the concerns in which people earn their living should claim too much from them. Perhaps the company town or executive suburb, the corporate welfare state, even the syndicalist dream of workers pouring themselves into their 'own' factory, are dubious guides to fulfilment. Nor is it necessarily right that people should work all their lives in a single sector, perhaps oblivious and even hostile to others. Business and public sector parochialisms have been frequently berated in this book. Nor does it seem right that people should be caught between a large employer, a tiny nuclear family and a gargantuan state, with no effective network of social organisations in between. Perhaps European developments will encourage more cross-fertilisation of ideas on small social organisations, notably those designed to promote co-operation, local communities and charitable action, care for children and old people and a strengthened family life. A society that seeks more social responsibility from its decision makers – whether in boardrooms, union offices or council chambers – should not forget that it is in the prime institutions of family, neighbourhood and local community that the lesson of social interdependence is first learnt if it is going to be learnt at all. The provisioning problems of such small social organisations – and the grassroots of the micro-gifts economy – may call for increasing attention in the future.

CONCLUSION

This last chapter has ranged very widely and reflects the author's personal points of view. He does not necessarily expect readers to agree with his selection of contemporary critiques and proposals. He does believe that it is better to bring out such value judgements clearly rather than let them creep in implicitly or even unawares. The important point is that it is not enough to analyse existing forces: micro-economics also contributes to the analysis of social improvements. It helps to clarify how much freedom of manœuvre in reforming organisations we really have. How we use that freedom is, of course, a matter of moral judgement on which differences of opinion are inevitable and healthy. But whatever one's moral presuppositions, the problem of trade-offs and priorities between social markets, democratic compulsion and induced social responsibility is inescapable. Whatever, too, the new organisational patterns, it is reasonable to assume that the double role of micro-economics emphasised in this book will still apply. That is to say, economics will still provide the basic principles of rational choice by which organisational choices can be made more efficient. And economics will provide, as before, an intellectual framework within which mankind's age-old problem, the choice of allocative systems to secure both organisational *and* social ends, will continue to be clarified and debated.

Notes

Chapter 1 What is Organisational Economics?

1 This last definition follows Peter M. Blau and W. Richard Scott, in *Formal Organisations: A Comparative Approach*, San Francisco, Chandler, 1962, Ch. 1.

Chapter 2 Markets, Bureaucracies, Gifts

1 Most recently in Kenneth E. Boulding, *The Economy of Love and Fear: A Preface to Grants Economics*, Belmont, California, Wadsworth, 1973.
2 A useful outline of the development of contemporary theories is contained in C. J. Hawkins, *Theory of the Firm*, Macmillan Studies in Economics, London, Macmillan, 1973.
3 For references to relevant books see Note on Further Reading.
4 P. Sargant Florence, *The Economics and Sociology of Industry*, 2nd edition, London, Watts, 1969, p. 249.
5 Neil W. Chamberlain, *Enterprise and Environment: The Firm in Time and Place*, New York, McGraw-Hill, 1968, Ch. 5.
6 Gardiner Means, *The Corporate Revolution in America: Economic Reality vs. Economic Theory*, London, Crowell-Collier Press, 1962, pp. 54–5.
7 Anthony Downs, *Inside Bureaucracy*, Boston, Little, Brown, 1967, p. 2.
8 See for example, A. Wildavsky, *The Politics of the Budgetary Process*, Boston, Little, Brown, 1964. And more recently, H. Heclo and A. Wildavsky, *The Private Government of Public Money*, London, Macmillan, 1974.
9 For example by J. S. Mill and Philip Wicksteed, and in more recent times by Lord Robbins, Sir Denis Robertson and Kenneth Boulding; also by some economic anthropologists, economic historians and social-economic theorists, notably Raymond Firth, R. H. Tawney, G. D. H. Cole and R. M. Titmuss.
10 Boulding, op. cit., p. 27.

Chapter 3 Economics and Decision Making

1 For a useful outline of profit maximising, sales maximising and other modern theories of the firm, see C. J. Hawkins, *Theory of the Firm*, Macmillan Studies in Economics, London, Macmillan, 1973. See also Robin Marris and Adrian Wood, *The Corporate Economy*, London, Macmillan, 1971, especially the chapters by Marris, Wood and Williamson; and W. J. Baumol, *Business Behaviour, Value and Growth*, revised edition, London, Harcourt, Brace and World, 1967.
2 The Open University, *Approaches to the Study of Public Administration*, Part 3, 'The administrative process as incrementalism', Milton Keynes, The Open University Press, 1974, p. 7.
3 Charles E. Lindblom, 'The science of muddling through', *Public Administration Review*, Spring, 1959.

4 Henry Mintzberg, *The Nature of Managerial Work*, New York, Harper and Row, 1973, p. 52.
5. ibid., p. 99.

Chapter 4 Marginalism

1 Professor G. Lawson, *The Accountants Journal*, 1964, pp. 226, 267, 268.
2 Richard Pryke, *Public Enterprise in Practice: The British Experience of Nationalisation over Two Decades*, London, MacGibbon and Kee, 1971, Ch. 15.
3 See, for example, D. C. Hague, *Pricing in Business*, London, Allen & Unwin, 1971.
4 Tony Eddison, *Local Government: Management and Corporate Planning*, London, Leonard Hill Books, 1973, p. 37.
5 *Accounting for Health*, Report of a King's Fund Working Party on the applications of economic principles in health service management, under chairmanship of Professor Brian Abel-Smith, King Edward's Hospital Fund for London, 1973, p. 21.
6 A. D. H. Kaplan and others, *Pricing in Big Business*, Washington, The Brookings Institution, 1958.
7 James S. Earley, 'Marginal policies of "excellently managed" companies', *American Economic Review*, Vol. XLVI, No. 1, March 1956.
8 Hague, op. cit.
9 For a discussion of this issue see Ralph Turvey, *Economic Analysis and Public Enterprises*, London, Allen & Unwin, 1971.
10 Alan Williams, *The Economics of Public Expenditure, Memorandum to the Select Committee on Procedure*, 1968–9, p. 141.

Chapter 5 Opportunity Cost

1 James Buchanan, *Cost and Choice: An Inquiry in Economic Theory*, Chicago, Markham Publishing Company, 1969, pp. 44–5.
2 G. F. Thirlby, 'The Subjective Theory of Value and Accounting Cost', *Economica*, Vol. XIII, February 1946.
3 For an introduction to the mathematical techniques of operational research see D. C. Hague, *Managerial Economics*, London, Longmans, 1973, Part 3.
4 For a relevant discussion of the objectives and efficiency of charities, see Benedict Nightingale, *Charities*, London, Allen Lane, 1973, especially Ch. 8.
5 See Peter F. Rudge, *Ministry and Management: The Study of Ecclesiastical Administration*, London, Tavistock Publications, 1968, p. 153.
6 See Jonathan Boswell, *The Rise and Decline of Small Firms*, London, Allen & Unwin, 1973, Ch. 9.
7 *Cost Benefit Analysis as applied to the Nationalised Industries*, Treasury Memorandum, Appdx. 8, Vol. III of the 1st Report of the Select Committee on Nationalised Industries, London, HMSO, 1968.
8 *Report of the Committee on Local Authority and Allied Personal Social Services* (the Seebohm Committee), Cmnd. 3703, London, HMSO, 1968, p. 152.
9 Henry Mintzberg, *The Nature of Managerial Work*, New York, Harper and Row, 1973, p. 86.

Chapter 6 Time, Risk and Uncertainty

1 Frank Knight, *Risk, Uncertainty and Profit*, 1st edn., Boston, Houghton Mifflin, 1921, Ch. 7.
2 G. L. S. Shackle, *Uncertainty in Economics and Other Reflections*, London, Cambridge University Press, 1968.
3 See G. T. Jones, *Simulation and Business Decisions*, Harmondsworth, Penguin, 1972.
4 Ruth Mack, *Planning on Uncertainty: Decision-making in Business and Government Administration*, Wiley, 1971, Ch. 11.
5 Quoted in David B. Hertz, 'Risk Analysis in Capital Investment', *Harvard Business Review*, Vol. 42, No. 1, 1964.
6 National Board for Prices and Incomes, *Report No. 102, Gas Prices* (Second Report), Appendix C, Investment in Distribution, pp. 97–101, London, HMSO, Cmnd. 3924, 1969.
7 *Fortune Magazine*, 'IBM's $5,000,000,000 gamble', September, October 1966.

Chapter 7 Size and Efficiency

1 For a useful summary of the evidence here, see, for example, F. M. Scherer, *Industrial Market Structure and Economic Performance*, Chicago, Rand McNally, 1970, Ch. 2 and 3. Also M. A. Utton, 'Mergers and Concentration in British Industry', Cambridge University Press, National Institute of Economic and Social Research, Occasional Paper No. 26, 1973.
2 Kenneth E. Boulding, *Economic Analysis*, 3rd edition, New York, Harper, 1955, p. 589.
3 For empirical studies of production and cost functions see Donald S. Watson, (ed.), *Price Theory in Action*, 2nd edition, Boston, Houghton Mifflin, 1969, Part 3, 'Production functions and cost functions'. For more detail see J. Johnston, *Statistical Cost Analysis*, New York, McGraw-Hill, 1960, and V. Gold, 'New perspectives on cost theory and empirical findings', *Journal of Industrial Economics*, Vol. 14, April 1966.
4 C. Pratten and R. M. Dean, *The Economies of Large-Scale Production in British Industry: An Introductory Study*, London, Cambridge University Press, 1965, p. 105.
5 The Chartered Institute of Public Finance and Accountancy, *Water, Sewerage, Pollution and Finance*, London, pp. 11–13.
6 Edith Penrose, *Theory of the Growth of the Firm*, Oxford, Blackwell, 1959.
7 W. J. Baumol, *Business Behaviour: Value and Growth*, revised edition, London, Harcourt, Brace and World, 1967. Robin Marris, *The Economic Theory of Managerial Capitalism*, London, Macmillan, 1964. Also, Marris and Wood (eds.), *The Corporate Economy*, London, Macmillan, 1971.
8 For Galbraith's theories see Chapter 2, A Note on Further Reading.
9 A. Singh and G. Whittington, in collaboration with H. T. Burley, *Growth, Profitability and Valuation: A Study of United Kingdom Quoted Companies*, London, Cambridge University Press, 1968, Ch. 8, 'Summary and conclusions'.
10 *Bolton Report*, Report of the Committee of Inquiry on Small Firms, London, HMSO, Cmnd. 4811, 1971, Ch. 4.

11 G. D. Newbould, *Management and Merger Activity*, Liverpool, Gutt-stead, 1970, Ch. 4, Section 2, and Ch. 5.
12 M. Z. Brooke and H. L. Remmers, *The Strategy of Multinational Enter-prise: Organisation and Finance*, London, Longman, 1970, Ch. 9.
13 For a summary of the evidence on these issues see F. M. Scherer, *Industrial Market Structure and Economic Performance*, Chicago, Rand McNally, 1970, particularly Ch. 17.
14 ibid., p. 280.
15 The findings on human 'size effects' from many of these studies, in social as well as industrial organisations, are summarised in Geoffrey K. Ingham, *Size of Industrial Organisation and Worker Behaviour*, London, Cambridge University Press, 1970.
16 See Ingham, op. cit., where this author also quotes some other socio-logists holding similar views.
17 P. M. Blau and R. A. Schoenherr, *The Structure of Organisations*, New York, London, Basic Books, 1971.
18 Anthony Downs, *Inside Bureaucracy*, Boston, Little, Brown, 1967.
19 Jonathan Boswell, *The Rise and Decline of Small Firms*, London, Allen & Unwin, 1973.
20 Alfred Marshall, *Principles of Economics*, 8th edition, London, Mac-millan, 1964, p. 263.

Chapter 8 Profits and Market Knowledge

1 Neil Chamberlain, *The Firm: Micro-economic Planning and Action*, New York, McGraw-Hill, 1962, p. 76.
2 D. C. Hague, *Pricing in Business*, London, George Allen & Unwin, 1971.
3 ibid., p. 133.
4 Joan Robinson, 'Imperfect competition revisited', *Economic Journal*, 1953.
5 See D. S. Watson (ed.), *Price Theory in Action: A Book of Readings*, Boston, Houghton Mifflin, 1969, Pt. 1.

Chapter 9 Big Business Budgets and Plans

1 Alfred D. Chandler, Jr, *Strategy and Structure, Chapters in the History of the Industrial Enterprise*, Cambridge, Mass., MIT Press, 1962.
2 Derek F. Channon, *The Strategy and Structure of British Enterprise*, Boston, Division of Research, Graduate School of Business Administra-tion, Harvard University, 1973.
3 See Edith T. Penrose, *The Theory of the Growth of the Firm*, Oxford, Blackwell, 1959, Ch. 7, on the 'economics of diversification'. For a detailed description of diversification in a large firm see Charles Wilson, *History of Unilever: A Study in Economic Growth and Social Change*, London, Cassell, 1968, Vol. 3.
4 Channon, op. cit., especially Chs. 3 and 7.
5 ibid., pp. 211, 217.
6 Bruce Scott, *The Stages of Corporate Development*, Part II, p. 4, un-published paper, Harvard Business School, Boston, 1971.
7 Neil W. Chamberlain, *The Firm: Micro-economic Planning and Action*, New York, McGraw-Hill, 1962, p. 397.
8 Michael Z. Brooke and H. Lee Remmers, *The Strategy of Multinational Enterprise: Organisation and Finance*, London, Longman, 1970, p. 69.

9 ibid., p. 103.
10 ibid., p. 118.
11 ibid., p. 119.
12 Neil W. Chamberlain, op. cit., p. 417.
13 ibid., p. 420.

Chapter 10   The Provisioning of Social Enterprises

1 Harvey E. Brazer, 'City Expenditures in the US', New York, National Bureau of Economic Research, *Occasional Paper 66*, 1959.
2 Bleddyn Davies, *Social Needs and Resources in Local Services*, London, Michael Joseph, 1968. See also Bleddyn Davies, A. Barton and I. McMillan, 'Variations in Childrens' Services among British Urban Authorities: A Causal Analysis', *Occasional Papers in Social Administration, No. 45*, London, G. Bell, 1972.
3 F. G. Dickinson, *The Changing Position of Philanthropy in the American Economy*, New York, National Bureau of Economic Research, 1970.
4 ibid., introduction by Solomon Fabrikant, p. 26.
5 Benedict Nightingale, *Charities*, London, Allen Lane, 1973.
6 For advocacy of pricing solutions, see particularly publications of the Institute of Economic Affairs. For the 'private affluence, public squalor' view, see J. K. Galbraith, *The Affluent Society*, London, Hamish Hamilton, 1958, and also the same author's, *Economics and the Public Purpose*, London, Hamish Hamilton, 1974.
7 For a basic exposition of consumers' surplus, see E. J. Mishan, *Cost-Benefit Analysis: An Informal Introduction*, 2nd edition, London, Allen & Unwin, 1975, Chs. 7 and 8.
8 For the theory of public goods see R. W. Houghton (ed.), *Public Finance: Selected Readings*, 2nd edition, Harmondsworth, Penguin, 1973, Part 2, 'The choice between private and public goods', especially articles by P. A. Samuelson and R. A. Musgrave.
9 See W. J. Baumol, *Performing Arts, the Economic Dilemma: A study of problems common to theater, opera, music and dance*, New York, Twentieth Century Fund, 1966.
10 For the economics of housing, see for example L. Needleman, *The Economics of Housing*, London, Stapler Press, 1965, and A. A. Nevitt (ed.), *The Economic Problems of Housing*, London, Macmillan, 1967.
11 On the relative roles of local authorities and the voluntary housing movement, see M. Harloe, R. Issacharoff and R. Minns, *The Organisation of Housing: Public and Private Enterprise in London*, London, Heinemann, 1974.
12 For a discussion of the money-raising methods of charities see B. Nightingale, *Charities*, London, Allen Lane, 1973, Ch. 5.
13 R. A. Schwartz, 'Personal philanthropic contributions', *Journal of Political Economy*, 1970.
14 F. G. Dickinson (ed.), *Philanthropy and Public Policy*, New York, National Bureau of Economic Research, 1962, pp. 114–15. See also W. J. Baumol, *Performing Arts, the Economic Dilemma*, op. cit.
15 Mary Morris, *Voluntary Work in the Welfare State*, London, Routledge & Kegan Paul, 1969, pp. 191–3, 250–60. See also M. Young and P. Willmott, *The Symmetrical Family*, London, Routledge & Kegan Paul, 1973, p. 216.

Chapter 11 Social Enterprises: Allocation Problems

1 For many practical examples, see Trevor Newton, *Cost–Benefit Analysis in Administration*, London, Allen & Unwin, 1972.
2 See, for example, N. Lichfield, *Cost–Benefit Analysis in Town Planning: a Case Study of Cambridge*, Cambridge and Isle of Ely Council, 1966.
3 Mancur Olson, 'On the priority of public problems', in Robin Marris (ed.), *The Corporate Society*, London, Macmillan, 1974.
4 ibid., p. 316.
5 Tom Berkshire, 'Developing a system of measurement in a metropolitan authority: early experiences of the Greater London Council', *Local Government Studies*, February 1974.
6 *Output Measurement Discussion Papers, 2*, 'Personal Social Services', The Chartered Institute of Public Finance and Accountancy, London, December 1972.
7 Some of the material for this section is drawn from the Institute of Local Government Studies, *Corporate Planning*, Vol. 1, No. 1, February 1974.

Chapter 12 Organisational Reform

1 Charles Levinson, *Capital, Inflation and the Multi-Nationals*, London, Allen & Unwin, 1971, p. 104.
2 J. H. Dunning, 'The Multinational Enterprise and UK Economic Interests', *Journal of Business Policy*, Vol. 1, No. 4, Summer 1971.
3 A variety of views is contained in J. H. Dunning (ed.), *The Multinational Enterprise*, London, Allen & Unwin, 1971.
4 Sidney M. Robbins and Robert B. Stobaugh, *Money in the Multinational Enteprise: A Study of Financial Policy*, London, Longman, 1974, Ch. 10.
5 Edith Penrose, 'The state and multinational enterprises in less-developed countries, in J. H. Dunning, (ed.), op. cit., p. 238.
6 R. Jones and O. Marriott, *Anatomy of a Merger: A History of GEC, AEI and English Electric*, London, Jonathan Cape, 1970, p. 156.
7 John Brooks, *Business Adventures*, Harmondsworth, Penguin, 1971, Ch. 7.
8 *Report of the Committee on Consumer Credit*, London, HMSO, Cmnd. 4596, 1971.
9 United States Environmental Protection Agency, *The Economics of Clean Air*, March 1972, Table 1–4. It has been argued that these estimates provide no more than a starting point for analysis.
10 Thomas Schelling, 'On the ecology of micro-motives', in Robin Marris (ed.), *The Corporate Society*, London, Macmillan, 1974, p. 63.
11 Wilfred Beckerman, *In Defence of Economic Growth*, London, Jonathan Cape, 1974, p. 102.
12 J. S. Mill, *Principles of Political Economy*, Vol. II, London, John W. Parker and Son, 1857, pp. 320–6.
13 Joseph A. Schumpeter, *Capitalism, Socialism and Democracy*, 3rd edition, London, Allen & Unwin, 1950, p. 131.
14 Charles Carter, *Wealth*, Harmondsworth, Penguin, 1971, p. 120.
15 Mancur Olson, 'On the priority of public problems', in Robin Marris (ed.), op. cit., p. 302.

16 Barbara Ward and Rene Dubos, *Only One Earth: The Care and Maintenance of a Small Planet*, Harmondsworth, Penguin, 1972, p. 174.
17 Richard A. Musgrave, 'On social goods and social bads', in Robin Marris (ed.), op. cit., pp. 282–3.
18 Milton Friedman, *Capitalism and Freedom*, Chicago, University of Chicago Press, 1962, p. 133.
19 Harry G. Johnson, 'The economic approach to social questions', an inaugural lecture delivered 12 October 1967, London, LSE, 1967, pp. 14–15.
20 Pope Paul VI, Apostolic Letter, *Octogesima Adveniens*, London, Catholic Truth Society, 1971, pp. 19–20.
21 Kenneth J. Arrow, 'The place of moral obligation in preference systems', in Sidney Hook (ed.), *Human Values and Economic Policy*, New York University Press, 1967, p. 118.
22 Joseph Bower, 'On the amoral organisation', in Robin Marris (ed.), op. cit., pp. 206 and 210.
23 Kenneth Arrow, 'On the Agenda of Organisations', in Robin Marris (ed.), op. cit., pp. 232–3.
24 Emmanuel Mesthene, 'On the ideal–real gap', in Robin Marris (ed.), op. cit., p. 16.
25 Marris, op. cit., p. 392.
26 ibid., p. 398.

Index